BYZANTINE
EMPRESSES

BYZANTINE EMPRESSES

CHARLES DIEHL

Translated from the French by
Harold Bell and Theresa de Kerpely

1963

ALFRED A. KNOPF / *NEW YORK*

L. C. catalog card number: 62–15576

THIS IS A BORZOI BOOK
PUBLISHED BY ALFRED A. KNOPF, INC.

FIRST BORZOI EDITION

Chapters I through VII first appeared in *Byzantine Portraits*, Alfred A. Knopf, 1927; originally issued in French as *Figures Byzantines*, Paris: Armand Colin, 1906. Chapters VIII through XIV originally appeared in French as parts of *Impératrices de Byzance*, © 1959, Max Leclerc et Cie, proprietors of Librairie Armand Colin.

CONTENTS

BYZANTINE
EMPRESSES

Chapters I through VII of this book were translated by Harold Bell, and Chapters VIII through XIV by Theresa de Kerpely.

THE LIFE OF A BYZANTINE EMPRESS

I

In the most secluded part of the Imperial Palace of Byzantium, far beyond the guardrooms and the apartments of state, in the midst of shadowy gardens and running waters, which, to quote a contemporary chronicler, made of it "a new Eden," "another Paradise," arose the private dwelling of the Greek Emperors of the Middle Ages.

From the descriptions of Byzantine historians we can still obtain some idea of the exquisite, splendid abode which many generations of Princes had embellished from age to age, and where, far from the noise of the world, and the tedium of ceremonial, the *Basileis*, representatives of God on earth, were able from time to time to become men for a space. Precious marbles and glittering mosaics abounded. In the great hall of the New Palace, constructed by Basil I, above the magnificent colonnade of green marble alternating with red onyx, were vast compositions, monuments of that secular art, which the Byzantine masters practiced far more commonly than one imagines, representing the sovereign enthroned among his victorious generals, and unfolding the glorious epic of his reign: "the Herculean labors of the Basileus," as a contemporary chronicler has it, "his solicitude for his subjects, his deeds on the battlefield, and his God-awarded victories." But above all, the imperial bedchamber must, it seems, have been a marvel. Below the high ceiling, studded with golden stars, in the midst of which, in green mosaic, was a cross, the symbol of salvation, the whole of the vast chamber was magnificently decorated. In the mosaic floor a central medallion enclosed a peacock with spreading plumage, and in the corner were four eagles—the imperial bird—framed in green marble, with wings outstretched ready to take their flight. On the lower part of the walls, the mosaic made, as it were, a border of flowers. Higher up, against a background of glowing gold, still other mosaics represented the entire imperial family in state costume: Basil crowned and seated on his throne, near him his wife Eudocia, and grouped around them, very much as they may be seen in the faded miniatures of a fine manuscript in the Bibliothèque Nationale, their sons and daughters, holding books on which were written pious verses from the Scriptures. They all raised their hands solemnly toward the redeeming cross; and long inscriptions carved on the walls invoked upon the dynasty God's blessing and the assurance of eternal life.

The Pavilion of the Pearl, with its golden vault upheld by four columns of marble and its mosaic wainscot with hunting scenes, contained the summer bedchamber of the sovereigns, and opened through porticoes on two of its sides upon cool gardens. There was the winter bedchamber in the Carian Pavilion, so called from being constructed throughout of Carian marble, protected from the violent winds that blew from the Sea of Marmora; there was the Empress's wardrobe, wainscoted in the white marble of Proconnesus, and covered with pictures of the saints. And, finest of all, there was the bedchamber of the Empress, a wonderful room whose marble pavement seemed like "a meadow of enameled flowers," the walls of which, lined with porphyry, Thessalian breccia, and white Carian, were such rare and happy combinations of color that it was known as the Pavilion of Harmony. There was the Pavilion of Love also, and that of the Purple, wherein, according to custom and tradition, the imperial children must be born, and from which they derived their title of Porphyrogenitus. And everywhere was the splendor of silver and ivory doors, purple curtains sliding on rods of silver, tapestries embroidered in gold with fantastic animals, great golden lamps swinging from the domes, precious furniture wonderfully incrusted with mother of pearl, ivory, and gold.

It was in this marvelous Palace, in the midst of her court of eunuchs and women, far from the tedium of ceremonies, far from the tumults of the capital, in the quiet peacefulness of flowery gardens, amid the clear sparkle of fountains, that she lived whose life I shall attempt to describe in the following pages; "the Glory of the Purple, the Joy of the World," as the people of Constantinople hailed her; "the Most Pious and Most Happy Augusta, the Christ-loving Basilissa," as she was officially styled—in short, the Empress of Byzantium.

II

One is apt to form a rather false notion of the life of these Greek Empresses of the East. By an unconscious association of ideas—the life of women in ancient Greece, in medieval

Russia, in the Mohammedan Orient—one is too ready to assume that the Byzantine Empresses were perpetual recluses, carefully cloistered in the Gynaeceum and guarded by armed eunuchs; seeing none but women, "beardless men," as eunuchs were called in Byzantium, and old priests; appearing in public only on very rare occasions, and even then closely veiled from the public eye. One is apt to imagine them reigning over a court of women carefully separated from that of the Basileus—living, in short, a harem life in a Christian world.

This notion, though widespread, is very questionable. Under few governments have women had a better position, or played a more important part, or had a greater influence upon politics and government, than under the Byzantine Empire. It is, as has been justly remarked, "one of the most striking characteristics of Greek history in the Middle Ages." [1] Not merely did many of these Empresses dominate their husbands by their beauty, or by their superior intelligence: that alone would prove little, and harem favorites have done as much. But under the monarchy founded by Constantine, in almost every century of its history, one meets with women who either have reigned themselves or, more frequently, have with sovereign power disposed of the crown and made Emperors. And these Princesses looked neither the outward and visible signs of authority, nor the substance of it. We find evidence of this legitimately wielded power not only in the life of the Gynaeceum, but even more definitely in public affairs, in which its legality is expressly admitted by contemporaries. And therefore, those who wish to know and understand the society and civilization of Byzantium must learn

[1] A. N. Rambaud, "Impératrices d'Orient," *Revue des Deux Mondes,* 1891, tome i, p. 829.

some unexpected things about the life of these forgotten Princesses of long ago.

III

Throughout the vast extent of the Imperial Gynaeceum the Empress reigned supreme. Besides her women, she too, like the Emperor, had a numerous retinue of palace officials. At the head of her household was a Praepositus, or Lord Chamberlain, in supreme command of all the chamberlains, referendaries, ushers, and silentiaries, attached to the service of the Basilissa, all, together with the halberdiers, or protospatharii, of her bodyguard, carefully chosen from among the eunuchs of the Palace. To serve her at table the Empress, as well as the Emperor, had a Grand Master and a Chief Taster. At the head of her women was a Grand Mistress of the Palace, on whom was generally bestowed the high dignity of Patrician of the Girdle, and who, with the Protovestiarius, managed the innumerable throng of maids of honor, ladies of the bedchamber, and ladies-in-waiting. As a rule, the Emperor appointed those who were to serve the Augusta, and he especially reserved to himself the privilege of personally investing the Grand Mistress with the insignia of her office, as well as that of receiving the homage of newly appointed maids of honor. But for the majority of her attendants the Empress held a special investiture in order to emphasize the fact that they were in her service. And although, on the day of their installation, when assuming their official robes—golden tunic, white mantle, and high, tower-like headdress (the *propoloma*) with long white veil—the women of the Basilissa were admonished by the Praepositus to fear God and be sincerely faithful and wholly devoted to the Basileus and the Augusta, there is reason to believe that, once admitted to the imperial chamber, they soon forgot the Emperor in their loyalty to the Empress.

Since she could rely upon the fidelity of her servants, the Empress was free to act as she chose within the Gynaeceum, and she used this freedom in accordance with her character and temperament. For many of these fair Princesses their toilet was one of their chief occupations. It is said that Theodora, accomplished coquette as she was, took great care of her beauty; she slept far into the morning so that her face might appear serene and lovely; she took frequent and prolonged baths in order to preserve the striking freshness of her complexion; she loved splendid robes of state, the dazzle of great purple-violet mantles embroidered in gold, the glittering jewels, and the precious stones and pearls: for she knew that her beauty was the best guarantee of her absolute power. Other Princesses had simpler tastes; except in state ceremonies, Zoë wore only soft, light dresses, which were better suited to her fair beauty; but on the other hand, she was addicted to the use of perfumes and cosmetics, and in her apartments great fires were kept going summer and winter for the preparation of unguents and perfumes, so that they were rather like an alchemist's laboratory. And there were others who despised all such refinements of luxury, preferring, in the words of a contemporary, "to adorn themselves with the beauty of their virtues," and scorning as unworthy and futile "the cosmetic art beloved of Cleopatra."

Some, like Theodora, thought an exquisitely served table an inalienable privilege of supreme power; while others spent but little on themselves, and took delight in storing money away in great strongboxes. Many were pious; devotional exercises, long vigils before the holy icons, and serious conversations with austere monks, took up much of an Empress's time. Many had a taste for books, and gathered about them a group of men of letters, who composed to their order works in prose and in verse, for which they were always well paid. Occasionally some of these Empresses, such as Athenais and Eudocia, condescended to authorship; and the Princesses of the Comnenian dynasty in particular have the merited reputation of being well educated, scholarly, and learned. Others took pleasure in buffoons and clowns: notwithstanding her intelligence, the great Theodora herself, with her native genius for staging, occasionally got up amusements in doubtful taste, often at the expense of her guests. And, finally, court intrigues and love affairs occupied much of their time, and often even worried the Emperor.

It must not be supposed, however, that a Byzantine Empress divided all her hours between religion, the toilet, receptions, festivities, and holidays. Higher matters often engaged the attention of many of them, and more than once the government felt the power of the Gynaeceum. The Augusta had her private fortune, which she managed as she chose without consulting or even notifying the Basileus; she had her own political opinions, which were not infrequently at variance with those of the sovereign. It is even more surprising in such an autocracy to find that the Emperor gave the Basilissa complete liberty in certain respects, and often was quite ignorant of what went on in her part of the Palace. For the Gynaeceum was the scene of strange and mysterious happenings. When Anthemius, Patriarch of Constantinople, was cited under strong suspicion of heresy to appear before the Council and was excommunicated by the Church and exiled by Justinian, it was in the Palace itself, in Theodora's apartments, that he found refuge. There was some astonishment at first at his sudden disappearance; he was thought to be dead, and finally was forgotten. Great, therefore, was the general amazement when, after the Empress's death, the Patriarch was discovered in the depths of the Gynaeceum; he had lived twelve years in this safe retreat unknown to Justinian and—what is perhaps even more admirable—unbetrayed by Theodora. It was also in the Gynaeceum that the plot was hatched to murder the Emperor Nicephorus Phocas. Without any suspicion on the part of the Basileus, Theophano was able to receive her accomplices, to introduce armed men into the women's quarters, and to hide them so well that when the Emperor, who had been warned at the last moment by an anonymous letter, ordered a search of the Gynaeceum, no one was found, and it was thought that someone had tried to play a practical joke. Two hours later in a stormy night the chief conspirator was hoisted up to the Empress's chamber in a wicker basket, and the Basileus, attacked defenseless in his bedchamber, fell dead, his skull split open by a mighty sword stroke, and his body riddled with wounds.

One obviously must not draw very far-reaching conclusions from such exceptional occurrences. But the extraordinarily significant point is that there was no such impassable barrier as one is apt to imagine between the court of the sovereign and the Empress's apartments. Just as, on the one hand, the Augusta's women received investiture at the hands of the Basileus in the presence of all his courtiers, so the Basilissa permitted many of the high dignitaries, who were by no means "beardless officers," to visit her in her own quarters; and that same Byzantine etiquette which has been represented as so strict and prudish demanded that on certain solemn occasions the Gynaeceum should be open to everyone.

For example, when the new Empress, three days after her wedding, left the bridal chamber to take her bath in the Palace of Magnaura, courtiers and people lined the paths of the garden through which she went with her suite. And as the Basilissa passed along, preceded by attendants bearing dressing gowns, perfumes, boxes, and vessels, and escorted by three maids of honor holding red apples encrusted with pearls, as a symbol of love, the organs played, the people cheered, the court players made coarse jests, and the high officers of state accompanied the Empress to the baths, and waited for her at the door to conduct her back again in pomp to the nuptial chamber.

And several months later, when the Empress gave birth to a son, a week after her delivery the entire court filed past the young mother. In the room, hung for the occasion with gold-embroidered tapestries and glittering with the light of innumerable lamps, the Basilissa lay in a bed covered with golden coverlets, and near her was the cradle of the young heir to the throne. One by one the Praepositus presented to the Augusta the officers of the imperial household, and afterward, according to their rank, the wives of the great court dignitaries, and even the widows of high officials. Last of all came the aristocracy of the Empire, senators, proconsuls, patricians, and officials of all kinds; and each, as he made his obeisance to the Empress, offered his congratulations, and left a little present near the bed for the newborn child.

One can readily see that these are not harem customs; and, in the face of such testimony, is it fair to speak of the strict seclusion of the Gynaeceum, and of the inflexible prudery of Byzantine ceremonial?

IV

A Byzantine Empress spent by no means all her life within the narrow confines of her private dwelling. Official rules of procedure regulated her position in public life, and defined her part beside the Basileus both in the state ceremonies and in the government of the monarchy.

The importance of court ceremonies in the life of a Byzantine Emperor is well known. One of the most curious works transmitted to us from that distant period, and one of the most useful in reconstructing the strange and picturesque aspects of that vanished society, is the *Book of Ceremonies*, written toward the middle of the tenth century by the Emperor Constantine VII. It is entirely devoted to descriptions of the processions, festivals, audiences, and state banquets, which a heavy and inflexible etiquette imposed as duties upon the sovereign. Although the importance attached to these official acts has been often misunderstood, like so many other things in connection with Byzantium—St. Louis, for instance, and even Louis XIV, heard Mass more often than a Basileus—it is nevertheless certain that they constituted a very large part of the business of being Emperor. Now the Empress took part in them constantly. "When there is no Augusta," says a Byzantine historian, "it is impossible to celebrate the festivals and to give the entertainments prescribed by etiquette."

Thus, in the public life of the monarchy, the Empress had her part and her share of royalty. The Emperor naturally left in her hands nearly everything connected with the ladies of the court. On Easter, while the Basileus in the nave of St. Sophia was receiving the high dignitaries of the Empire, who solemnly gave him the kiss of peace in memory of Christ's resurrection, the Empress, enthroned in the women's gallery of the Great Church, surrounded by her chamberlains and bodyguards, received the wives of the high officials according to their husbands' rank; and each in full court dress of silk, covered with jewels and gold, and crowned with the *propoloma*, came and kissed the Empress.

Ceaselessly the recurring festivals gathered this brilliant throng of ladies around the Empress. In November, on the feast of the Brumalia, an ancient pagan survival, the Basilissa in the Pavilion of the Purple presented rich silks to the ladies of the court. On the evening of the same feast day she entertained them elaborately, while the choir from St. Sophia and the Holy Apostles recited poems in her honor, and the court comedians and buffoons amused the company with interludes, and toward the end of dinner representatives of the circus factions with some of the highest state officials performed a slow and stately torch dance before the Augusta and her guests. It was the Empress, again, who assisted the Emperor in the receptions given to foreign Princesses when they visited the Palace at Byzantium. She, as well as the Basileus, gave them audience; she invited them and the women of their suites to dine with her; she showered them with gifts and attentions. In this way she had a certain part in the foreign policy of the monarchy, and on the graciousness of her welcome depended many of the successes of the imperial diplomacy.

But official etiquette by no means limited the Basilissa to the reception of ladies. She often assisted the Emperor her husband still more directly. On Palm Sunday she received with him. At court banquets she sat at table with him, among the senators and high dignitaries honored by a command to the imperial entertainment. And since, according to etiquette, she had her share in the prescribed acclamations with which the populace were in the habit of saluting their rulers, she did not hesitate to show herself in public with the Basileus. In the Hippodrome on the occasions of the principal races, and in front of the Sacred Palace at the performance of certain political ceremonies of great importance, the multitude chanted: "Appear with the Augustae, O God-crowned Em-

perors!" and again: "O God-protected pair, O Basileus, and
thou, Glory of the Purple, come and enlighten your slaves,
and rejoice the hearts of your people!" and again: "Come
forth, Empress of the Romans!"—all of them meaningless
phrases if the Basilissa was not in the habit of showing herself on those days in the box in the Hippodrome or on the balcony of the Palace. It was even so little the custom for her to
confine herself to the imperial residence that she often appeared in public without the Emperor. Thus, she used to go
without him in solemn procession to St. Sophia; she made her
state entrance into the capital without him; she went to meet
him on his return from military expeditions. For a Byzantine
Empress was something more than the consort and associate
of the Emperor: the great part which she so often played in
politics is due to the fact that from the day that she was first
enthroned upon the throne of Constantine she received the
fullness of imperial power.

V

In Byzantium reasons of state had, as a rule, little effect
upon the Emperor's choice of a consort. The monarch selected his wife in a more original and somewhat extraordinary fashion.

When the Empress Irene wished to find a wife for her son
Constantine, she sent messengers up and down the Empire
to seek out the most beautiful girls in the monarchy and bring
them to the capital. With a view to limiting the choice and
facilitating the task of her envoys, the Empress indicated
carefully what she considered the suitable age of candidates
to be, as well as their height and their size in shoes. After receiving these instructions the messengers set out, and one
evening arrived in a Paphlagonian village. Seeing in the dis-

tance a large and splendid mansion which had the appearance of belonging to a rich landowner, they decided to pass
the night there. Their choice was unfortunate; the proprietor
was a saint, who had completely ruined himself by his alms-
giving to the poor. Nevertheless, he welcomed the Emperor's
envoys with great hospitality, and calling his wife said:
"Serve us up a good dinner." Her resources being somewhat
limited, she answered: "How can I? You have managed your
affairs so well that we haven't so much as a single fowl in the
yard." "Go light your fire," the saint replied, "get ready the
great dining hall, and set the old ivory table; God will provide our dinner." God did provide; and when the envoys, who
were delighted at the way in which they had been made welcome, questioned the old man over the dessert about his family, they found that he had three granddaughters of marriageable age. "In the name of the God-crowned Emperor,"
they exclaimed, "show them to us, for there is not in all the
Roman Empire a young girl whom we have not seen." The
girls were sent for and proved to be charming; and it happened that one of them, Mary, was of the required age and
proportions and wore shoes of the specified size.

The messengers were delighted with their find, and took
the whole family with them to Constantinople. About a dozen
other young girls had been assembled there, all very pretty,
and most of them of rich and noble families. At first these
beautiful creatures rather despised the newcomer; but she,
who was by no means a fool, said one day to her companions:
"Girls, let's make an agreement that whichever of us shall be
chosen by God to be Empress shall help the others to find
husbands." Whereupon a general's daughter scornfully answered: "Oh, indeed! I am the richest, the best born, and the
most beautiful; the Emperor will undoubtedly marry me.
None of the rest of you need have any hopes, for you have no

families to speak of, and nothing but your pretty faces."
Needless to say, she was punished for her disdain. When the
candidates were brought before the Empress, her son, and
the Prime Minister, she was immediately told: "You are
charming; but you are not the wife for an Emperor." Mary,
on the other hand, instantly won the young sovereign's heart,
and he chose her.

There are other similar anecdotes to show that this was
the usual manner of choosing a Byzantine Empress, though
sometimes the sovereign simplified matters even more by
taking a fancy to some beautiful adventuress, as did Justinian to Theodora. One can see at all events that the Basileis
did not insist upon noble birth, and that in their eyes any
pretty woman might make a suitable Empress. But it is also
noteworthy that the solemn ceremonies accompanying the
coronation and marriage gave the future Empress an entirely
new character, and made of the poor girl of yesterday a superhuman being, the incarnation of power and holiness.

I shall not describe in detail the pompous ceremonies—for
all these Byzantine functions are somewhat alike in their mo-
notonous magnificence—with which the future Empress was
conducted veiled into the great hall of the Augustaeum to be
invested by the Emperor with the purple chlamys, which the
Patriarch had already blessed; nor shall I tell how the sovereign placed upon her head the crown with long diamond
pendants; nor of the court reception in the Palace Chapel of
St. Stephen; nor shall I describe the wedding, when the Patriarch placed the nuptial crown upon the heads of the newly
married pair. Out of all the complicated ritual it will be
enough to point out a few salient features, which will clearly
indicate the complete sovereignty implied in the glorious title
of Empress of Byzantium.

In the first place, the marriage follows the coronation instead of preceding it. It is not as the Emperor's wife that the Empress shares the autocratic power; it is no reflected authority that she receives from her husband. By a premarital and independent act she is invested with sovereign powers; and this sovereignty, to which she, like the Emperor, is raised by God's actual choice, is equal in plenitude to that of the Basileus. And so true is this, that it is not the Emperor who presents the new Empress to the people. After the imposition of the crown has conferred supreme power upon her, she goes forth unaccompanied by the sovereign, and escorted only by her chamberlains and her women. Slowly, between the ranks of guardsmen, senators, patricians, and high dignitaries, she passes through the Palace and goes out upon the terrace, beneath which are stationed the members of the high public services, the soldiers, and the people. Aloft in her rich imperial robes, glittering with gold embroideries, she shows herself to her new subjects and makes herself solemnly known to them. Before her the colors are dipped, grandees and people prostrate themselves, their heads in the dust, and the factions raise the time-honored acclamations. Very reverently, a candle in either hand, she first bows before the cross; then she greets her people, while a unanimous cry goes up: "God save the Augusta!"

Here is another instance. The coronation of the Empress, indeed, is surrounded with somewhat more mystery than that of the Emperor, for instead of being celebrated in St. Sophia it takes place in the Palace. But one should not imagine this to be the effect of certain so-called Byzantine notions "which imposed," we are told, "a life of seclusion upon the wife, and accorded ill with much publicity." As a matter of fact, all the courtiers, men and women alike, are present at her coronation; and, when at the conclusion of the ceremony the sovereigns hold a reception in St. Stephen's Church, there are not, as is sometimes thought, two separate receptions, the Basileus receiving the men, and the Augusta the women. First all the men and then all the women of the court pass before the thrones on which the Emperor and Empress are seated side by side. And after being presented, each in turn, men as well as women, supported under the arms by two silentiaries, prostrates himself and kisses the knees of the Basileus and of the Augusta.

Here is yet another instance. After their marriage in St. Stephen's the imperial pair are escorted to the bridal chamber by the entire court, both men and women. The people make a lane for them as they go, and salute the new Basilissa as follows: "Welcome, God-chosen Augusta! Welcome, God-protected Augusta! Welcome, Wearer of the Purple! Welcome, thou whom all desire!" The crowd is admitted into the nuptial chamber itself, before the imperial bed of gold, and the newly married couple have to listen to the acclamations and congratulations all over again. And in the evening at the wedding banquet, the greatest nobles of the court—those who are styled Friends of the Emperor—and the greatest ladies dine with the sovereigns in the Triclinium of the Nineteen Couches. What strikes one most in all these ceremonies is the freedom of association between men and women in this court which has been stigmatized as prudish; and also how little secluded is the life of such an Empress, who is required by official etiquette as the first act of her reign to show her face to all the people of Byzantium.

We must, of course, guard against overstating the case. In these delicate matters, custom and etiquette naturally varied with the times. It seems, indeed, that toward the end of the ninth century and during the tenth, perhaps under the influence of the Mohammedan East, a stricter etiquette confined the Empress more closely to the Gynaeceum, that she veiled

herself more, that she appeared less frequently in public ceremonies. But between the fifth and ninth centuries there is no
trace of anything of the sort; and when, from the end of the
eleventh century onward, Byzantium came day by day into
closer contact with the West, when Western princesses sat
upon the throne of Constantine, this rigidity of etiquette, if it
had ever existed, broke down, and the ancient ceremonial
perished.

One last example will serve to illustrate fully the rights
which law and custom conferred upon a Byzantine Empress.
When the Emperor Zeno died in the year 491, his widow, the
Empress Ariadne, seized the power firmly in her own hands,
and, going forth from the Palace to the Hippodrome with the
great dignitaries of court and monarchy, stood up in the imperial box in her robes of state and addressed the assembled
people. She told them that by her order the Senate and the
high officials were about to meet, and that under her presi-
dency, they, together with the army, would choose a successor to the deceased Emperor. As a matter of fact, the supreme
council of the Empire did meet in the Palace; but its first act
was to leave in Ariadne's hands the choice of the new sovereign. Extraordinary as such procedure may seem, one must
be careful not to regard it as revolutionary. The Augusta, legitimately invested with supreme power from the day of her
coronation, exercises it legitimately in all its fullness, and
transmits it as it pleases her. The people in ratifying her
choice formally recognize her rights. "Thine is the imperial
power, Ariadne Augusta," cried the multitude. And the experienced minister who in the sixth century edited the ceremonial code from which this story is taken says explicitly
that the question of the succession becomes extraordinarily
difficult "when there is neither Augusta nor Emperor to
transmit the power."

And therefore it is that in every act involving a change in the government of the monarchy, the election or the association of a new Basileus, the Basilissa always appears officially, showing herself in the Hippodrome, haranguing the people, energetic and active, without anyone's being at all astonished or scandalized. Since the power was vested in her, she could as her fancy directed either create a new Emperor, or rule as Regent in the name of her young children, or even reign herself. At a time when the Germanic West would have been indignant at the idea of a woman reigning, oriental Byzantium accepted peacefully an Empress who in her official documents proudly styled herself as a man: "Irene, great Basileus and Autocrat of the Romans."

Byzantine miniatures have preserved the portraits of many of these Princesses of long ago. They are of many different physical types, for as a matter of fact every nation gave Empresses to Byzantium—Europe and Asia, the Caucasus and Greece, Constantinople and the provinces, Syria and Hungary, France and Germany, and even the barbarous Khazars and Bulgars. In like manner they show equally profound differences of character: "Among those Augustae," as has been well said, "was every conceivable type of woman—politicians, like Theodora or Irene of Athens; writers, like Eudocia or Anna Comnena; women of pleasure, like Zoë the Porphyrogenita; and others pure and devout, like her sister Theodora; some who cared only for concocting new combinations of perfumes and elegancies of toilet, or for inventing gowns and coiffures to revolutionize Byzantine feminine society; some whom no one ever talked of and others about whom there was too much talk; some whose doors were opened only to pious monks and zealot priests; others who welcomed buffoons and storytellers; and some whose windows opened now and again to drop out a human body sewn in a sack into the silent waters of the Bosphorus." [2] To understand them, we must therefore not be deceived either by the sumptuous uniformity of the imperial costume that they wore, or by the apparently rigid ceremonial which may seem to have regulated their lives. Their natures differed, and so did the parts they played; and it is precisely this which constitutes their interest for us.

In the history of a vanished society it is not the wars, picturesque as they may be, nor the palace revolutions and barrack mutinies, though they were often tragic enough, which should engage our chief attention. The most fruitful procedure is to endeavor to reconstruct the varying aspects of daily life, the different ways of living and thinking, the manners and customs—the civilization, in short. On all of these the life of a Byzantine Empress may perhaps shed some new light; and, in restoring her to the historical setting and in reconstructing the surroundings in which she lived, we may have accomplished a not wholly useless task. From these seemingly restricted studies there will emerge a more general impression, and with it some vivid, picturesque scenes from the little-known society of distant Byzantium.

[2] A. N. Rambaud, loc. cit., p. 838.

ATHENAIS

I

On the 7th of June 421, the Most Pious Emperor Theodosius, then about twenty years of age, married a young girl who came from Athens, where her father had been a professor in the university. She was born of pagan parents; but in order to ascend the throne of Constantine she had become a Christian, and on the day of her baptism had changed her pretty name Athenais to Eudocia, a name at once more Christian and more suited to her imperial rank.

How did this astonishing marriage between a little provincial girl and the all-powerful Basileus come about? The answer is simple. It was a love match, and the Byzantine chroniclers have fortunately given us the whole romantic story. The young Theodosius, from the time he had reached man's estate, had contemplated marriage. He pestered his eldest sister Pulcheria, who had brought him up and governed the Empire in his name, and insisted that she should find a wife for him. Neither birth nor wealth mattered; but he insisted that she should be beautiful, supremely beautiful, with a beauty such as Byzantium had never before beheld. And so to please him Pulcheria searched all the East without finding anyone possessed of the requisite perfections. Paulinus, the friend of her childhood, the Emperor's crony, also made investigations, when chance unexpectedly threw in their way the longed-for beauty.

Leontius, a professor at the University of Athens, had two sons and a daughter. He was a rich man. But when he came to die, he left his fortune, by a curious whim, to his sons Valerius and Gesius. "To my beloved daughter Athenais," he wrote in his will, "I bequeath one hundred pieces of gold. To succeed in the world she will have her good luck, which is better than any other woman's." In vain Athenais begged her brothers to share their father's estate with her; she was obliged to leave home and seek refuge with her mother's sister, who took her to Constantinople, where another aunt, Leontius's sister, lived. These two women persuaded the girl to invoke the help of the Palace against her brothers, and she obtained an audience of the Augusta Pulcheria. Athenais was twenty years of age. She was very beautiful, being rather tall, with a wonderful figure, and curly blond hair that framed her features in a golden aureole and enhanced the brilliancy of her fair complexion. Her lovely eyes were intelligent and full of life, and she kept them modestly lowered. She had a pure Greek nose, and she carried herself with grace and dignity. Furthermore, she could express herself well, and stated her request to perfection. She made an immediate conquest of Pulcheria, who was enthusiastic about her. The Augusta asked the girl a few questions about her family and her past life, and soon ran to tell her brother of the marvelous creature she had discovered. Theodosius in great excitement was smitten with Athenais from his sister's description, and begged the Augusta to show him the young enchantress at once. So he hid himself behind a tapestry with his friend Paulinus, and waited for the young petitioner to enter the room. The effect she made upon the two young men was prodigious; Paulinus was delighted, and the Emperor fell completely in love with her. A few weeks later, after the Patriarch Atticus had instructed her in the Christian religion and purified her in the waters of baptism, Athenais-Eudocia became Empress of Byzantium.

It is difficult to say how much truth there is in this charming tale. The outlines of it do not appear before the eleventh century and are greatly elaborated by the fancy of later periods. Contemporary historians know nothing of the details I have just given. The only undoubted fact is that the new Empress was born an Athenian and a pagan, and that she was very pretty and perfectly educated. That was sufficient to captivate Theodosius, who was in any case anxious for political reasons to perpetuate the dynasty; and one can understand, moreover, that the ambitious Pulcheria, who was supreme, and anxious to preserve her supremacy, should wish to further a marriage in which the bride would owe everything to her. She was her godmother; she wished to adopt her; and she may well have thought that in the circumstances there would be no changes in the Sacred Palace.

II

At the time when Athenais-Eudocia became the consort of Theodosius, life in the Imperial Palace at Byzantium presented a peculiar appearance. For seven years Pulcheria, a young woman of twenty-two, the eldest sister of the Basileus, had ruled over it with complete authority. She was astute, energetic, ambitious, and essentially a politician. After the death of Arcadius, she, as the oldest member of the family, had carried on the government during her brother's minority, and in 414, at the age of fifteen, had taken the title of Augusta, thereby regularizing her assumption of power. Being anxious to devote herself without hindrance to her task— also, perhaps, not wishing to share the authority with another —she had made a vow, at the age of sixteen, never to marry, and as a memorial of her promise had dedicated in St. Sophia a golden table adorned with precious stones. And, as she was very religious, she had reformed the court and turned the Palace into a monastery. Under the influence of the Patriarch Atticus, Pulcheria's two sisters, Arcadia and Marina, had followed her example and taken the vow of celibacy. And the suites of these pious Princesses so modeled themselves upon them that, night and day, hymns and religious exercises were constantly in progress in the imperial dwelling. Instead of gorgeous ceremonies and splendid costumes, military processions and the cheers of the multitude, nothing was heard but the intoning of the offices, nothing seen but the somber habit of priests and monks. The Palace, now purged of the licentious courtiers who had dishonored it, and carefully ruled in every detail according to grave and holy precepts, presented a totally new appearance. Disdaining luxury, beautiful clothes, and the idleness characteristic of high rank, these Princesses worked with their own hands, spinning and sewing for the poor, extending their charities and their good works. Pulcheria founded churches and gave vast endowments to hospitals and charitable institutions; her sisters imitated her. A great gust of piety, charity, and renunciation reinvigorated the Sacred Palace and swept away the old atmosphere of intrigue.

It was in this atmosphere that Pulcheria had brought up the young Theodosius. Highly educated herself—she knew

both Greek and Latin, an accomplishment already rare at
that period—she had surrounded him with excellent masters
and carefully chosen companions. He profited by his good
teaching, and was really a very learned young man. He had
been taught Greek and Latin, astronomy, mathematics, natural history, and many other things; he could draw and paint,
and was fond of illuminating his manuscripts with beautiful
miniatures. He had a taste for reading, and had formed a
large library, and in the evening liked to work very late by
the light of a lamp that he had invented. His reward is to be
known in history as Theodosius the Calligrapher. But Pulcheria had watched even more carefully over her brother's
moral education. He was very devout, he took pleasure in
singing hymns with his sisters, he fasted regularly twice a
week, and he liked to dispute with theologians. Pulcheria herself had even given him lessons in deportment; she had
taught him how an Emperor should wear his clothes, how he
should receive people, when to smile and when to appear
grave and serious—in short all the refinements of ceremonial
that an Emperor was obliged to know. And thus, at the time
of his marriage, Theodosius was a nice young fellow, of
medium height, fair, with black eyes, very well brought up,
very polite, quiet, gentle, and amiable, and somewhat of a
bore and a pedant. Of physical exercises, he cared only for
hunting, and, not being particularly energetic, was not in the
least attracted by war and fighting. He was of a sedentary
disposition and preferred to stay in the Palace; and, as his
character was feeble, he was easily influenced. In short, he
was a conscientious and mediocre Emperor, good enough
perhaps for quiet times, but totally unsuited for the troubled
century in which he lived.

Between her imperious sister-in-law and her easy-going
husband, what would become of Athenais? It must not be

forgotten that she too was a clever woman. At the time of her birth Athens, her native city, was still the great university town of the Hellenic East, the finest museum of ancient Greece, the last refuge of pagan learning. As a professor's daughter she naturally had received an incomparable education. Her father had taught her rhetoric; had made her learn the masterpieces of ancient literature, Homer, the tragic poets, Lysias, and Demosthenes; had trained her, in the manner of the schools, to improvise brilliantly on given subjects, to compose pretty verses, to speak with elegance. Furthermore, she had been initiated into the mysteries of the Neoplatonic philosophy, whose most illustrious exponents had been made welcome in Athens; she also knew astronomy and geometry, and succeeded equally in everything. She pleased Pulcheria by her intelligence and her gift of expression, and one may well believe that she delighted Theodosius as much by her erudition as by her beauty.

The education that Athenais had received was an altogether pagan one, and the thin veneer of Christianity which the Patriarch had applied to her soul failed, in all probability, to impair in any way the teachings of her youth. Moreover, among people who remained faithful to ancient ideas, the Emperor's marriage with the young Athenian may well have appeared as a victory for paganism, or, at the least, as a promise of toleration. And, in fact, the Empress did not at first differ materially from the daughter of Leontius.

Indeed, Constantinople in the fifth century, notwithstanding its position as a Christian capital, retained a strong impress of paganism. It had been enriched by Constantine and his successors with the finest spoils of ancient sanctuaries; its squares and its palaces were adorned with the most renowned masterpieces of Greek sculpture; and in this incomparable museum the dethroned gods seemed still to retain their prestige and their glory. At the court, in spite of the dominant tone of religion and bigotry, many ceremonies and festivals preserved the memory of pagan traditions; and, although pious folk considered any dealings with the Graces and the Muses a mortal sin, poetry was by no means exiled from the Imperial Palace. Eudocia was fond of verses and took pleasure in composing them, and she found about her people to share her tastes and encourage her in them. One of her first acts immediately after her marriage was to compose a poem in heroic verse upon the Persian War, which had just been brought to a successful conclusion. She could have done nothing better calculated to please Theodosius and win completely the love of her studious husband. When, toward the end of the year 422, she in addition bore him a daughter, her influence increased still more; on the 2nd of January 423, the Basileus gave her, as a New Year's present, the title of Augusta, thus making her officially the equal of Pulcheria. And in the privacy of the imperial family her ascendancy over her weak husband grew steadily greater.

It is not unlikely that she had a voice in the foundation, in the year 425, of the University of Constantinople. In it we can see the preponderating position given to Greek: whereas thirteen professors taught the Latin language and literature, fifteen were appointed to teach Greek; one chair was created in philosophy; and the most eminent men of the times, some of them very recent Christians, were invited to lecture at the new university. It should, however, be observed that, if the foundation of a university and the consideration thereby shown to letters are characteristic of the taste of the period, the new institution had in general a Christian tone—witness the subordinate position given to philosophy—and was intended by its founders to be in a sense a rival to the too pagan University of Athens. And this illustrates vividly the evolution which was slowly taking place in the soul of the Empress Eudocia.

Living in the devout atmosphere of the court, she felt unconsciously the influence of her surroundings. Her marriage may have seemed a victory for paganism, but as a matter of fact she had done nothing for her former co-religionists; and in 424, the Emperor Theodosius, in renewing the edicts of proscription against the worship of the false gods, declared solemnly that he "thought there were no longer any pagans." A further significant fact is that Eudocia, like a true Byzantine, developed a passion for theological disputes. When in 428 Nestorius, Patriarch of Constantinople, taught the heresy which bears his name, and the ambitious Cyril, Patriarch of Alexandria, more from jealousy of a rival than from devotion to Orthodoxy, thereupon started a serious quarrel in the Eastern Church, Eudocia joined with her husband in championing the Patriarch of the capital against his enemies, and tried to checkmate the turbulent successor of Athanasius, whose chief aim was to establish a primacy for his see over all the Eastern bishoprics. This episode is valuable not only as an illustration of the part which Athenais-Eudocia played in religious quarrels, but also as a proof of her increasing influence and of the breach that was widening between her and Pulcheria.

In arranging her brother's marriage, the imperious Augusta had had no intention of resigning the power that Theodosius had permitted her to exercise. Nevertheless, Eudocia's star waxed ever more powerful. She advanced her friends and relatives in the sovereign's favor; she used her influence on behalf of Paulinus, the Master of the Offices, and also the Egyptian Cyrus of Panopolis, who, like her, was fond of books and wrote verses; she had her flatterers and her party at court, and soon she was not afraid to oppose her sister-in-law. Rumors of this underground rivalry spread beyond the Palace, and clever intriguers egged the two women on in the hope of gaining some personal advantage. Cyril, especially, made use of it in his quarrel with Nestorius; when writing to the Emperor and his wife, he wrote also to the Augusta Pulcheria, whom he knew to be hostile to his rival, and whose influence with the weak Basileus he counted upon. But even though Theodosius reproved him in very energetic terms for his conduct, saying: "Either you thought that my wife, my sister, and I, were not in harmony with one another, or Your Piety hoped that your letters might sow dissension between us"—notwithstanding this protest, the results proved that Cyril had not been mistaken in his calculations. Theodosius, after having convoked the Council of Ephesus with the firm intention of upholding Nestorius, allowed himself finally to be imposed upon by Cyril's illegal audacity, by the clamor of the monks of Constantinople, by the advice of the high dignitaries whom the Patriarch of Alexandria had won over, and above all by the influence of Pulcheria. The gathering of 431 was a victory for the Alexandrians and a triumph for the imperious Augusta. For Eudocia it was a serious reverse; she was later to suffer even more cruelly from the consequences of these court rivalries, and from the struggle for influence in which she was engaged.

III

The journey which Athenais-Eudocia made in the year 438 to Jerusalem provides interesting testimony regarding the outstanding feature of her personality: the mixture in her soul of pagan memories and Christian preoccupations.

In 423 the court of Constantinople had received an important visitor. The celebrated Galla Placidia, half sister of

Honorius and aunt of Theodosius II, having been obliged to
leave the Palace at Ravenna, had come with her daughter
Honoria and her young son Valentinian to take refuge in
Byzantium. A marriage had been proposed between the imperial children, the newborn Eudoxia and the five-year-old
Caesar, who was now, by the death of Honorius, heir to the
Western Empire. Theodosius II spared no pains to procure
the recognition of his future son-in-law in Italy, under the
guardianship of Galla Placidia. Fourteen years later, in 437,
the cherished scheme was fulfilled. Athenais-Eudocia had
ardently desired this alliance, which would set her daughter
upon the glorious throne of the West, and had vowed, if the
marriage took place, to make a pilgrimage to Jerusalem, like
St. Helen before her, to give thanks to God in the very place
where His divine Son had died for mankind. Her necessary
separation from a child whom she adored made her perhaps
the more willing to undertake the journey, and in 438 the
Empress set out for the Holy City.

The first place she visited was Antioch. This city, which
was still full of the traditions and monuments of ancient civilization, awoke within her the memories of her pagan youth.
In the Senate House, seated on a golden throne that glittered
with precious stones, she received the civic magistrates and
the principal inhabitants, and, recalling her father's teachings, improvised a brilliant speech in honor of the city whose
guest she was. She alluded to the distant age when Greek col-
onies had carried Hellenic civilization throughout the archi-
pelago as far as the coasts of Syria, and ended by quoting a
line of Homer:

I claim proud kinship with your race and blood.

The Antiochenes were too cultivated and too fond of letters
not to be wildly enthusiastic about a Princess who thus in-

voked the purest traditions of Hellenism. And, as in the
splendid days of ancient Greece, the municipal senate voted
her a golden statue in the Curia, and deposited in the museum
a bronze stele inscribed with a record of the imperial visit.

Her stay in Jerusalem is in striking contrast with this vision of antiquity. Jerusalem was essentially a Christian city,
full of pious memories of the Saviour, peopled with religious
of both sexes, and covered with churches and monasteries
built over all the spots which the Passion of Christ had hal-
lowed. Eudocia remained there an entire year devoting herself to religion and good works, visiting the Holy Places,
attending the consecration of churches, and distributing rich
gifts among the most venerated sanctuaries. In return, she
obtained precious relics—some of the bones of St. Stephen
and the chains with which the Apostle Peter had been bound.
These she brought piously from Jerusalem to Constantinople
and deposited them with ceremony in the Church of St. Law-
rence. Half of the chains she sent to her beloved daughter in
Rome, the young Empress Eudoxia, the thought of whom
had inspired and accompanied her on her voyage, and the
Church of San Pietro in Vincoli was built to receive them.

A few years later Athenais-Eudocia was to return to the
Holy City of Jerusalem, and this time for the rest of her life.

In 439, at the time of her return to the capital, the Basilissa was at the height of her glory. Her daughter was married to an Emperor, and she herself had just made a royal
progress through the East amidst universal rejoicing. She
seems to have thought that the time was ripe for a more overt
struggle with her former benefactress and present rival, the
Augusta Pulcheria. At all events, between 439 and 441, her
friends became increasingly influential in the Palace; the office of Praetorian Praefect of the East was given to her protégé Cyrus of Panopolis, a poet and man of letters whose es-

sentially Hellenic culture had been for some time past a bond
between him and the Empress. Such a man could never commend himself to Pulcheria and the religious party, and it was
thus a personal triumph for Eudocia to have won him the favor of Theodosius. This success encouraged her to go still
further. In the Sacred Palace at that period, the eunuchs had
great influence over the irresolute Emperor; Eudocia joined
forces with Chrysaphius, the favorite for the time being, in
order to effect the definite removal of Pulcheria from the government; and for a while she seemed to have won. The Augusta was obliged to leave court and retire to her own house;
but, while appearing to abdicate, Pulcheria never abandoned
the struggle. Her orthodox friends, disliking the new direction of affairs and the favor shown to statesmen of over-
liberal opinions, were in the end to make Eudocia pay dearly
for her ephemeral victory.

The story of her downfall is no less romantic than that of
her elevation to the throne. Paulinus, the Master of the Offices, was a great favorite of the Emperor's, with whom he
had played as a child and whose confidence he had won; and
he was equally a friend of the Empress's, since he had used
all his influence to bring about her marriage. The Basileus
had chosen him to be his "best man" at his wedding, and
thereafter had loaded him with honors. Paulinus was on
terms of the greatest intimacy with the sovereigns, whom he
visited freely whenever he chose, and his influence was powerful in the Palace. Now, Paulinus was handsome, elegant,
and of haughty carriage; he is said to have made an impression even upon the austere Pulcheria herself. The enemies of
Athenais were not slow in making capital out of all this; the
passionate devotion of the Master of the Offices to the Basilissa and the real friendship which she showed for him
became in their hands weapons to arouse the jealousy of

Theodosius and thereby to produce the most unfortunate results.

The Emperor, so runs the tale, went to church one day, and Paulinus, who was unwell, was excused from taking part in the solemn procession. On the way a beggar offered the Emperor a Phrygian apple of extraordinary size. Theodosius bought it, and, as he was still devotedly attached to his wife, sent it to her. She, in turn, made a present of it to Paulinus, and the Master of the Offices, not knowing who had given it to the Empress, offered it to Theodosius, thinking to please him. The Emperor was astonished, and, as soon as he had returned to the Palace, summoned the Empress and blurted out: "Where is the apple I sent you?" "I have eaten it," replied Eudocia imprudently. For the sake of her salvation, Theodosius adjured her to tell him the truth, but she gave him the same answer. Then, taking the apple out from under his cloak, the Basileus showed it to his untruthful wife. There followed a violent scene. Furiously jealous, the Emperor ceased to live with his wife; and Paulinus was completely disgraced and exiled to Caesarea in Cappadocia, where soon afterward Theodosius had him assassinated.

Here again it is difficult to determine with any degree of certainty what truth there may be in the story. The oldest accounts of it that we have date only from the sixth century, and contemporaries knew nothing of it, or at least did not record it. The main features, however, have an air of verisimilitude. It is not necessary to assume that Eudocia was guilty of anything other than imprudence; many years later, when on her deathbed and about to appear before her Maker, she swore that she and Paulinus had been absolutely innocent. But the fury and jealousy of Theodosius speedily resulted in the Empress's disgrace. Her enemies made good use of the affair to regain their influence over the Emperor. After the dis-

grace of Paulinus came that of Eudocia's other friend, the
Praefect Cyrus. At last, knowing that her influence was
gone, almost openly quarreling with her husband, alone, suspected in her own court, exasperated furthermore by the slan-
ders which were circulated about her, and justly outraged by
the odious murder of Paulinus, she sought permission of
Theodosius to retire to Jerusalem. The Emperor accorded it
gladly, and may even have urged her to go. He felt henceforth only hatred, suspicion, and bitterness for her, and
found it easy to separate forever from the wife he once had
loved so much.

It was about the year 442 that Eudocia returned to the
Holy City, and she lived there eighteen long years until her
death. This sad and melancholy end of her life seems to have
strangely altered the Princess's character. She had hoped, on
leaving Constantinople, to find peace and forgetfulness at the
tomb of Christ; but even in her distant exile she was pursued
by the rancor of enemies, and her husband's suspicions brutally invaded the calm of her retreat. In 444, two of her intimate friends, the priest Severus and the deacon John, whom
she had taken with her from Byzantium and who had great
influence with her, were denounced to the Emperor, arrested,
and put to death. The Empress, furious at the outrage, revenged herself by bloodshed: Saturninus, the governor of
Jerusalem, was murdered by assassins whom she had hired.
Afterward her passionate nature sought other means of satisfying its restlessness. She devoted herself to religion, living
among ascetics and monks, and became an adherent of the
most mystical form of Christian theology. The little pagan
girl of Athens took sides with the Monophysites, who at this
very period were winning a victory for their doctrine, under
Dioscorus of Alexandria, at the Conciliabulum of Ephesus
(449), and forcing their will upon Theodosius. It may be

that she hoped by associating with them to revenge herself in some way upon the Emperor, upon Pulcheria, and upon those who had brought about her disgrace. Whatever the reason, she threw herself heart and soul into the struggle, and put all that was left of her influence and wealth at the service of her friends. Even after the Council of Chalcedon in 450, concurrently with the Roman legates, had solemnly condemned her favorite heresy, she clung to it obstinately, perhaps because it still pleased her to oppose Pulcheria, whom she hated, and who, now that Theodosius was dead, shared Eudocia's throne with a Prince Consort. The Basilissa eagerly encouraged the dissenters, and incited them to armed resistance to the imperial forces. The representations of her daughter and of her son-in-law, and the entreaties of Pope Leo the Great himself, were necessary to bring Eudocia back to Orthodoxy.

She yielded at last to the pontiff's admonitions, and, to win the "eternal glory" which he promised her, she used all her remaining influence to pacify the Palestinian monks who had risen against their bishops, and to guide penitent heretics to the faith of Chalcedon (453). Every year as it passed brought fresh sorrows to the aged woman. Her husband Theodosius died in 450, and in 455 her sister-in-law Pulcheria followed him: her condition as a dethroned Empress remained unchanged. In the West, during the sack of Rome in 455, her daughter Eudoxia and her granddaughters had fallen into the hands of the Vandals, and one of them had been forced to marry Genseric. In the East, another dynasty had replaced the family of Theodosius the Great upon the throne of Byzantium. Eudocia, now no longer of any importance, was forgotten. In the Holy City, which she loved, she found consolation in building hospitals, convents, and churches, in repairing the city wall, and in writing verses— the last vestige of her early taste for letters. Thus engaged,

she died about the year 460, and was buried in the Basilica of
St. Stephen, which she had founded; and the grateful people
of Jerusalem gave to her who had done so much for their city
the title of "the New Helen."

IV

Athenais-Eudocia had indeed a strange career: she was
born in Athens a pagan; through a love match she became
Empress of Byzantium; and she died in exile at Jerusalem
near the tomb of Christ, a devoted and impassioned Christian
mystic. And it is just because of these contrasts in her romantic and melancholy life that she is of such interest to the historian. Placed on the borders of two worlds, at the meeting
point of two civilizations, combining in herself the dying traditions of pagan culture with the precepts of victorious Christianity, and having withal sufficient intelligence and education to understand the evolution in process around her, she
presents a curious and significant example of the way in
which the most contradictory ideas and the most violent contrasts could, in that century, exist side by side in a single
personality. Her life has already demonstrated the fusion
of these diverse elements; in her writings it is even more
apparent.

Eudocia had always loved poetry. In the period of her
greatness she had, as we have seen, celebrated in heroic verse
the victories won by the imperial armies over the Persians,
and her eulogy of Antioch may have been composed in verse.
In the last years of her life she once more diverted herself
with literary exercises, but this time she was inspired exclusively by religious subjects. She translated into heroic verse
parts of the Old Testament, the Pentateuch, Joshua, Judges,
and Ruth; even in the ninth century so good a literary critic

as the Patriarch Photius admired her work greatly, and considered it quite remarkable "for a woman, and an Empress at that." She also made similar translations of the prophecies of Zechariah and of Daniel which the grammarian Tzetzes highly commends, referring to the talent of "the golden Empress, the very learned daughter of the great Leontius." Moreover, she composed the *Homerocentra*, or Homeric Centos, in which she undertook to tell the episodes of the life of Christ by means of Homeric verses ingeniously assembled. That happened to be a style of composition greatly esteemed in her time, and Eudocia, as she herself acknowledged, was only continuing the work of one of her contemporaries, Bishop Patricius. It must, however, be admitted, in spite of the praises which Byzantine critics of later times bestowed upon the imperial labors, that her production was of no great value. At bottom it has no sort of originality of any kind, and, notwithstanding Eudocia's vaunt that she "had made the sacred stories harmonious," the form is no better. Her language is feeble and her versification mediocre. In short, the only interesting and characteristic feature of the work is the attempt to clothe the life of Christ with the rhythm and language of Homer, thus achieving a strange union of pagan and Christian elements. There would therefore be very little to say about the writings of Athenais-Eudocia if she was not the author of a more curious work—namely, a poem in three cantos on St. Cyprian of Antioch, which was much admired by Photius, and of which some important fragments have been preserved.

According to the legend, Cyprian of Antioch was a celebrated magician. One day a young pagan, Aglaidas, came to ask him to use his mysterious science on his behalf. He loved a Christian maiden, Justina, who did not reciprocate his affection, and saw no means other than diabolical of overcoming her resistance. Cyprian consented, and to vanquish the virgin put forth all his powers to such effect that he himself soon succumbed to Justina's radiant beauty. All the magician's attempts were in vain; the demons whom he invoked fled before the sign of the cross which the young girl made. At last, becoming convinced of the vanity of his horrid arts, Cyprian burned his books of magic, gave all his goods to the poor, and embraced Christianity. The defeated lover did likewise. Finally, the repentant magician became Bishop of Antioch, and with Justina bravely underwent martyrdom for his faith.

The most interesting part of the poem that I have briefly outlined is the second book, containing Cyprian's confession. When the time had come for him to abjure his errors, the learned pagan determined to make the story of his life public and to tell the assembled people all that he had gathered from the magic arts of paganism, all the sinful things he had done with the accursed help of the demons, and how in the end, when his soul was enlightened, he had come to repent and be converted. In the course of his long recital, Cyprian explains how he had been initiated in all the holy places of paganism: at Athens and at Eleusis; upon Olympus,

Where foolish mortals say the false gods live;

at Argos and in Phrygia, where the augur's art is taught; in Egypt and in Chaldaea, where one can learn the mysteries of astrology. Forcefully he tells how he had studied

Those fleeting forms that ape the eternal wisdom;

how he had fed upon that ancient and baneful science spread abroad by demons, to the undoing of the human race. By his accursed skill he had been able to raise up even the Prince of Demons, who had

Given the lordship of the world to him,
And power upon the legions of the damned.

But this Satan whom Cyprian describes is not the Devil of
the Middle Ages; in his sinister grandeur he is more sugges-
tive of the fallen archangel whom Milton was later to portray
in *Paradise Lost:*

His face was like to a flower of purest gold
Shining in the flame-radiance of his eyes.
Upon his brow a glittering crown was set;
His vesture was resplendent.
Earth trembled when he moved; about his throne
Numberless hosts kept vigil; like a god
He seemed, and like one thought to vie with God,
Nor feared to battle with the Lord Eternal.

This fallen god is the father of vanities, and builds of vain
shadows all that can deceive and destroy mankind:

Cities and palaces and shadowy streams,
Deep woods, and even the longed-for sight of home,
And all the illusions of night-wanderers—

deceptive mirages, wherewith the demons fool men and lead
them on to damnation.

Next, he tells the story of the temptation of Justina. Cyprian lets loose demon upon demon against her, even Satan
himself, but all in vain. Then the magician creates phantom
seducers for her undoing. To have the readier access to her,
so that he may tempt her even more sorely, he transforms
himself now into a young woman, now into a beautiful bird
that sings entrancingly; he even changes Aglaidas into a
swallow, so that he can fly to his sweetheart. But beneath the
pure and steadfast gaze of the maiden the lying bird falls

heavily to the ground. Cyprian then tries other means. Justina's family is overwhelmed with every kind of calamity, and the plague decimates her native city, but nothing can move the inflexible girl. In the face of so many failures, the defeated magician begins to doubt his own power; he curses Satan, and resolves to break the compact which binds him to the Prince of Devils. And like Justina he now opposes the sign of the cross to the onslaughts of the Enemy. But Satan ironically and implacably taunts the victim who would escape his clutches:

> *Christ will not snatch thee from my hands, he never*
> *Opens his arms to one who has obeyed me.*

And the wretch, terrified by the menace of eternal damnation, ends his confession with this pathetic appeal:

> *Such was my life; say now, will Christ be moved*
> *To grant my prayer?*

Throughout this poem there are passages of real and vigorous beauty, and it at once arouses in the mind a host of literary reminiscences and comparisons. Cyprian and Satan are Faust and Mephistopheles, and in the proud, splendid demon of the Greek writer, in the haughty speeches which are put into his mouth, there is already something of the fallen archangel of *Paradise Lost.* There are passages elsewhere which suggest *The Divine Comedy,* such, for instance, as that in which Eudocia describes vigorously the personifications of the vices which evil spirits spread throughout the world: Falsehood and Lust, Fraud and Hatred, Hypocrisy and Vanity. And indeed it is no small merit in a Greek work of the fifth century that it should thus recall Dante, Goethe, and Milton. Does this imply that Athenais-Eudocia is to be credited with great originality? Here again her personal contribution is but slight, for not one of these admirable inventions is of her creating. As early as the fourth century, probably in Syria, the legend of St. Cyprian of Antioch had become sufficiently popular to be rendered into Greek prose. This is the tale which the Empress put into verse, as she had versified the Scriptures and the life of Christ. The beauty of the subject she chose is no proof of her intellectual superiority.

But she deserves some credit, at least, for having chosen it; and it is by her very choice that her work is of importance for the study of her character. One may fancy that the story of Cyprian of Antioch had a very special interest for Athenais-Eudocia, for it was in a certain sense her own story. Her parents had wished her to learn, like the magician, "all that there is in earth and air and sea." Like him she had been initiated "into the foolish wisdom of the Greeks." Like him "she had thought she lived, though being in truth but dead." Then, like him, she had renounced "the impious faith of idols," and had broken "vain images of the gods." And like him, also having become a Christian and devout, she longed to convince "those who take pleasure still in perverse idols." And this is why one has a right to imagine that into her edifying story Athenais-Eudocia has put something of herself.

And yet it cannot be said that even this sincerity of hers has added any touch of genius to her performance. Here, as in her other poems, the form, her only contribution, is mediocre. The work itself, however, is full of interest when we come to study the psychology of our heroine. From the very beginning of her contact with Christianity, the new influence rapidly blotted out of her soul all the graces of pagan antiquity and all the charm of the recollections of her youth. Athens, Eleusis, and Argos, all those holy places where her early years had been spent, were to her from henceforth only cities of refuge for the false gods. The learning in which she had

been brought up seemed an illusion sent by malevolent demons; the beautiful legends that had delighted her childhood
meant no more to her now than old wives' tales. As Renan
says in a celebrated passage of his *Saint Paul:*

> Ah! beautiful, pure images, very gods and very god-
> desses, tremble, all of ye! The fatal word has gone
> forth: ye are idols. The error of this ugly little Jew is
> your death-warrant.

It was thus that in a day triumphant Christianity completely
transformed Athenais. The learned young pagan girl-
philosopher of yesterday vanishes, and in her place we have
only the Most Pious Empress Eudocia. And when some
vague echoes of her classical training sounded in her soul,
when she found that her Hellenic education still kept alive
within her the worship of form and the memory of Homer,
perhaps she feared that she was yielding once again to the
frauds and deceits of Satan—if it were not rather that she
thought, like a good Christian, that by consecrating the glories of paganism to the service of the Divine Majesty she had
thereby made them to become sanctified.

❦❦❦ III ❦❦❦

THEODORA

The adventurous life of Theodora, Empress of Byzantium, who, beginning her career behind the scenes in the Hippodrome, rose to the throne of the Caesars, has always aroused curiosity and excited the imagination. During her lifetime her extraordinary good fortune so greatly astonished her contemporaries that the idle tongues of Constantinople invented the most incredible stories to explain it— hence all that mass of gossip that Procopius has gathered together painstakingly in *The Secret History* and has handed down to posterity. After her death the legend grew to still greater dimensions: Orientals and Occidentals, Syrians, Byzantines, and Slavs added more and more touches to the romantic incidents of her romantic story; and because of this rowdy fame Theodora, alone out of so many Princesses who sat upon the throne of Byzantium, has been well known down to our own times, and is almost popular.[1]

[1] For the details of Theodora's life I refer the reader to my monograph: *Théodora, impératrice de Byzance*, Paris, 1904. I have felt, nevertheless,

I do not feel, however, that we have the right to assume
any very exact knowledge of this famous Empress, whom so
many regard as simply an illustrious adventuress. Down to
the present time, the majority of those who have attempted to
describe her have used chiefly, almost exclusively, the anecdotes that Procopius retails. I am far from maintaining that
his work is of no value; I even think that by a careful study of
it one could become better acquainted than heretofore with
the psychology of Theodora during her stormy youth. But it
must always be borne in mind that *The Secret History* is not
our only source of information. Other, newer documents have
been discovered, mainly in the last few years, from which we
can gather more material for a character study of the celebrated Empress. *The Lives of the Blessed Orientals*, which
was compiled about the middle of the sixth century by an intimate friend of the Empress, John, Bishop of Ephesus; the
unpublished fragments of the same author's great *Ecclesiastical History;* the anonymous chronicle attributed to Zacha-
rias of Mytilene; and other contemporary works, such as
the biographies of the Patriarch Severus and Jacobus Baradaeus, the Apostle of the Monophysites, have all been published or translated from the Syriac manuscripts in which
they lay forgotten, and they shed a curious light upon the
part that Theodora played in questions of religion and politics. There are other writers as well, longer known to us but
rarely enough consulted, such as Johannes Lydus; there are
the new fragments of Malalas, not to speak of the Imperial
Novels, whose tiresome verbosity has, in spite of the great
amount of important material they contain, damped the ardor of many; and even Procopius himself, who, happily for
us, has left other works besides *The Secret History*. And

---

the necessity of including a sketch of this celebrated Empress among my
portraits of Byzantine Princesses.

from all these writings, if one takes the trouble to read them carefully, certain facts emerge which place the people of Justinian's court in a different light from that in which they are generally presented to us.

I

In the early years of the sixth century the notoriety of the actress and dancer Theodora was widespread throughout Constantinople.

Little is known of her origins. Some of the later chroniclers say that she was born in Cyprus, the hot, passionate land of Aphrodite. Others, with greater likelihood, bring her from Syria. But, whatever her birthplace, she came while still a child to Byzantium with her parents, and it was in the corrupt and turbulent capital that her youth was spent.

Her family is equally obscure. In the legend, out of reverence for the imperial rank to which she attained, she is given an illustrious, or at least a presentable, ancestry in the person of a steady and respectable father of senatorial rank. As a matter of fact, she seems to have been of humbler origin. Her father, if *The Secret History* may be trusted, was a poor man named Acacius, by profession guardian of the bears in the amphitheater; her mother was no better than she should be, like many connected with the stage and the circus. Into this professional household three daughters were born, the second, the future Empress, about the year 500.

Early in life Theodora came in contact with the people whom she was later to charm as an actress before governing as Empress. Acacius had died leaving his widow and his three daughters in very straightened circumstances. To retain her late husband's position, the family's only means of support, the mother saw no better way than to take up with

another man, who should obtain the guardianship of the
bears, and thus look after both the family and the animals.
But the success of her plan depended upon the consent of
Asterius, the head of the Greens, and Asterius had accepted
money to support a rival candidate. In order to overcome opposition, Theodora's mother thought she might be able to interest the people in her cause, and, one day when the crowd
was assembled in the circus, she appeared in the arena thrust-
ing before her her three little daughters, crowned with flowers, who held out their hands in supplication to the spectators. The Greens merely laughed at the touching request.
But fortunately the Blues, who were always delighted to oppose their adversaries, hastened to grant the prayer which the
Greens refused, and awarded Acacius's family an employ-
ment similar to that which it had lost. Theodora never forgot
the scornful indifference with which the Greens had received
her entreaties; and from that moment began in the child the
tendency toward long-cherished rancor, and the implacable
desire for vengeance, which became so strong in the woman.

Thus Theodora grew up in the casual society of the Hippodrome, and in the course of time was ready for her future
career. The elder of her sisters had made a success on the
stage, and Theodora followed in her footsteps. She went on
the boards with her big sister and played the part of lady's
maid; she also accompanied her to entertainments, where, in
the mixed company of the more public apartments, she came
across much impurity and indiscreet familiarity. Then she,
in her turn, became a full-fledged actress, but she had no desire to be a flute-player, a singer, or a dancer, like so many
others; she preferred to appear in living pictures, in which
she could display undraped the beauty of which she was so
proud, and in pantomimes wherein her vivacity and her feeling for comedy could have full scope.

She was pretty and rather small, but extraordinarily graceful; and her charming face, with its pale, creamy coloring,
was lighted up by large, vivacious, sparkling eyes. Little of
this all-powerful charm is left in her official picture in San
Vitale at Ravenna. Beneath her imperial mantle she appears
stiff and tall; under the diadem that hides her forehead her
delicate small face, of a narrow oval shape, and her large,
thin, straight nose, invest her with a sort of solemn gravity,
almost with melancholy. One feature alone remains unal-
tered in this faded portrait, and that is the beautiful black
eyes that Procopius speaks of, under the heavy, meeting eyebrows, which still illumine her face and seem almost to en-
gulf it.

But Theodora had something else besides her beauty. She
was intelligent, witty, and amusing: she had Bohemian high
spirits which were often exerted at the expense of her fellow
actresses, and a pleasing and comic way with her that kept
even the most volatile adorers firmly attached. She was not
always kindly, and she did not stop at hard words if they
would provoke a laugh, but when she wanted to please, she
knew how to put forth irresistible powers of fascination.
Bold, enterprising, and audacious withal, she was not content to wait for favor to seek her out, but set forth consciously
and joyously to provoke and encourage it; and having but little moral sense—it is difficult to see where she could have acquired it—as well as to a rare degree the perfect amorous temperament, she became an immediate success, both without
and within the theater. Belonging to a profession of which
virtue is not a necessary attribute, she amused, charmed, and
scandalized Constantinople. On the stage she indulged in the
most audacious exhibitions and the most immodest effects.
Off it she soon became celebrated for her wild suppers, her
adventuresomeness, and the number of her lovers. Soon she

became so compromised that respectable people passing her
in the street drew aside lest they should sully themselves by
contact with a creature so impure, and the very fact of meeting her was considered an ill omen. At this time she was not
yet twenty years of age.

Suddenly she disappeared. She had a Syrian lover, Hecebolus by name, who was appointed governor of the African
Pentapolis; Theodora decided to accompany him to his distant province. The romance, unfortunately, did not last long.
For reasons unknown, Hecebolus brutally sent her away, and
penniless, without the necessities of life, the unfortunate
Theodora for some time roamed all the East in misery. In
Alexandria at last she settled down for a while, and her sojourn there was not without its effect upon her future. The
capital of Egypt was not merely a great commercial center, a
rich and splendid city, of loose habits, corrupt, the favorite
abode of many celebrated courtesans. From the fourth century onward it was also one of the capitals of Christianity.
Nowhere else were religious quarrels more bitter, nor theological disputes more subtle and heated, nor fanaticism more
easily excited; nowhere else had the memory of the great
founders of the solitary life produced a richer flowering of
monasteries, of mystics, and of ascetics. The suburbs of
Alexandria were studded with religious houses, and the Lib-
yan desert was so full of hermits as to be worthy of its name
—"the Desert of the Saints."

In her moral distress, Theodora was not insensitive to the
influence of the sphere into which circumstances had cast
her. She approached such holy men as the Patriarch Timo-
thy and Severus of Antioch, who preached especially to
women; and it is not improbable that owing to them the penitent courtesan may, momentarily at least, have entered upon
a purer and more Christian mode of life. By the time of her

return to Constantinople, she had become more sensible, more mature, and was weary of her wandering existence and of her wild adventures. Whether sincerely or not, she was careful to lead a more virtuous, retired life. According to one tradition she was very respectable and proper, and lived in an unpretentious little house, staying at home and spinning, like the matrons of good old Roman times. It was under these circumstances that she met Justinian. We cannot tell how she managed to enslave and hold this man, no longer young—he was nearly forty—this politician in so delicate a situation, with a future which must not be compromised. Procopius talks of magic and philters, but that really complicates matters too much, and leaves out of account the consummate intelligence, the easy grace, the humor and wit, with which Theodora had conquered so many hearts. Above all, it omits her clear, inflexible courage, that was to influence so powerfully her lover's feeble and undecided character. At all events, we know that the Prince was completely enslaved. Being madly in love, he refused his mistress nothing. She was fond of money, so he loaded her with wealth. She coveted honors and distinctions, so he persuaded his uncle, the Emperor, to raise her to the high rank of patrician. She was ambitious and keen for power, so he allowed himself to be swayed by her advice and was the docile instrument of her likes and of her hates. Soon he came to the point of insisting upon marriage. The good Emperor Justin was not worried by her lack of noble birth, and does not seem to have grudged his consent to his beloved nephew. The opposition to Justinian's scheme came from an unexpected quarter. In her peasant mind the broad common sense of the Empress Euphemia was shocked at the thought of having a Theodora as her successor; and, in spite of all her affection for her nephew, in spite of her usual compliance with his every wish, on this point she stood firm. Very fortunately, Euphemia died in 523, in the nick of time. Henceforth it was plain sailing. Senators and high dignitaries were forbidden by law to marry women of servile condition, innkeepers' daughters, actresses, or courtesans. To please Justinian, Justin abrogated the law. He went even further. When in April 527, he associated his nephew with him officially in the imperial power, Theodora shared in her husband's elevation and triumph. With him on Easter day in St. Sophia, gleaming with candlelight, she was solemnly crowned. Afterward, according to the custom of Byzantine sovereigns, she went to the Hippodrome and received the acclamations of the people in the place where she had made her first public appearance. Her dream had come true.

II

Such is the history of Theodora's youth—at least, that is how Procopius tells it; and for some two centuries and a half since the discovery of the manuscript of *The Secret History* this scandalous narrative has received almost universal credence. Must it therefore be accepted without reserve? A pamphlet is not history, and one may well inquire into the truth of these amazing adventures.

Gibbon declared long ago that no one would invent such incredible things, and that therefore they must be true. Of late years, on the other hand, intelligent scholars have at various times doubted the authority of Procopius's unsupported statements, and there has been serious talk of the "Theodora legend." Without wishing to reopen the question, or to belittle the value of some of the comments that have been made, I should hesitate to whitewash too thoroughly her whom *The Secret History* has so outrageously blackened. It is a pity that

John, Bishop of Ephesus, who had access to Theodora and knew her well, should, out of respect for the great ones of the earth, have omitted to give us full particulars concerning the insults which the pious but brutally outspoken monks more than once, so he tells us, directed against the Empress. It is certain, at all events, that Procopius was not alone among her contemporaries in criticizing her, and that there were persons attached to the imperial court, such as the secretary Priscus and the Praefect John of Cappadocia, who knew the joints in her armor. I do not know whether, as Procopius states, she really had a son in her youth, whose birth was, it appears, such an unfortunate accident; it is certain, at all events, that she had a daughter of whom Justinian was not the father. This reminder of her stormy past does not seem, however, if we may judge by the success that this girl's son had at court, either to have worried the Empress very much or to have troubled the Emperor. Certain of Theodora's characteristics fit in fairly well with the stories that are told about her youth: the interest she took in poor girls of the capital, who had been led astray, more often through want than through viciousness, and the steps she took to rescue these unfortunates and to free them, as a contemporary writer puts it, "from the yoke of their shameful slavery"; and also the rather contemptuous harshness with which she always treated men. And if all this that is undeniable is admitted, it will be impossible to reject *The Secret History* in its entirety.[2]

But are we therefore obliged to believe that Theodora's

---

[2] It must be added that in an unfortunately somewhat obscure passage in *The Lives of the Blessed Orientals*, John of Ephesus, who knew the Empress well, calls her rather brutally, but without otherwise seeming to cast reproach upon her, "Theodora the strumpet." If the translation ἐκ τοῦ πορνείου, by which Land renders the Syriac text, is accurate, the passage would confirm in one word the essence of what Procopius relates in such detail.

adventures had the blazing notoriety that Procopius invests
them with; that she was, as in his account, a courtesan on the
heroic scale, an angel of evil, whom the Devil permitted to go
flaunting her lusts to and fro upon the earth? It must not be
forgotten that Procopius has a habit of investing his char-
acters with an almost epic perversity; and, although he tries
hard to determine to a hair's breadth the lowest point to
which Theodora fell, I for my part regard her—though her
interest may thereby be diminished—as the heroine of a less
extraordinary tale. She was a dancer who, having led the
same life as the majority of her kind in all ages, tired suddenly of her precarious amours, and, finding a sensible man
who could provide her with a home, settled down to married
life and conjugal devotion—an adventuress, perhaps, but at
the same time astute, quiet, and clever enough to be able to
keep up appearances; one who could marry even a future
Emperor without a fearful scandal. Ludovic Halévy, I know,
created just such a character and named her Virginie Cardi-
nal. But it is not this Theodora who is of importance to us.
For there is another, a less well-known and far more interesting Theodora: a great Empress, closely associated in all
Justinian's work, who often played a decisive part in the
government, a woman of high courage, of exceptional intelligence, energetic, despotic, proud, violent and passionate,
complex and baffling, but always extraordinarily fascinating.

III

In the apse of San Vitale at Ravenna, glowing with golden
mosaics, we may still see Theodora in all the splendor of her
majesty. The costume she is wearing is of unparalleled magnificence. Clad in a long purple-violet mantle with a broad
border of gold embroidery flowing in glistening folds, she

wears on her aureoled head a lofty diadem of gold and precious stones; in and out through her hair are wound twisted
strands of gems and pearls, while other jewels fall in sparkling streams upon her shoulders. Thus she appears in this
official portrait to the eyes of posterity, and thus in her lifetime she desired to appear to her contemporaries. Seldom has
upstart accustomed herself more rapidly to the exigencies of
her newly acquired majesty; seldom has highborn sovereign
loved and appreciated more thoroughly the many pleasures,
the delights of luxury, and the little gratifications of pride,
which the exercise of supreme power can bestow. Very feminine, always elegant and eager to please, she loved sumptuous apartments, magnificent clothes, marvelous jewels, and
an exquisite and delicate table. She took careful and constant
care of her beauty. To keep her face calm and serene, she
lengthened her hours of sleep by endless siestas; to preserve the freshness of her complexion, she took frequent
baths followed by long hours of rest. For she felt that her
charm was the surest guarantee of her influence.

Even more tenacious was she of the circumstances of
power. She would have her own court, her own following,
her own guards and processions; like the upstart she was, she
loved the complications of ceremonial, and added to them. To
win her approval one had to be constantly paying court to
her, to prostrate oneself at her feet, and to dance attendance
interminably every day in her antechambers at her hours of
audience. Her theatrical experience had given her a taste for
stage effects as well as the knowledge of how to obtain them;
but above all, being very haughty, she insisted jealously upon
her rank, and it doubtless gave her a secret delight to see so
many great nobles, who in former days had treated her with
more familiarity, bending low over her purple buskins.

It would be somewhat ingenuous, however, to imagine

that all this display, this apparent insistence upon etiquette, must necessarily have excluded such adventures as those that Sardou has invented for his Theodora. It is certain that many mysterious things about which Justinian knew nothing could take place in the Imperial Gynaeceum; the story of the Patriarch Anthemius which I have already related is proof of this. Nor would I be so foolish as to insist upon Theodora's post-marital virtue. Although, as is well known, it is always difficult to be certain on such points, I am not ready to believe that the Augusta's life was without reproach. I am fully convinced that during her youth she went the pace, and I do not feel called upon to be scandalized if she kept it up in later life; Justinian would have been the only person entitled to complain. But facts are facts and one must take them as one finds them.

Now, it is certain that no contemporary writers nor any historians of a later age—and it is these last who have strongly censured Theodora for her cupidity, her despotic and violent temper, her excessive influence over Justinian, and the scandal to which her heterodox views gave rise—not one of them records anything which casts doubt upon the correctness of her private life after her marriage. Even Procopius, who has so calumniated her, relating so fully the adventures of her youth, and telling with his notorious wealth of detail of her perfidies, her cruelties, and her infamies, as a grown woman, even he—however little attentively one may wish to read the text—does not hint at the shadow of an amorous adventure after her marriage on the part of this absolutely corrupt woman. I think it will be readily allowed that, if the Empress had given the slightest occasion, the pamphleteer would not have been backward in describing her adulteries in detail. He has told of nothing of the sort because there was really nothing to tell.

But this reflects no credit upon Theodora's moral qualities. Aside from the fact that she was no longer young when she ascended the throne—an Eastern woman at thirty is almost on the threshold of old age—she was too intelligent and too ambitious to risk compromising by love intrigues the position she had won for herself. Supreme power was worth taking some pains to preserve, and the dignity of her life reflects credit quite as much upon her common sense as upon her moral qualities. But chiefly, this courageous and ambitious woman, so eagerly desirous of power, had other interests than the pursuit of vulgar amours. She was endowed with several of the principal qualities which justify the striving for supreme power: a proud energy, a stern fixity of purpose, and a serene courage that never failed her even in the most difficult circumstances. It was owing to these qualities that, during the twenty-one years that she shared Justinian's throne, she exercised a profound—and legitimate—influence over her adoring husband.

IV

One incident that must never be forgotten in writing of Theodora is the part she played on that tragic 18th of January 532, when the triumphant rebels stormed at the gates of the Imperial Palace, and the distracted Emperor completely lost his head and thought only of flight. Theodora was present at the council; in the midst of the general discouragement she alone was brave and self-controlled. At first she said nothing; suddenly, in the silence, she arose, disgusted with the universal cowardice, and recalled the wavering Emperor and his ministers to their duty. "If there were left me no safety but in flight, I would not fly," said she. "Those who have worn the crown should never survive its loss. Never will

I see the day that I am not hailed Empress. If you wish to fly, Caesar, well and good; you have money, the ships are ready, the sea is clear; but I shall stay. For I love the old proverb that says: 'The purple is the best winding-sheet.' " On that day, when, to quote a contemporary, "the very Empire seemed upon the brink of destruction," Theodora saved Justinian's throne; and in this supreme struggle, when her crown and her life were at stake, ambition inspired her to real heroism.

At this decisive moment, Theodora, by her coolness and energy, showed herself a statesman; and, as has been well said, she proved herself worthy of her place in the Imperial Council which until then she had owed to the Emperor's weakness. Henceforth she never lost it, and Justinian did not begrudge it her. To the very last he was passionately devoted to the woman he had adored in his younger days; and as he was completely under the influence of her superior intelligence and of her strong and resolute will, he never refused her anything, either the outward show or the real exercise of supreme power.

Upon the church walls of that time and over the gates of citadels, Theodora's name may still be read alongside of the Emperor's; in San Vitale at Ravenna her portrait is a pendant to that of her imperial husband; and, in the mosaics that decorated the apartments of the Sacred Palace, Justinian had in like manner associated Theodora with him in connection with his military triumphs and the brightest glories of his reign. The people erected statues to her, and officials did homage to her, as they did to Justinian, for throughout her life she was the equal of the Emperor. Upon the most momentous questions Justinian was pleased to take the advice of "the most reverend spouse whom God had given unto him," whom he loved to call "his sweetest delight"; and her contemporaries are unanimous in declaring that she used unscrupulously her boundless influence over the sovereign, and that her power was quite as great as his, and perhaps greater.

During the twenty-one years of her reign she interfered in everything: she filled the administration with her protégés; she meddled in diplomacy, in politics, and in the Church, and managed things to suit herself; she created and deposed popes and patriarchs, ministers and generals, as her fancy dictated; she was as eager to advance her favorites as she was to ruin the influence and power of her adversaries; nor did she even hesitate, whenever she thought proper, to countermand openly the sovereign's orders and substitute her own for them. In all matters of importance she was her husband's active assistant; and, although her influence was sometimes unfortunate, although her cupidity, her violence, and her pride, by arousing the pride and cupidity of the Emperor, inspired unwise acts, it must be remembered that she had often a truer insight than he into the interests of the State, and that the political ideas that she had at heart, if the times had permitted of their full realization, would have solidified and strengthened the Byzantine Empire and perhaps even have altered the course of history.

Whereas Justinian, carried away by the splendor of Roman antiquity, reveled in fancies now magnificent, now hazy, dreaming of the restoration of the Empire of the Caesars and the triumph of Orthodoxy through union with Rome, Theodora, with a clearer and more penetrating vision, turned her eyes to the East. She had always been in sympathy with the monks of Syria and Egypt, such as Zooras, Jacobus Baradaeus, and many others, receiving them in the Palace, and entreating their prayers in spite of their ugly rags and their uncouth manners. Like all good Byzantines she was sincerely devout. But besides this she was too acute and had too keen a political sense not to understand the importance of religious questions in a Christian State, and the danger of ignoring them. Now, she felt that the rich and flourishing provinces of Asia, Syria, and Egypt, constituted the real strength of the monarchy; she realized the danger that was brewing for the Empire in the religious differences by which the peoples of the East from this time forth began to manifest their separatist tendencies; she felt the need of pacifying the dangerous unrest by opportune concessions and by broad toleration; and, in trying to divert the imperial policy to the attainment of this end, she may without paradox be considered to have shown better judgment and a clearer insight into the future than her imperial colleague.

Whereas Justinian, a theologian at heart, gave up his time to religious questions out of a love of controversy for the sterile pleasure of dogmatizing, Theodora, by her realization of the deep political problems which underlay the shifting and changing quarrels of the theologians, proved herself of the race of the great Byzantine Emperors. And that is why, in the interests of the State, she went on her way unswerving, openly protecting heretics, boldly challenging the Papacy, carrying the irresolute Justinian along with her, throwing herself with her whole soul into the struggle, and never acknowledging defeat. It was to her protection that heretic Egypt owed many years of toleration; it was through her that heretic Syria was able to put its persecuted national church upon a firm foundation; she it was who made it possible for the dissenters first to be restored to favor and to resume freely the spreading of their doctrines, and afterward to withstand the excommunications of many councils and the harshness of the secular arm; and it was to her that the Monophysite missions in Arabia, Nubia, and Abyssinia owed their success. To the day of her death, she kept up a tenacious, impassioned struggle for her beliefs, like a statesman, and yet like a true woman. She could be yielding or brutal according to circumstances; she had the boldness to cause the arrest and deposition of one Pope, and the ability to bend another to her will; she had the courage to protect her persecuted friends and to furnish them with the means of reforming their church, and the adroitness often to make the Emperor carry out her policies whether he would or no.

The Church has never pardoned Theodora the brutal deposition of Pope Silverius, nor the tenacity with which she clung to Monophysitism, nor the overbearing violence with which she settled scores with ecclesiastics—with Vigilius in particular. Century after century, ecclesiastical historians have hurled curses and insults at her. But Theodora is worthy of being judged with less violence and more justice. Doubtless she carried out her plans with a too passionate eagerness, a too imperious brutality, a too obstinate rancor, even with a too cold-blooded cruelty; but she had great gifts as well: she was keenly alive to the needs of the government and saw clearly what was capable of accomplishment. The policy she had at heart does honor to her clarity of vision, and, taken all in all, was worthy of an Emperor.

V

But her great interest lies in the fact that under her statesmanlike qualities Theodora was a woman. She shows it by her love of luxury and elegance, and much more by the fierceness of her passions and the strength of her hates. When her interests were at stake, she had no hesitations and no scruples. Mercilessly she got rid of everyone whose influence might outweigh her own; pitilessly she broke all whose ambition showed signs of affecting her power or of undermining her influence. To avenge herself and to preserve her power she would stoop to anything, force and craft, falsehood and bribery, intrigue and violence. And if she felt at times that the feeble Justinian was escaping from her grasp, if circumstances and influences beyond her control caused her momentarily to give way, she always contrived by means of her audacity and her pliancy to stage a striking revenge; ambitious and subtle, she always insisted upon having the last word on everything—and she always succeeded.

The gossips of Constantinople told dark stories of secret executions at Theodora's orders, of underground dungeons, of prisons, silent and terrible, where her victims were incarcerated and tortured. One must be careful not to take these tales too literally. Some of the Empress's most illustrious victims did not fare so badly on the whole, and succeeded, in spite of short periods of disgrace, in making creditable careers for themselves; it is a fact, moreover, that her most dangerous adversaries were sent not to death but merely into exile.

But, without enlarging unnecessarily the list of her cruelties, one must not make Theodora out too merciful and too good. When she hated, she was not the sort of woman to stop at anything, whether at the scandal of an unjust disgrace, or even, perhaps, at an assassination. The stories of the Emperor's nephew Germanus, of Priscus the secretary, and of Photius, the son-in-law of Belisarius, are enough to show the strength of her hatred. The fall of the Praefect John of Cappadocia, the bold and formidable minister who held her in his grip for a moment and made her fear for her power, illustrates even better the unscrupulous energy of her ambitious soul and the incredible resources of her perfidy. In like manner, and by a similar mixture of adroitness and violence,

she made so great a general as Belisarius pay for his rare outbursts of independence, and, through her ascendancy over
Antonia, the patrician's wife, contrived to make him her very
humble and docile servant. Here again one is forced to ad-
mire both the Empress's great ingenuity in managing an
intrigue, and her indifference to the means and instruments
employed. Antonia, after a stormy youth, constantly deceived her doting husband; but she was astute and bold, consummate in intrigue, and capable, says Procopius, who knew
her well, of accomplishing the impossible. Theodora quickly
saw that by veiling this woman's love affairs she could make
her the devoted slave of her schemes and the best guarantee
of Belisarius's fidelity. They formed an alliance. Antonia put
all her cleverness at the Basilissa's disposal, and in the deposition of Pope Silverius, as well as in the disgrace of John
of Cappadocia, played an important part, and demonstrated
the extent of her ability. In return, Theodora covered up her
follies and her slips, and on several occasions reconciled
her to Belisarius and made him pardon her. And thus, having
her favorite at her mercy, the Empress through her kept the
general under her thumb.[3]

From the favor she showed Antonia, must we conclude,
with *The Secret History*, that Theodora tolerated women's
failings and concealed many lapses under her imperial robe?
The facts give a contrary impression. It may be that, owing
to her highhanded impulses and her habit of subordinating
everything to her schemes, Theodora did at times interfere
indiscreetly in the family affairs of others, and arranged
marriages in the same despotic way that she governed the
State. But by the laws which she caused to be made on di-

---

[3] Upon these two incidents the reader may consult two chapters in my
book previously cited: "Théodora et Jean de Cappadoce," pp. 173–90,
and "Théodora et Bélisaire," pp. 191–216.

vorce and adultery, as well as by her actions, she showed a
constant interest in strengthening the ties of marriage—"that
holiest of all things," as a law of the period terms it—and in
making this lawful and holy estate respected by everyone.
The truth is that she was, as an historian says, "naturally
anxious to help unfortunate women," and this anxiety is
shown in the measures she caused to be adopted with regard
to women who were badly treated or unhappily married, and
also in those which she advised for comedy actresses and
fallen women. She knew from experience the slums of the
capital, and realized all the misery and shame that they contained, and early in her reign she used her influence to im-
prove them. But she was nonetheless very strict, a watchful
guardian of public morals, and she undertook the task of
making her capital purer and more moral.[4]

Are we to believe that some memory of her own experiences and a measure of sorrow for her past were responsible
for these measures? On the whole it is probable, if not certain, and it cannot but enhance our opinion of her. There is a
singular nobility in the following words from an imperial
edict, which she undoubtedly inspired: "We have set up
magistrates to punish robbers and thieves; are we not even
more straitly bound to prosecute the robbers of honor and
the thieves of chastity?"

It would indeed be puerile to try to conceal Theodora's
defects and vices. She loved money and she loved power; she
showed perhaps too much family affection in providing for
her relatives; and, to preserve the throne she had ascended,
she was unscrupulous, perfidious, violent, cruel, implacable,
bitter, and adamant, to those who had incurred her hatred.
She was a woman of great ambition, who by her intrigues

[4] See the chapter, "Le Féminisme de Théodora," pp. 217–30, in my
book.

troubled the Palace and the Empire profoundly. But she had
her good qualities as well. Her friends called her "the faithful
Empress," and she deserved the name. She had other, more
eminent virtues: a masculine vigor, a lofty energy, and a
statesman's clear and powerful intelligence. Her influence
was not always good, but she made a deep impress upon
Justinian's government. After her death, there followed a
period of decadence in which the once-glorious reign drew
sadly to a close.

When on the 29th of June 548, Theodora, after a long
illness, died of cancer, Justinian mourned bitterly a loss
which he rightly felt to be irreparable. During her lifetime
he had adored her, and after her death he piously treasured
her memory. As a memorial to her, he desired to keep in his
service all who had been near her; many years later, whenever he wished to make a solemn promise, he was in the habit
of swearing by the name of Theodora, and those who desired
to please him would talk to him about "the excellent, beautiful, and wise sovereign" who, after helping him faithfully in
this world, was now praying to God for her husband.

It must be admitted that this apotheosis is somewhat excessive. Theodora the dancer did not have precisely those
virtues which carry one straight to Paradise. Theodora the
Empress, in spite of her piety, was possessed of faults and
vices hardly consistent with the halos of the saints. But the
point is worthy of notice, for it shows the incomparable fascination and charm that this very ambitious, but thoroughly
feminine, woman was able to exert even from beyond the
grave.

❧❧❧ IV ❧❧❧

IRENE

Toward the end of the year 768, Constantinople was in festive array: the Byzantine capital was celebrating the marriage of the heir apparent of the Empire, Leo, son of Constantine V.

On the morning of November 1st, a flotilla of boats, sumptuously spread with brilliant silks, had gone to the Palace of Hieria, on the Asiatic shore of the Bosphorus to fetch the young bride across for her solemn entry into Byzantium. Several weeks later, on the 18th of December, in the triclinium of the Augustaeum in the Sacred Palace, before the assembled court, the two Basileis had crowned the new sovereign. Seated on golden thrones, Constantine and his son, in the presence of the Patriarch, had lifted the veil that hid the face of the future Empress, had vested her with the silken chlamys over her long golden robe, had set the crown upon her head, and had fastened the jeweled pendants in her ears. Then, in St. Stephen's Church, the new Augusta had re-

ceived the homage of the high officials of the monarchy; from
the terrace of the Hall of the Nineteen Couches she had
shown herself to the people and had been acclaimed by them.
Lastly, she had returned to St. Stephen's, with her brilliant
following of patricians, senators, cubicularies, and maids of
honor, and there the Patriarch Nicetas had solemnized the
marriage, and had placed the nuptial crown upon the heads
of bride and bridegroom.

The old Emperor Constantine V, that energetic iconoclast,
never dreamed when he arranged these festivities and when
he set the diadem of the Caesars upon the young woman's
head, that this delicate Basilissa was to destroy his life's work
and lose the throne for his dynasty.

I

Like Athenais-Eudocia, Irene was by birth an Athenian;
like her, she was an orphan, when circumstances of which
we know nothing, and in which her beauty was doubtless the
essential factor, made her an Emperor's daughter-in-law.
But there the resemblance between the two Princesses stops.
Athens in the eighth century was wholly different from what
it had been in the fifth. It was no longer the home of pagan
letters, a university town, full of the glory of ancient writers
and the memory of illustrious philosophers. It no longer preserved religiously the memory of its exiled gods in the
shadow of its temples. In the time of Irene it was a pious,
quiet, little provincial town, where the Parthenon had been
converted into a church, where St. Sophia had driven Pallas-
Athene from the Acropolis, and where the saints had replaced the gods. In such surroundings, education, and, above
all, feminine education, could no longer be what it had been
in Athenais's time. Like the majority of her contemporaries,

Irene was devout and pious, with an intense, burning piety, that was aggravated by the events of the troubled times in which she lived.

A serious religious conflict had been disturbing the Byzantine Empire for more than forty years, and the struggle, called the Iconoclastic Controversy, was now at its height. The strictly theological nature of the term must not blind one to the real character of this formidable crisis; it was quite other than a mere trifling question of discipline or worship. Undoubtedly the Iconoclastic Emperors, devout as were all the men of their age, were inspired by the most ardent and sincere religious motives; one of the objects of their reform was to raise the moral plane of religion by stripping it of such a renascence of paganism as the excessive veneration of the images of the Virgin and the saints seemed to them to be. Another point troubled them even more: above all else, they were dismayed at the power that the monks, the chief defenders of the images, had, by their wealth and influence, acquired in the State. Beginning with the eighth century, there was in fact—strange as it may appear in so Christian an Empire as Byzantium—a struggle between the State and the monks.

Against the latter, the Emperor Constantine V, a passionate, violent, energetic man, had carried on the war with peculiar severity. By his orders, brutal and often terrible executions had taken place. The monasteries had been secularized, and the religious driven out, imprisoned, or exiled. Constantinople had scarcely any monks left in it. All Byzantine society had joined in the struggle in one or the other camp. On one side was officialdom: the court clergy, the functionaries, the upper classes, and the army, utterly devoted to so victorious a general as Constantine V. On the other side were the lower clergy, the middle classes, the people, and the women, whose mystical piety was enthralled by the splendors of ritual, whose devotion was kindled by the magnificence of the churches, and who could not bring themselves to give up the miraculous and venerated icons.

Irene was a woman, and came besides from a province ardently devoted to the images. Her sympathies were thus not to be doubted. But at the time when she became a member of the imperial family, the persecution was at its height, and it would not have been wise for her to show too decided an opposition in the neighborhood of the formidable Constantine V. Irene, therefore, carefully dissimulated her real beliefs. She even, at her father-in-law's request, went to the extent of swearing a solemn oath never to accept image worship; and at this moment some part of her lying and unscrupulous spirit, later to show itself so forcibly, makes its appearance.

However, despite this apparent submissiveness, the young woman's piety was not without its results. This became clear when in 775, upon the death of Constantine V, the new Emperor, Leo IV, perhaps under Irene's influence, which was very great at the beginning of his reign, relaxed to some extent the former penalties. The Basilissa was determined. Many women harbored the proscribed images; it is said that in the Palace itself Anthusa, a daughter of Constantine V, fearlessly kept up her devotion to the forbidden icons. Irene imagined she could imitate her sister-in-law, and fancied she might be able to restore the prohibited worship secretly in the imperial residence. Her attempt was destined to a tragic outcome. In April 780, several of the Empress's intimate friends were arrested and put to torture by order of Leo IV, under suspicion of Iconodule sympathies. The Basilissa herself was compromised. It was reported that one day her husband discovered in her apartments two images of saints hidden under the cushions. At sight of them he became violently angry; and although Irene, who was always ready to swear to anything, vowed she had no idea who had put them there, her influence with the Emperor was seriously impaired. She was in a sort of disgrace when, happily for her, Leo IV died suddenly in September of the same year. The heir to the throne, Constantine VI, was a child of ten; and Irene, his governor and regent, was Empress.

II

Few historical personages are more difficult to estimate correctly than the celebrated sovereign who restored Orthodoxy in Byzantium. She is known to have been beautiful; there is every reason to believe that she was chaste and that, although thrown while still in her youth into a corrupt and dangerous court, she always kept herself above reproach. And, lastly, she was devout. But besides this what do we know of Irene? What was the temper of her mind? What was her character? The acts of her government, to be sure, give us glimpses; but were these acts the result of her own will? During her reign, did she have ideas of her own, or was she only an instrument in the hands of astute advisers? These are a few of the difficult problems to be decided, and they are the more difficult from the fact that the writers of her time exhaust all the expressions of unbounded admiration in speaking of this devout, orthodox Princess.

It would be possible, by following their lead, to describe Irene in the most flattering terms; and some writers of our own times have not failed to do so. A celebrated novelist who amused himself in his younger days by making a sketch of this most pious Empress, and who has just portrayed her more fully in a picturesque and masterly novel,[1] describes her as initiated into the mysteries of Platonic philosophy, into the dogmas of "cosmopolitan Hermetism," as knowing "the power-bestowing theurgical incantations," and as using this power, when she had mastered it, for one end alone, the greatness of Byzantium and the restoration of the ancient hegemony of the Roman Empire. Let him who would see her through the eyes of Paul Adam read this: "Seated beneath the imperial canopy at the extreme point of the promontory overlooking the rapid waters of the Bosphorus, she spent her evenings under the deathless beauty of the Levantine sky watching her reflection in the polished metal basins, splendid as the Mother of God in the shrine-like majesty of her garments that caught the glimmer of the twinkling stars in every facet of their matchless jewels. Thoughts of victory thrilled within her. She called to mind the mysterious teachings of the schools. The love of making a people vibrate to the breath of her soul left her panting and exhausted." [2] And such is the author's sympathy for this remarkable woman that her very crime finds excuse in his eyes, and seems to him almost justified. She dethroned her son and had him blinded, says the novelist, "because she preferred to suppress the individual for the benefit of the race. And she was absolutely right." [3]

These, of course, are poetic imaginings. But even serious historians have portrayed Irene in no less seductive guise. One praises her talents, her great ability, her resourcefulness, her clear-sightedness, and her force of character.[4] An-

---

[1] Paul Adam, *Irène et les eunuques*, Paris, 1906.

[2] Paul Adam, *Princesses byzantines*, pp. 33–4.

[3] Ibid. p. 80.

[4] A. Gasquet, *L'Empire byzantin et la monarchie franque*, pp. 252, 287.

other regards her as an altogether remarkable woman, who gave the Byzantine Empire "the best and most reconstructive government that it probably ever had." And he adds: "She was a woman really born to rule, for she had a masculine intellect, she was admirably endowed with all the qualities of a great sovereign, she knew how to speak to the people and make them love her; she was excellent in her choice of advisers, and was possessed of perfect courage and admirable presence of mind." [5]

I must confess that to me Irene is much less attractive. She was overwhelmingly ambitious—her admirers remark that her dominating characteristic was the love of power ($\tau\grave{o}$ $\phi\acute{\iota}\lambda\alpha\rho\chi o\nu$)—and all her life she was devoured by a consuming passion, the desire to rule. She was young and beautiful, but she never took a lover for fear of acquiring a master. She was a mother, but ambition stamped out even her maternal affection. To attain her self-appointed ends she allowed no scruples to stand in her way; she considered all means worthy, dissimulation and intrigue, cruelty and treachery. She directed all the powers of her mind and all the strength of her pride toward one single object, the throne. And this was her entire life. Even her very real and deep piety helped her ambitious schemes; for it was a narrow, superstitious piety, which made her fancy that she was God's chosen instrument, that she had a work to accomplish in the world, a work that she must defend and never permit others to overthrow. She thus successfully combined religious promptings with ambition and love of power; and, being consequently always convinced that she was in the right, and certain of her duty, she pressed sincerely on to her goal without pausing at any obstacle or allowing any difficulty to turn her aside from the path. She was proud and passionate, violent,

[5] G. Schlumberger, *Les Iles des Princes*, p. 112.

brutal, and cruel; she was tenacious and obstinate, and followed up her schemes with extraordinary and untiring perseverance. She was subtle and dissembling, and brought an unprecedented resourcefulness and an incomparable genius for plotting and intrigue to the fulfillment of her designs. There is, decidedly, an element of grandeur in this familiar habit of supreme power which ultimately gains a complete mastery of the soul and so transforms it that all natural feeling is abolished and nothing is left but ambition.

It is well to bear in mind that, in externals, Irene was admirably suited to the part of a woman of great ambition. She was majestic, she had the dramatic sense, she loved splendor and magnificence, and she loved to build—in all of which she reveals her femininity. In addition, her friends maintain that she governed well, that the people loved her and regretted her downfall, and that her reign was an era of unmixed prosperity. We shall see presently what to think of this praise. In any case, I am unable to distinguish the great intelligence, the vigorous intellect, the masculine courage, and the strength of soul in adversity, that her adherents attribute to the Empress. One thing that makes me doubt her statesmanlike qualities and her clearness of insight is the fact that she was always too quick to think she had succeeded, and that several times she encountered obstacles which she ought to have foreseen. She was able and powerful, perhaps, at intrigue; but in her methods of operation I see rather a petty trickiness and slyness, which, while it sometimes undoubtedly succeeded, in no way implies genius. I grant that she was pertinacious, and that she kept hammering at obstructions until she had broken them down. But, in spite of her much-vaunted greatness of soul ($\tau \grave{o}$ $\kappa \rho \alpha \tau \alpha \iota \acute{o} \phi \rho o \nu$) and masculine spirit ($\tau \grave{o}$ $\mathring{\alpha} \rho \rho \epsilon \nu \omega \pi \grave{o} \nu$ $\phi \rho \acute{o} \nu \eta \mu \alpha$), she appears to me neither truly energetic nor really brave.

In 797, when she was on the point of carrying out the *coup d'État* that overthrew her son, she lost her head at the critical moment; she took fright, thought of humiliating herself, believed the business had miscarried, and wanted to abandon the whole project. In 802, when some conspirators brought about her downfall, she allowed herself to be dethroned without even attempting resistance. She was weak in defeat, and in victory pitiless. The treatment she inflicted on her son makes it superfluous to mention her heart. Undoubtedly she did some great things during the twenty-odd years of her reign: she dared bring about a political and religious revolution of unparalleled importance. But she herself had neither greatness of soul nor greatness of will.

But, whatever Irene was like, the times in which she lived still remain strangely interesting and dramatic. As has been truly said: "In all Byzantine history, full as it is of incredible events, the reign of Irene is perhaps one of the most astonishing." [6]

III

When the death of Leo IV gave into Irene's hands the substance of supreme power, there were many rival ambitions in the field. At court she was confronted by the silent hostility of her brothers-in-law, the five sons of Constantine V, popular and ambitious men, from whom she had everything to fear. Their father, before he died, had vainly made them swear never to conspire against the legitimate sovereign; as soon as Leo IV had ascended the throne they had broken their oaths; and even though, after this attempt, the eldest of them, the Caesar Nicephorus, had been stripped of his dignities and exiled to far-off Cherson, a numerous

[6] E. Molinier, *Histoire des arts appliqués à l'industrie*, tome i, p. 84.

following undertook to work on their behalf. Moreover, all the chief posts in the government were occupied by zealous Iconoclasts. The Master of the Offices, or Chancellor, and the Domestic of the Scholae, or Commander-in-Chief of the Army, were old and tried servants of the dead Basileus Constantine V. The Senate and the high provincial officials were no less devoted to the policies of the preceding reign. The Church, under the administration of the Patriarch Paul, was full of enemies of the images. With such men Irene could undertake nothing, while they in their turn rightly suspected the Basilissa's tendencies, and feared lest she should attempt some reactionary measures. To realize her pious projects and her ambitious dreams the Empress would have to look elsewhere for advice and support.

And here appears her skill in preparing the way. Some of her opponents she broke mercilessly by sheer force; others she ousted more gently from positions where they hampered her. A plot having been formed to elevate the Caesars to the throne, she grasped the opportunity to force them into holy orders; and, so that no one should be in ignorance of their final downfall, she compelled them to take part in the solemn Christmas services of the year 780 in St. Sophia, in the presence of all the people of the capital. At the same time, she little by little changed the personnel of the Palace. She advanced her own family, and gave positions to her brother, her nephew, a female cousin, and other relatives. She disgraced Constantine V's old generals, in particular the terrible Michael Lachanodraco, Strategus of the Thracians, who had made himself notorious by his savage hatred of the monks, and by his jovial brutality in forcing marriage upon them. Their places she filled with her own creatures, particularly with the eunuchs of her household, who were her especial friends. It was to them that she entrusted all the great offices in the Palace and in the administration, and it was from their number that she finally selected her Prime Minister, Stauracius.

This man, the Basilissa's chief favorite, became patrician and Logothete of the Dromos, and was soon the acknowledged and all-powerful master in the Sacred Palace. As diplomatist he negotiated a peace with the Arabs; as general he crushed the Slavic rebellion; and, to enhance his prestige still further, Irene allowed him a solemn triumph in the Hippodrome. The army, discontented under such a commander, vainly manifested its hatred of the upstart; he was certain of the Empress's favor, and increased in pride and insolence. Indeed, he attached himself faithfully for twenty years to Irene's fortunes, always falling with her, and with her returning to power. And perhaps this energetic, active, ambitious man, whose merits cannot be denied, often directly inspired the sovereign's measures; but it is obvious what a private character—of the nature of a *camarilla*—this seizure of all the machinery of the administration by the eunuchs of the household gave from the outset to Irene's government.

Irene, while filling the public services with new men, modified the general policy of the Empire. She brought to an end the war in the East, and in the West sought a reconciliation with the Papacy, and began negotiations for an alliance with Charlemagne. Above all, she restored a long-abandoned policy of toleration. "Pious men," says a contemporary chronicler, "began to speak freely; once more the Word of God could spread without hindrance; those who sought eternal salvation could retire unmolested from the world, and God's glory was once more celebrated; the monasteries flourished again, and prosperity was universal." Monks reappeared in Constantinople, and the cloisters were opened at last to many who had long been forbidden to have vocations.

The Empress ostentatiously took measures to repair the sacrileges of the former régime; she went in great pomp to restore to St. Sophia the valuable crown that Leo IV had removed, and she replaced solemnly in their sanctuary the relics of St. Euphemia, which had been thrown into the sea by order of Constantine V and miraculously recovered. The religious party was delighted at these developments, greeting the accession of this pious sovereign as an unexpected miracle; and they gave thanks to God who "by the hand of a widow and a fatherless child would now overthrow sacrilege and put an end to the Church's enslavement."

An ably managed intrigue gave into Irene's hands the only power she lacked—the Patriarchate. Suddenly, in 784—without consulting the government, says Theophanes, though it is more probable that the suggestion emanated from the Palace—the Patriarch Paul resigned his office and retired to a monastery, declaring to all who cared to listen that he was full of remorse for his sins, and desirous of expiating his crimes against the images, in the hope at least of dying at peace with God. This decision of his, which made a great stir in the capital, Irene very cleverly exploited, and chose the imperial secretary Tarasius, a layman, a man she was sure of, to be head of the Church in Paul's place. He was an astute, pliable politician, who played admirably the part the sovereign had doubtless mapped out for him. When his name was proposed, and when the Empress herself begged him to accept the nomination and allow himself to be elected, he refused, declining the charge which he was asked to undertake and requesting permission to explain to the people the reasons for his refusal. In a long discourse he reviewed in detail the deplorable condition of the Church, the discords that rent it, and the schism that separated it from Rome, and, very adroitly, naming it as the price of his acceptance, he

launched the idea of an Ecumenical Council to restore peace
and concord to the Christian world. At the same time, by a
clever sidethrust, he disavowed the Iconoclastic synod held
in 753, denying that it had any canonical authority, on the
ground that it had done nothing but register illegally pro-
mulgated decrees of the civil authority concerning the
Church. And, having thus prepared the way for the Basilissa's schemes, he finally gave in, received all the sacred orders
at one and the same time, and ascended the patriarchal
throne.

Provided with so valuable an ally, Irene felt able to throw
aside the mask. Writs were sent throughout the Empire calling upon the prelates of Christendom to meet in Constantinople during the spring of 786, for the Empress was sure
of victory. But she had left out of account the opposition of
certain bishops, as well as that of the regiments of the
Imperial Guard, which was faithful to the memory of Constantine V and firmly attached to the policy of that glorious
Emperor. The error was obvious from the moment the Council opened in the Church of the Holy Apostles. The bishops
were solemnly seated in their chairs; Irene and her son were
in the Porch of the Catechumens; Plato, Abbot of Sakkudion, one of the most ardent defenders of the images, had
the floor and was delivering an appropriate homily, when
suddenly the soldiers, sword in hand, burst into the church
and threatened the prelates with death. Irene, not lacking in
courage, tried in vain to interpose and calm the uproar: her
efforts were useless and her authority unrecognized. The
Orthodox bishops were insulted, hustled, and driven out,
seeing which the Iconoclastic bishops joined with the army,
applauding and crying: "We have won! We have won!"
Irene herself escaped not without some difficulty "from the
lion's claws," as an ecclesiastical chronicler says; and though

she was unscathed, her partisans ostentatiously proclaimed her a martyr.

She had gone too fast, and all was to do over again. This time a tortuous policy was adopted. The Basilissa and her Prime Minister brought to the task all their wiles and all their capacity for intrigue. The government by money and promises won over the Asiatic army corps, which were always jealous of the troops on garrison duty in the capital. A great expedition against the Arabs was then announced. The guard regiments were the first to leave for the front, and they were immediately replaced in Constantinople by divisions whose fidelity was assured. At the same time, to force the recalcitrants to obedience, the wives and children of the soldiers in the field were arrested and their property was seized. With these precious hostages in their hands, the government was able without danger to break, furlough, and disband the ill-disposed guard regiments. Irene had now the necessary support for her schemes—namely, an army of men of her own choosing under leaders devoted to her. Nevertheless, having her failure of 786 in mind, she did not risk reopening the Ecumenical Council in Constantinople itself. It met in 787 at Nicea; and under the all-powerful influence of the court, the Patriarch, and the monks, it unhesitatingly anathematized the Iconoclastic decisions of 753, and completely re-established image worship and Orthodoxy. Then, in November 787, the Fathers crossed over to Constantinople, and at a last solemn session in the Palace of Magnaura, Irene, in the presence of Pope Hadrian's legates, subscribed her name to the canons that restored her cherished beliefs.

Thus, by seven years of patient skill, Irene had, in spite of some precipitancy, made herself all-powerful. She had gratified the Church and her own piety; above all, she had crushed under foot everything that interfered with her ambition. And her friends, the religious party, proud of such a sovereign, hailed her pompously as "the Christ-supporting Empress, whose government, like her name, is token of peace" (χριστοφόρος Εἰρήνη, ἡ φερωνύμως βασιλεύσασα).

IV

At the very moment that Irene was winning this victory, when her triumph seemed most complete, her ambition was seriously threatened.

Constantine VI was growing up; he was seventeen years of age. Between the son, eager to reign, and the mother, passionately desirous of supreme power, a conflict was inevitable; and it was destined to surpass in horror anything that can be imagined. Accordingly, the pious historians of the period are unable to account for this infamous struggle except by diabolical inspiration, and, in their anxiety to excuse the most devout Empress, have so far as possible cast the blame for her misdeed upon her sinister counselors. But these excuses will not stand investigation: from what we know of Irene it is certain that she was fully aware of her actions and was completely responsible for them. She was bound to safeguard the work that had just been accomplished and to retain her usurped power: to do so she halted neither at strife nor at crime.

Irene, domineering and passionate, continued to treat her son like a child. At the beginning of her reign, from political motives, she had begun negotiations for a marriage between Constantine VI and one of Charlemagne's daughters; and a palace eunuch had been dispatched to Aix-la-Chapelle to instruct the young Rotrude in the language and customs of her future country; the learned men of Charlemagne's Palatine Academy, in their pride at the prospective alliance, were inspired with a longing to learn Greek. But politics undid what they had done. After peace had been re-established with Rome, the Frankish alliance seemed less necessary to Irene; it is said that she feared chiefly lest the mighty Charles should become too strong a support to his son-in-law and help him be master of the Empire. Thus she abandoned the cherished plan, and in spite of Constantine's protests—for he had conceived from afar an affection for the young Western Princess—forced another marriage upon him. I have already given the charming tale out of the *Life of St. Philaret* of how the imperial envoys, according to established custom, traveled throughout the provinces to discover a bride worthy of the Basileus, and how, from among the candidates for Constantine's hand, Irene and her minister chose a young Armenian girl from the Paphlagonian Theme, Mary of Amnia. She was pretty, intelligent, and devout, and came, moreover, from a family of modest origins; above all, Irene felt that she would submit with docility to her benefactress's wishes, and that from such a daughter-in-law she need have no fear of inconvenient ambitions. The marriage was thus determined upon, and Constantine, in spite of himself, had to obey. This was in November 788.

Irene, furthermore, was careful to keep her son out of all public business. The Emperor was practically isolated in his own court, without friends or influence; while the all-powerful Stauracius, on the other hand, insolent and haughty, governed as he chose, and everyone humbled himself before the favorite. At last the young Emperor revolted against this tutelage, and with some of his intimates conspired against the Prime Minister. But misfortune overtook him. The plot was discovered, and Irene realized at once that she had been directly threatened. From that day forth ambition stifled her maternal affection. She retaliated brutally.

The conspirators were tortured, exiled, or cast into prison; the Emperor himself was beaten with rods, like a disobedient child, roundly rebuked by his mother, and kept for several days in close confinement. After this the Empress thought herself safe. Her flatterers also encouraged her illusion, proclaiming that "even God did not wish her son to reign." Being superstitious and credulous, like all her contemporaries, she allowed herself to be convinced by their words and by soothsayers who promised her the throne; and, in order to make sure of it, she risked everything upon a single throw. The army was asked to take a new oath of allegiance, and the soldiers were obliged to swear in the following unusual way: "So long as thou shalt live we will never recognize thy son as Emperor." And henceforth, in the official acclamations, Irene's name was put before Constantine's.

As in 786, so again this time, the eager and ambitious Princess had proceeded too quickly. In 790, a manifesto was suddenly issued by the Asiatic regiments in favor of the young Emperor. The revolt spread from the Armeniac army corps to the other themes, and soon all the troops gathered together and demanded that Constantine VI should be set at liberty and recognized as the one and only Basileus. Irene was frightened and gave in. She consented to free her son and abdicate; raging but powerless, she witnessed the disgrace of her closest friends. Stauracius, the Prime Minister, was tonsured and exiled to Armenia, and Aëtius, another of her intimates, shared his downfall. She herself was obliged to retire to her magnificent Eleutherian Palace, and she beheld in the enjoyment of the favor of the young Prince, now solemnly proclaimed, all those whom she had fought, all the enemies of the images that she had restored. Among the foremost was old Michael Lachanodraco, on whom was bestowed the high dignity of Master of the Offices.

But Constantine VI bore no grudge against his mother. Hardly a year had elapsed since Irene's downfall, when, in January 792, the young monarch granted her petitions, restored to her the title of Empress, brought her back to the Sacred Palace, and associated her in the government. At the same time the Basileus weakly recalled her favorite, Stauracius. Irene returned thirsting for vengeance, determined to punish those who had betrayed her, and more eager than ever to fulfill her ambitious desires. But this time she acted more circumspectly. In 790 she had been too certain of success; she had wished to hurry matters and win the throne at one stroke, and by her cruelty toward her son had scandalized public opinion and caused the army to revolt. Her failure taught her to be more careful; this time she took five long years in the slow preparation of her triumph by the most subtle and ingenious intrigues.

Constantine VI had undoubted qualities. Like his grandfather he was brave, energetic, intelligent, and capable; his very adversaries praise him, recognizing his merits as a soldier and his aptitude for government. The accusations brought against him, chiefly that of debauchery, are not to be taken as literally as one might imagine, for in the minds of their authors they are all inspired by the scandal of his second marriage. His Orthodoxy being beyond dispute, he was extremely popular with the lower classes and in good odor with the Church; and as he was a brave and active general, quite willing to resume hostilities against the Bulgarians and the Arabs, he satisfied the army. It was Irene's masterstroke to embroil this estimable sovereign with all his best friends in turn, to make him appear at once ungrateful, cruel, and cowardly, to lose him the goodwill of the army, to turn popular feeling against him, and, finally, to ruin him with the Church.

Her first use of the influence which she had regained was
to excite Constantine's suspicions against Alexius Muselé,
the general who had issued the manifesto of 790; him she
managed to compromise so thoroughly that the Emperor disgraced and imprisoned him, and then had him blinded. This
was a double victory for Irene, for she not only revenged herself upon the man who had betrayed her confidence, but also
stirred up against Constantine his best support, the Armeniac troops. At the same time, since there was still a party
that continued to plot on behalf of his uncles, the Caesars,
the Emperor, on Irene's advice, sentenced the eldest to be
blinded and had the tongues of the four others cut out—a
useless cruelty that made him very unpopular, especially
with the Iconoclasts, who cherished in the persons of the
victims the memory of their father, Constantine V. Finally,
to arouse public opinion against her son, the Empress de-
vised one last scheme, the most Machiavellian of all.

Constantine VI, as is well known, did not love his wife,
although she had borne him two daughters, Euphrosyne and
Irene. And he kept mistresses. After Irene's return to the
Palace, he soon developed a lively affection for one of the
Empress-mother's maids of honor. Her name was Theodota.
She belonged to one of the great families of the capital, and
was related to some of the most celebrated men of the Orthodox party, Plato, Abbot of Sakkudion, and his nephew
Theodore. Irene complacently encouraged her son's passion
for her lady-in-waiting, and it was she herself who urged
him to divorce his wife and marry the young girl; for she
knew quite well the scandal that such a step would arouse,
and the help it would afford to her plans. Constantine listened
eagerly to her advice; and there then began in the Palace a
very curious intrigue to get rid of Mary—an intrigue to which
I must later return, for it is altogether characteristic of con-

temporary Byzantine customs. In the end, despite the Patriarch's opposition, the Emperor put his wife in a convent, and, in September 795, married Theodota.

Irene's expectations were realized. From all Byzantine Christendom, even from the farthest provinces, there went up a cry of horror at this adulterous marriage. The religious party were utterly scandalized and made an uproar; the monks, fanning the flame, thundered against the debauched, bigamous Emperor, and clamored at the weakness of Tarasius, the Patriarch, who, with characteristic diplomacy, allowed such abominations to exist. Irene quietly helped and encouraged their revolt, "because," as a contemporary chronicler says, "they were resisting her son and bringing shame upon him." One should read the ecclesiastical writers to see to what a paroxysm of fury the religious party attained in their righteous wrath against the disobedient and shameless son, against the debauched and corrupt Prince. "Woe to thee," said Theodore of Studion, quoting the words of the Preacher, "woe to thee, O land, when thy king is a child!" Constantine kept his head, and exerted himself by means of compromise to allay this terrific outburst. The principal center of opposition being the monastery of Sakkudion in Bithynia, he went on pretext of a holiday to Prusa, the watering-place, and from there made all sorts of courteous overtures to the monks of the celebrated monastery. In the hope of placating them by such a mark of consideration, he even paid them a visit. But nothing came of it. "If we have to shed our blood," said Theodore of Studion, "we will shed it gladly."

In the face of this intransigence the Emperor was so misguided as to lose patience, and he determined to employ force. Arrests were made; some of the religious were beaten with rods, imprisoned, or exiled; the remainder of the community was dispersed. But such rigorous punishments served only to complicate the situation. The monks everywhere fulminated against the tyrant, "the new Herod"; and in the very Palace the Abbot Plato came and insulted him to his face. Constantine had himself in hand. To the abbot's invectives he answered coldly: "I have no desire to make martyrs," and let him have his say. Unfortunately for him, he had already made too many. Public opinion was exasperated, and Irene knew how to profit by it.

During the court's sojourn in Prusa, the Empress-mother had played her cards very cleverly, and circumstances were as favorable as could be desired. Theodota, the young Basilissa, had had to return to the Sacred Palace for her accouchement, and Constantine, who was devoted to her, became restless in her absence. Therefore when, in October 796, he was told that she had borne him a son, he made haste to depart for Constantinople. He thus left the ground clear for Irene's intrigues. By gifts and promises and by her personal charm, she quickly won over the principal officers of the guard to her side, and persuaded them to consent to a *coup d'État* making her sole Empress. The conspirators, acting as usual under Stauracius's orders, arranged to await a favorable moment. But there was still one reef upon which the whole scheme might suffer shipwreck. If Constantine were to achieve some brilliant military success, it would probably serve to restore his tottering prestige; and, as a matter of fact, in March 797, he had just begun the campaign against the Arabs. His mother's friends did not scruple to turn the expedition into failure by means of a lie very like treason, and the Emperor was obliged to return to Constantinople, having neither encountered the enemy nor accomplished anything.

The crisis was drawing near. On the 17th of July 797,

Constantine was returning from the Hippodrome to the Palace of St. Mamas. The traitors surrounding him thought their chance had come, and attempted to take him prisoner. He, however, succeeded in escaping, and jumping into a boat hurried across to the Asiatic shore, counting on the fidelity of the troops of the Anatolic Theme. Irene, who upon the news of the attempted arrest had immediately taken possession of the Great Palace, was terrified and lost her head; seeing her friends waver, and learning that the people were inclined to favor Constantine, she decided to humble herself and send some bishops to him to intercede for her, when suddenly the passion for supreme power inspired her to play a last card. Many of the courtiers had compromised themselves very deeply with her in the plot; she threatened to denounce them to the Basileus and to turn over to him the incriminating documents. Terrified at this, and seeing no other means of averting certain destruction, the conspirators plucked up their courage and seized their unfortunate sovereign. He was brought back to Constantinople and shut up in the Sacred Palace; and there, in the Purple Pavilion where he had been born, the executioner came by his mother's orders and put out his eyes. However, he did not die. He was kept in seclusion in a splendid residence where later his wife Theodota, who had stood bravely by him during the crisis, was allowed to join him. She even bore him a second son, and thus he passed the remaining years of his life in quiet obscurity. But his days as Emperor were over.

Very few mourned the unfortunate Prince. The religious party in their narrow fanaticism looked upon his disgrace as the righteous, divinely ordained punishment of his adulterous marriage, as the due reward of his stern treatment of the monks, as a memorable example whereby, says Theodore of Studion, "even Emperors will learn not to violate God's laws, nor to unchain impious persecutions." Pious souls once more acclaimed with gratitude and admiration the enfranchisement wrought by the Most Christian Empress Irene. The chronicler Theophanes, in spite of his devotion to the Basilissa, alone seems vaguely to have felt the horror of her crime. "For seventeen days," says he, "the sun veiled himself and gave forth no light, so that vessels went astray upon the sea; and all men said that it was by reason of the Emperor's blinding that the sun forbore to shine; and thus ascended the throne Irene, mother to the Emperor."

V

Irene's dream was realized. From henceforth she seems to have been drunk with success and power. For she dared to do an unheard of thing, a thing Byzantium had never seen before and was never to see again: she, a woman, assumed the title of Emperor. At the head of the *Novels* that she issued, she styled herself proudly: "Irene, great Basileus and Autocrat of the Romans." Upon her coins and upon the ivory diptychs that have preserved her portrait [7] she appears in all the pomp and circumstance of sovereignty. Thus, and more splendidly still, she showed herself to her people. On Easter Monday of the year 799, she returned from the Church of the Holy Apostles to the Palace in solemn procession, in a golden chariot drawn by four white horses, each led by a high official. Wearing the splendid imperial robes that glittered with purple and gold, she, like the Consuls of Rome, threw money by the handful to the assembled multitude. It was her apotheosis, and the climax of her splendor.

At the same time, adroit as ever, she nursed her popu-

[7] One is preserved in Vienna, the other in the Bargello at Florence. Cf. E. Molinier, loc. cit., tome i, pp. 81–4.

larity and strengthened her power. Her brothers-in-law, the Caesars, whose ambition survived their disgrace, intrigued against her once more. She put down their attempts cruelly and exiled them to distant Athens. To her friends the monks, on the other hand, she was attentive and beneficent, building them new monasteries and endowing restored ones lavishly. Owing to her favor, the great monastic establishments of Sakkudion in Bithynia and of the Studion in the capital attained to unprecedented prosperity. Finally, to conciliate the people, she undertook a whole series of liberal reforms— large remissions of taxation, reform of the financial administration, a lowering of customs duties both at frontiers and at ports and of taxes upon foodstuffs and articles of manufacture; and she pleased the poor by her charitable foundations. Constantinople was enchanted, and hailed her as its benefactress.

Nevertheless, veiled intrigues were in progress at court around the aged sovereign; her favorites were wrangling over the succession. At her death the throne would be vacant, for only two daughters were born on Constantine VI's first marriage. As for the children of his second marriage, the elder son, Leo, had died a few months after birth, and the second, born after his father's downfall, was considered a bastard, the issue of an illegitimate connection, and disqualified for the throne. The two eunuchs who governed the Empire, Stauracius and Aëtius, both hoped to obtain the power for their relatives, whom they helped to high positions. Irene's failing health, moreover, seemed to warrant the approaching fulfillment of their hopes. Jealous to the end, nevertheless, of her supreme power, and keenly suspicious of anyone who appeared to threaten her crown, the old Basilissa held tenaciously to the throne her crime had won.

For more than a year the Sacred Palace was the scene of

continual denunciations and violent quarrels, of sudden downfalls and unexpected returns to favor. Aëtius inveighed against the plots and ambitions of Stauracius, and Stauracius stirred up revolts to ruin Aëtius, while between the two drifted Irene, disturbed and irritated, now punishing, now pardoning. There is something really tragic in this struggle between the old, worn-out Empress, clinging desperately to her throne, and the all-powerful minister, ill likewise and spitting blood, in the care of physicians and on the brink of death, but conspiring still, and hoping for the crown against all hope. He was the first to succumb, about the middle of the year 800. While the Byzantine court was wasting its time in such fruitless quarrels, at that very moment, in St. Peter's in Rome, Charlemagne was restoring the Empire of the West.

It is said that a grandiose idea was entertained by the Teutonic Cæsar and the aged sovereign of Byzantium—namely, a marriage that would unite their monarchies under their joint rule, and restore even more gloriously and more fully than in the time of Augustus, of Constantine, or of Justinian, the ancient unity of the *Orbis Romanus*. It does not seem probable, but, at all events, negotiations were set on foot to establish a *modus vivendi* between the two States. Frankish ambassadors were present in Constantinople when the final catastrophe occurred in which Irene was overthrown.

As the old Empress grew more feeble, the intrigues became keener and bolder. Aëtius, all-powerful since the death of his rival, openly encouraged his brother and endeavored to assure him the support of the army. Others of the great nobles were aroused against the favorite's haughtiness and insolent ambition, and one of the ministers, Nicephorus, the Grand Logothete, took advantage of the general unrest to conspire in his turn against the Basilissa. The Iconoclastic party silently prepared its revenge. On the 31st of October 802, the revolution broke out. "God, in his wisdom that passeth understanding," says the pious Theophanes, "permitted it to happen, in order to punish the sins of mankind."

Irene was taking a holiday at her favorite residence, the Eleutherian Palace. The conspirators—among whom were former friends of Aëtius who had become discontented with the favorite, former intimates of Constantine VI, several Iconoclastic officers eager for revenge, high civil officials, courtiers, and even some relatives of the Empress, all of whom she had loaded with gifts—took advantage of her absence. At ten o'clock in the evening they appeared at the gates of the Sacred Palace and showed the guards of the Chalce forged orders, purporting to come from the Basilissa, in which she commanded Nicephorus to be proclaimed Emperor without delay, so that he might help her to withstand the intrigues of Aëtius. The soldiers allowed themselves to be persuaded, and surrendered the Palace.

In every Byzantine revolution the Palace was the essential point which had to be gained at the outset, as the token and symbol of victory. And, as a matter of fact, the night had not passed before messengers had announced to the whole city Nicephorus's achievement and the success of the *coup d'État.* No resistance was offered. At the same time, Irene was taken by surprise and arrested at Eleutherion, sent heavily guarded to Constantinople, and shut up in the Sacred Palace; while on the following morning in St. Sophia, the new Basileus caused himself to be crowned in haste by the Patriarch Tarasius, who seems to have forgotten his benefactress. Nevertheless, nothing was settled. Irene was popular, and the mob, recovering from their first surprise, were openly hostile to the conspirators. They insulted the new master and cursed

the Patriarch; and many people, remembering the protesta-
tions of loyalty with which the plotters had tricked the Empress, taxed them vigorously with their ingratitude. They
sighed for the old order that had been overthrown and for
the prosperity it had brought, and dreaded what the future
might have in store. The multitude, unable to believe what
had happened, wondered if they were not the victims of a
nightmare. Consternation and grief were universal, and the
cold, foggy autumn morning made the dawn of the new reign
even more desolate.

A woman of real energy might perhaps have profited by
this situation: Irene did not. Between ambition and piety, the
two sentiments that divided her soul and had governed her
life, piety this time proved the stronger. Not that her downfall in any way weakened her courage, for she showed no
weakness; but in the face of an accomplished fact, "as a wise
and God-fearing woman," to quote a contemporary, she
yielded without a murmur. Nicephorus, on the day after his
coronation, went to visit her, his eyes filled with hypocritical
tears, and, showing her, with his customary feigned good
nature, the black shoes he wore instead of the imperial red
buskins, assured her that his hands had been forced, and almost apologized for being Emperor. But Irene, with Christian resignation, humbled herself before the new Basileus as
before God's Anointed, blessing the mysterious decrees of
Providence, and acknowledging her sins as the cause of her
downfall. She made no reproach and uttered no complaint.
Upon Nicephorus's request, she even surrendered him her
wealth, asking only that she should be allowed free use of
the Eleutherian Palace.

The usurper promised all that she asked, and assured her
that during her life she should be treated "as becomes a
Basilissa." But he lost no time in forgetting his promises.

The aged sovereign was removed from Constantinople and
exiled at first to the monastery she had founded on the island
of Prinkipo. But even there she seemed too near. In November 802, despite the unusual severity of the winter, she was
sent to Lesbos. There she was kept closely guarded, and no
one was allowed to approach her—to such an extent were her
intrigues and the tenacity of her ambition still feared. In this
captivity she died miserably, in the month of August 803,
deserted by all. Her body was brought back to the monastery
on Prinkipo, and later to Constantinople, where she was
buried in the Church of the Holy Apostles, in the mortuary
chapel where so many Emperors slept.

Irene was so pious and orthodox a sovereign that the
Church has forgiven her everything, even her crimes.[8] The
Byzantine chroniclers of her time call her the Blessed
Irene, the New Helen, "she who fought for the true faith
like a martyr." Theophanes mourns her loss as a catastrophe,
and looks back upon the years of her reign as upon an era of
unusual prosperity. Theodore of Studion, a saint, addressed
the basest flatteries to her, not finding words rapturous
enough to describe "the wholly good sovereign," "so pure a
spirit, so holy a soul," who by her piety and her desire to
please God had delivered her people from slavery, and whose
deeds "shine like stars." Irene deserves of history less indulgence and more justice. One can understand, and, if one
wishes, forgive, the error of sincere folk whom party spirit
has blinded in regard to her, but one must beware of sharing
their error. Rightly regarded, this famous sovereign was a
politician, ambitious and devout, whom the passion for power

---

[8] It must, however, be noted that some Byzantines felt the horror of
Irene's crime keenly enough, and tried to relieve her of the responsibility
of it. The chronicler George the Monk, writing in the ninth century, declares that Constantine was blinded "without her being present, or even
being privy to her ministers' plans."

drove to crime, and whose achievements were totally insufficient to compensate for the horror of her deed. For by her intrigues, she reopened in Byzantium for a period of eighty years, to the great detriment of the monarchy, the era of palace revolutions to which for nearly a century her glorious predecessors the Iconoclastic Emperors had put an end.

V

THE BLESSED
THEODORA

I

In the year 829, Michael II the Amorian, Emperor of Byzantium, died, leaving the throne to his son, Theophilus. The new sovereign was unmarried; and at first, therefore, the Empress-dowager Euphrosyne took the place in the court ceremonies reserved by etiquette for the Augusta. But Euphrosyne detested the world. Daughter of the unfortunate Constantine VI, who was so cruelly blinded by order of his mother Irene, and of his first wife, Mary, she had retired after the downfall of her family to one of the convents of Prinkipo. There she had lived in quiet seclusion until, not without some scandal, the Basileus Michael had taken the beautiful nun, whom he loved passionately, out of her convent and set her upon the throne of the Caesars. But as soon as her husband was dead, Euphrosyne's one wish was to return immediately to some holy retreat; she therefore bent all her endeavors to finding a wife for the young Emperor, her step-son, without delay.

In accordance with the traditional custom of the Byzantine
court, messengers scoured the provinces to find the most
beautiful girls in the Empire and to bring them to Constantinople; and they were gathered together in the great Pavilion
of the Pearl so that from among them Theophilus might
choose the future Empress. He first selected the six most
attractive, but, finding himself unable to decide, postponed
his definite choice until the morrow. On the following day he
appeared among the girls holding, like Paris among the
three goddesses, a golden apple, to be given to her whom he
should choose, and thus equipped he began his inspection.
He stopped in front of a very lovely, highborn maiden named
Kasia, and being rather embarrassed, perhaps, and not quite
knowing how to start conversation, began sententiously
with the following dubious compliment:

> *A woman was the fount and source*
> *Of all man's tribulation.*

Kasia was witty, and retorted undismayed:

> *And from a woman sprang the course*
> *Of man's regeneration.*[1]

This answer ruined her chances. Theophilus was terrified
by her quick repartee and her emancipated point of view,
and, turning his back upon her, gave the apple and the Empire to an equally beautiful candidate, Theodora.

In characteristic Byzantine fashion, Kasia consoled herself for the loss of the throne by founding a convent to which
she retired; and, being a clever woman, passed her time composing religious poems and secular epigrams that have come

[1] This metrical translation is taken from J. B. Bury, *A History of the
Eastern Roman Empire from the Fall of Irene to the Accession of Basil I*
(*A.D. 802–867*), 1912, p. 82 and note (2). [Translator's note]

down to us and that are not without interest. Meanwhile her successful rival had been crowned with great ceremony in St. Stephen's Church in the Palace of Daphne, and, as usual, all her family shared her good fortune. Her mother, Theoctista, received the much coveted dignity of Patrician of the Girdle, her three sisters were married to high dignitaries, and her brothers, Petronas and Bardas, moved rapidly from one honor to another. They were destined to show but little gratitude to her whose unforeseen elevation and sisterly affection had brought them to the very steps of the throne.

The new Empress was an Asiatic, born in Paphlagonia of a family of officials. Her relatives were pious folk, much attached to the worship of the images, against which the successors of the most pious Irene had resumed the struggle, and it seems that her family had given proof of considerable zeal for their faith. Having been brought up in such an environment, Theodora was naturally devout and entertained great respect for the holy icons; wherefore at first she was not a little disconcerted by the court life into which her marriage had suddenly translated her.

The Iconoclastic controversy had been reopened about twenty years before, and was perhaps even bitterer than in the eighth century, since to the religious question a political motive had been added: the State advancing the right of interference in matters ecclesiastical, and the Church defending its liberties. Michael II had persecuted his opponents openly and unscrupulously, and Theophilus, an intelligent, masterful, energetic Prince, followed his father's example and continued his policy. Theodora tried in vain to use her influence in her friends' favor and to temper by her entreaties the rigor of the persecution. Theophilus was not a very good-natured monarch; when he frowned and raised his voice, his wife became terrified and dared not press the point, and she herself was obliged carefully to dissimulate her sentiments and her private sympathies. She had to conceal under her clothes the holy images that she insisted upon wearing, she had to take innumerable precautions in hiding away the forbidden icons in chests in her room, and she sometimes ran considerable risk in performing her secret devotions.

One day the Emperor's jester, a dwarf who used to amuse the whole Palace by his malicious witticisms, surprised the Empress at her prayers. Being of an inquisitive turn of mind, he asked to see the objects that so absorbed her attention. "These are my dolls," said Theodora. "They are pretty, and I love them dearly." The dwarf ran as fast as he could and told the Emperor about the beautiful dolls that the Basilissa kept under her pillow. Theophilus instantly understood what was going on, and, furious at finding his orders flouted in his Palace, hurried off to the Gynaeceum and began to make a violent scene. But Theodora was a woman, and knew how to get herself out of the difficulty. "It is not what you suspect at all," she said to her husband. "I was simply looking at myself in the mirror with my attendants, and your dwarf thought that the faces he saw reflected were religious images, and stupidly went off and told you so." Theophilus quieted down, or pretended to be convinced, but Theodora lay in wait for the taleteller. A few days later she had the dwarf soundly whipped for some peccadillo, and then warned him never again to talk about dolls in the Gynaeceum. And when, after drinking, the Emperor would occasionally revert to the subject and question the dwarf, the latter would make a significant gesture, putting one hand on his mouth and the other upon that part of his person which had been flogged, and say hurriedly: "No, no, Sir, let's not talk about dolls."

In the high society of the capital there was a general conspiracy in favor of the icons. The old Empress Euphrosyne, in the convent where she was spending the last years of her life, shared Theodora's sentiments, and whenever the small daughters of the Basileus came to pay her a visit, she talked constantly to them about the holy images. Theophilus, who suspected as much, always questioned the children on their return, without, however, obtaining any definite information. But one day the youngest of the imperial Princesses gave it away. After telling her father about the lovely presents they had received at the convent and the wonderful fruits they had eaten, she went on to explain that her grandmother had a chest all full of beautiful dolls, that she often touched them to the children's foreheads, and made them kiss them devoutly. Theophilus once more became angry and forbade his little daughters to visit the old Basilissa any more. But even among the courtiers many, including statesmen, held the same beliefs as the two Empresses. Ministers and privy counselors were quietly but deeply devoted to image worship, and matters had reached such a pass that even the astrologers, whom the Emperor was in the habit of consulting, prophesied openly to him the approaching overthrow of his work. He himself felt it so strongly that on his deathbed he made his wife and his Prime Minister, the Logothete Theoctistus, swear a solemn oath not to alter his policy, nor to interfere with his friend the Patriarch John, who had been its chief instigator. Final precautions have rarely been so useless.

II

The successor of Theophilus, his son Michael III, was a child; in 842, at the time of his father's death, he was not more than three or four years old. So, like Irene, Theodora assumed the regency during the minority of the young sovereign. She retained the principal ministers of the late reign, the Logothete Theoctistus, who had great influence with her, and the Magister Manuel. Both were devout men, secretly attached, like the Basilissa herself, to image worship; and being, moreover, men of sense, who were rightly worried at the long continuance of a useless and dangerous conflict, they naturally entertained the idea of restoring Orthodoxy. Nevertheless, in spite of their suggestions, the Empress seems at first to have hesitated. Theodora had loved her husband very much, she was devotedly attached to his memory, and dreaded, furthermore, the difficulties of the undertaking. But all the courtiers did their best to convince her; her mother and brothers were constantly giving her advice. In vain the Basilissa objected, saying: "My husband, the late Emperor, was a wise man; he knew what was expedient; we really cannot ignore his wishes." The danger of the situation was pointed out to her, the unpopularity she would incur if she were to persist in carrying out Theophilus's policy; she was worried by suggestions of a revolution in which her son might lose his throne. Her piety, moreover, prompted her to heed the advice that was given her so freely. She yielded.

A synod was assembled at Constantinople. But in order that it should accomplish its task satisfactorily the Patriarch had first to be removed. John, whom Theophilus had made Patriarch in 834, had been the Emperor's tutor. He was an intelligent, active, energetic man, and had lent his powerful aid to the sovereign's purposes; wherefore the opponents of the Iconoclastic party detested him. They represented him as a magician, nicknaming him Lecanomantis, or the Sorcerer, the new Apollonius, the new Balaam. They circulated the most horrid stories about him: how he had been able to destroy the Emperor's enemies by magic; how he had come by night, muttering mysterious charms, and cut off the head of the bronze serpent in the Hippodrome. And how in his suburban house he had fashioned a subterranean and diabolical cave, where in the company of fallen women, generally of wonderful beauty—several of whom by a refinement of scandal were said to be nuns consecrated to God—he conjured up demons by impure sacrifices and questioned the dead to learn the secrets of the future. But, whether or not this gossip was well founded, John was a man of high intelligence and strong will, and therefore very embarrassing. To get rid of him, the Emperor ordered him either to consent to the re-establishment of Orthodoxy or to resign; and it seems that the soldiers sent to convey this ultimatum did it rather roughly. At all events, the Patriarch was deposed and shut up in a monastery; and when, in a fury at his overthrow, he ventured to display his temper by mutilating the images in the monastery, the Regent ordered him to be severely flogged.

One of the victims of the former administration, Methodius, was put in his place, and a general reaction began at once. The bishops undertook the restoration of image worship; those who had been exiled and proscribed were called home and received in triumph; prisoners were set at liberty and honored as martyrs. Upon the walls of the churches religious pictures reappeared, and once more the figure of Christ, solemnly replaced over the Chalce Gate, bore witness to the piety of the masters of the Imperial Palace. At last, on the 19th of February 843, clergy, court, and people, united in a solemn and magnificent ceremony. All night long in the church of Blachernae the Empress prayed devoutly with the priests. In the morning a triumphal procession wound through Constantinople; amid an enthusiastic crowd Theodora, surrounded by bishops and monks, went from Blachernae to St. Sophia and gave thanks in the Great

Church to the Almighty. Adherents of the defeated party were made to march in this procession that celebrated their downfall, carrying candles and bending low under the anathemas that were hurled at them. That evening, the Basilissa gave a banquet to the prelates at the Sacred Palace, and rejoiced with them over the success of her undertaking. This was the Feast of Orthodoxy. And thereafter, in recollection of this great event and in memory of the Blessed Theodora, the Greek Church held a stately festival every year on the First Sunday in Lent to celebrate the restoration of the images and the discomfiture of their enemies. It is still celebrated with pious and grateful devotion.

In the revolution even the dead had a place. The remains of the illustrious confessors Theodore of Studion and the Patriarch Nicephorus, who had suffered for their faith and had died in distant exile, were brought back in triumph to the capital. The Empress and the entire court considered it an honor to go, candle in hand, to receive the venerated relics, to escort with reverence the reliquary borne on the shoulders of priests, and to accompany it through an enormous multitude, to the Church of the Holy Apostles. By way of contrast the tomb of Constantine V was violated, and, regardless of his Imperial Majesty, the remains of the great opponent of the images were cast into the gutter; his sarcophagus of green marble was cut up into thin slabs and used to decorate one of the rooms in the Palace.

The Byzantine historians to whom we owe these details have unfortunately omitted to explain how this great revolution could have been accomplished so quickly, and, to all appearance, without encountering very serious difficulties. It would seem that the most important factor was the universal weariness that resulted from the interminable struggle. But another consideration may have induced statesmen to favor the decision that Theodora succeeded in carrying out. Although from the doctrinal point of view the Church was completely victorious, it was obliged in return to renounce those leanings toward independence manifested by some of its most illustrious defenders. It was now absolutely subject to the State; imperial control in religious matters was more complete than ever before. To this extent, notwithstanding the re-establishment of Orthodoxy, the policy of the Iconoclastic Emperors had borne its fruit.

For the great work that she accomplished, Theodora has been canonized by the Eastern Church. In carrying out her task, however, she was troubled by many pangs of conscience. One thing worried her above all others. As we know, she had loved her husband passionately, and she was unable to endure the thought that he was included in the terrible anathemas that had been hurled against the persecutors of the images. Therefore, when the Fathers assembled in the synod came to beseech her favor to restore the holy icons, she in turn made a request of them—namely, that they should absolve the Emperor Theophilus. And when the Patriarch Methodius objected that, while the Church had the incontestable right to pardon living penitent sinners, it could do nothing for a man well known to have died in mortal sin, Theodora invented a pious falsehood. She asserted that in his last moments the Basileus had repented of his errors, had devoutly kissed the images that she had offered to his lips, and had commended his soul like a good Christian into the hands of God. The bishops readily accepted this edifying story, realizing that it was the price of the restoration of Orthodoxy; and at the Regent's request they decided to offer prayers for a whole week in all the churches of the capital for the repose of the dead Emperor's soul. Theodora herself took part in these devotions, and trusted that she had thus won the mercy of God for the sinning but penitent Prince.

Legend in later times added many details to the touching story of Theodora's love for her husband. It was told how the Empress had learned in terrible dreams of the fate that threatened him. She had beheld the Virgin with Christ in her arms, enthroned among the angels, summoning the Basileus Theophilus before her tribunal and having him cruelly flogged. On another occasion she had dreamed that she was in the Forum of Constantine when suddenly a great mob surged into it, and a procession of men carrying instruments of torture passed through, dragging in their midst the wretched Theophilus, naked and in chains. Theodora had followed the crowd to the square in front of the Palace, before the Chalce Gate. There she had beheld, seated upon a throne, a tall man of terrible aspect, in the awful guise of a judge. The Empress, throwing herself at His feet, implored mercy for her husband, and the man answered: "Woman, great is thy faith. Because of thy piety and thy tears, and because of the prayers of My priests, I pardon Theophilus, thy husband." And He commanded the Emperor to be released. Simultaneously, the Patriarch Methodius made an experiment of his own to satisfy himself as to the designs of Providence. Upon the high altar of St. Sophia he laid a roll of parchment whereon he had written the names of all the Iconoclastic Emperors; then he went to sleep in the church and saw in a dream an angel who told him that the Emperor had found mercy with God; and he affirmed that when, upon awaking, he had removed the parchment from the holy table, the place where he had written the name of Theophilus had become white again, in token of pardon.

Several men, however, proved more implacable than God.

Lazarus, one of the most celebrated painters of icons, had had his right hand cut off by order of the deceased Emperor; and although, according to the legend, his hand had miraculously grown again, the martyr cherished a bitter hatred for his torturer. And to all that the Empress said, he answered obstinately: "God is not so unjust as to forget our sufferings and honor our persecutor." At the court banquet with which the Feast of Orthodoxy ended, another confessor proved no less intractable. This was Theodore Graptus, so called because Theophilus had had four defamatory verses stamped on his forehead with red-hot irons. The Empress, anxious to flatter the martyrs, asked the holy man who had inflicted so horrible a torture upon him. "For this inscription," he replied solemnly, "the Emperor your husband shall answer to me at God's judgment-seat." At this unexpected reply, Theodora burst into tears, and, turning to the bishops, asked if it was thus that they intended to keep their promises. Fortunately the Patriarch Methodius intervened, and not without some difficulty managed to calm the irascible confessor and to reassure the Empress. "Our promises stand," said he. "And if they weigh lightly upon some, that is of no importance." What is important, however, is the evidence that these anecdotes afford, both of the various considerations of policy and humanity that entered into the restoration of Orthodoxy, and of the compromises which the holy bishops and the most pious Theodora arranged with equal facility with their conscience.

III

"Orthodoxy," says a chronicler of the time, "is the greatest virtue." Theodora possessed this virtue in its fullness. But she had other qualities as well. Byzantine historians praise

her political astuteness, her energy, and her courage. They
put into her mouth heroic speeches, such as the one that
stopped an invasion begun by the Bulgarian King: "If you
triumph over a woman, you will reap no glory thereby;
but if you are beaten by one, you will be the laughingstock
of the whole world." At all events, she governed well during
her fourteen years of rule. Her government had, to be sure,
a religious color. She was very proud of having restored Orthodoxy, and was no less anxious to combat heresy; by her
order the Paulicians were given their choice between conversion and death, and, as they refused to yield, blood flowed
freely in the parts of Asia Minor where they were established.
The imperial inquisitors who were sent to crush their resistance did wonders: they succeeded in putting more than one
hundred thousand of them to death by torture—a serious matter, destined to have still more serious consequences. For by
throwing these desperate men into the arms of the Moham-
medans, the imperial government was preparing many troubles for itself in the future.

But in other ways the Regent's pious zeal inspired her to
happier undertakings; it was she who laid the foundations
of the great missionary enterprise which a few years later
carried the Gospel to the Khazars, the Moravians, and the
Bulgars. She had also the glory of inflicting several lasting
defeats upon the Arabs, and of repressing vigorously the insurrection of the Slavs of Hellas. But her chief concern was
the financial administration of the Empire. She is said to
have had a talent for money-making, and an amusing anecdote is told in this connection. One day, as the Emperor
Theophilus was standing at a window of the Palace, he saw
a large and splendid merchant-vessel entering the Golden
Horn. Upon inquiring the name of the owner, he was told
that it belonged to the Empress. He said nothing; but the

next day, as he was going to Blachernae, he went down to the harbor, had the vessel unloaded, and ordered the cargo to be set on fire. Then, turning to his friends, he remarked: "You were not aware that the Empress my wife had made a merchant of me! Never before has a Roman Emperor been a shopkeeper." Whether or not the story is true, Theodora managed the wealth of the State as successfully as her own. When she stepped down from the throne, she left a large balance in the Treasury. And on this account she would doubtless have been reckoned a great sovereign, had it not been for court intrigues and palace rivalries, always of rapid growth under a woman's government, and for the miserable son that Heaven had sent her.

IV

During the reign of Theophilus, the Imperial Palace, for so many centuries the residence of the Byzantine Basileis, had acquired new splendor. The Emperor was fond of building, and to the old constructions of Constantine and of Justinian had added a series of magnificent edifices, luxuriously decorated with the most elegant and exquisite ornaments. He loved pomp and splendor, and, to enhance the magnificence of the Palace receptions, he had ordered miraculous products of the goldsmith's and the mechanic's arts. Among them were the Pentapyrgion, a celebrated golden cabinet in which the crown jewels were exhibited; the golden organs that were played on days of solemn audience; the golden plane-tree standing near the imperial throne, on which mechanical birds fluttered and sang; the golden lions crouching at the Prince's feet, which at certain times rose up and lashed their tails, and roared; and the mysterious golden griffins which seemed to watch over the ruler's safety as in the palaces of Asiatic kings. Furthermore, he had entirely renewed the imperial wardrobe—the beautiful costumes glittering with gold that the Basileus wore in the court ceremonies, the splendid vestments of golden tissue studded with precious stones in which the Augusta arrayed herself. He was a patron of letters, science, and art. He had showered favors upon the great mathematician, Leo of Thessalonica, and in the Palace of Magnaura had founded a school where that scholar imparted the teaching that was one of the glories of Byzantium. He himself, Iconoclast though he was, had become very tolerant of the confessor Methodius from the moment that he proved his ability to solve certain scientific problems in which the Emperor was absorbed. Arabic architecture was much to his taste, and, as he was very anxious to replace religious painting by a freer, more secular style, he had turned the Byzantine art of his time into new channels. Owing to his efforts and intelligent protection, court life in the marvelous Sacred Palace, full of the refinements of splendor and rare luxury, with its incomparable pavilions and terraces, its gardens grandly opening upon the luminous reaches of the Marmora, had taken on a new effulgence. But now that the Emperor was dead, this glorious Palace was the scene of quarrels and intrigues.

Under the regency of Theodora, the real head of government was the Logothete Theoctistus. He was a man of no great merit, an incapable and always unfortunate general, a statesman of but moderate acumen, by temperament cold, melancholy, and harsh. He was unsympathetic and unloved, and maintained himself in power by the Empress's favor. Apartments had been assigned to him in the Palace itself. He exercised an enormous influence over Theodora, and scandalous reports were current in Byzantium concerning his relations with her. He was known to be ambitious, and people remembered the feverish haste with which he had left the army in Crete at the false news of a palace revolution, in order to observe events in the capital. He was suspected of aspiring to the throne, and it was even reported that Theodora approved his desires, and that she intended either to marry him herself or to give him one of her daughters in marriage. It was said that, in order to smooth his path to power, she was quite prepared, like the great Irene, to dethrone and blind her own son. At all events, being deeply devoted to the Regent and having unbounded influence over her, the Logothete did his best to arouse her distrust against all the counselors who shared the power with him.

By his intrigues he speedily rid himself of rivals. The Magister Manuel, tutor with Theoctistus of the young Michael III, was accused of conspiring against the imperial family and was forced to resign office. The Empress's brothers, Petronas and Bardas, were more formidable, especially the latter, whose great intelligence was combined with a total absence of scruples and morals. With Theodora's own consent, Bardas was, on some pretext, exiled from court, and the Logothete imagined that his own power was definitely established. He had not realized that he should have to reckon with the young Emperor.

For Michael III was growing up, and as he grew he showed himself utterly worthless. In vain his mother and the minister had done their utmost to give him an excellent education; in vain he had been entrusted to the best masters, surrounded by the most carefully chosen companions—legend includes among the Prince Imperial's comrades Cyril, later the Apostle of the Slavs. All had been useless, for Michael was fundamentally corrupt. He was now fifteen or sixteen years of age, and cared chiefly for horses, hunting, racing, shows, and athletic contests, and he even stooped to the point of making an exhibition of himself before his associates by driving a chariot in the palace hippodrome. His private life was still worse. He frequented the lowest society, spending part of his nights in drinking; and he had an acknowledged mistress, Eudocia Ingerina.

Theodora and Theoctistus decided that the only thing to be done was to find him a wife as soon as possible. Palace envoys once more searched the provinces for the most beautiful girls in the Empire, and brought them to Constantinople; from among them, Eudocia, a girl of the Decapolis, was chosen and at once crowned Basilissa. But in a few weeks, Michael tired of his wife and of marriage, returned to his former habits, his friends, and his mistress, and launched once more into excesses. All the ridiculous and odious tales that Byzantine historians tell about Michael III must be accepted with reserve; for the chroniclers of the Macedonian dynasty were all too anxious to excuse and justify the assassination by which Basil I won the throne. But, notwithstanding this reservation, undoubted facts testify to the insanity of the wretched Emperor's behavior. Constantly surrounded by actors, debauchees, and clowns, he and his unworthy familiars amused themselves by playing grotesque or filthy jests, he scandalized the Palace with his shocking practical jokes, and he respected neither his family nor his faith. A favorite amusement was to dress himself and his friends as bishops. One took the part of the Patriarch, and the others represented metropolitans; he himself assumed the title of Archbishop of Colonaea, and thus they went masquerading through the city, singing disgusting songs and parodying the holy ceremonies. One day, in imitation of Christ, Michael went to dine at the house of a poor woman, all aghast at receiving the Basileus so unexpectedly. Another time, meeting the Patriarch Ignatius in the streets with his clergy, the Emperor improvised a sort of vaudeville entertainment, and with his retinue of actors he accompanied them for some distance, singing them licentious songs to the sound of cymbals and tambourines.

His mother was the next victim of his disgusting jokes. He sent her word one day that the Patriarch was calling at the Palace, and that she would doubtless like to receive his blessing. The pious Theodora came in haste, and in the great Golden Triclinium found the prelate in full canonicals sitting on a throne beside the sovereign; his cowl was pulled down over his face, and he apparently was lost in deep thought. The Regent fell at the holy man's feet and begged him to remember her in his prayers, when all of a sudden the Patriarch got up, made a few pirouettes, presented his back to the Empress . . . one must consult the chroniclers to discover what he emitted in Theodora's face. Then he turned around and remarked: "You can hardly say, Madam, that even in this we have not tried our best to do you honor." Then, throwing back his cowl, the Patriarch proved to be none other than the Emperor's favorite jester. Michael burst into fits of laughter at this charming pleasantry, while Theodora called down curses upon him, saying: "You wicked child! God has this day withdrawn his help from you!" and left the room in tears. But, in spite of so many evidences of boorish impropriety, his tutors dared not interfere, and, whether from excessive indulgence, or because they hoped to curry favor, were careful not to reprimand him.

But it was Bardas, chiefly, who tolerated his nephew's amusements and so acquired an ascendancy over him. Through the good offices of his friend, the Lord Chamberlain Damianus, he had succeeded in having the Emperor recall him from exile, and very soon ingratiated himself into Michael's favor. Naturally, he detested Theoctistus, who

stood in his way, and he was constantly playing upon the
Basileus's distrust of the minister. He hinted that the Logothete was preparing some *coup d'État*, and he did not hesitate
to slander his sister, the Regent Theodora, by presenting her
conduct in the worst possible light. He succeeded so well that
an unimportant incident (the minister had refused advance-
ment to some friend of the sovereign's) grew into a violent
quarrel between Michael and Theoctistus. This was in 856.
Bardas took advantage of it to inflame Michael's bitterness
still further; he told him that he was being kept out of politics, and nettled his vanity by cynical remarks. "So long as
Theoctistus and the Augusta are together," he used to say,
"the Basileus will be powerless"; and he contrived to persuade the Emperor that his life was threatened. A plot was
formed against the Logothete. A great number of the courtiers were won over to Bardas's side, the Prince agreed to
everything, and even a sister of the Empress joined with
Bardas, her brother, against Theodora and her favorite.
Thus the conspiracy succeeded without great difficulty.

One day, when in the discharge of his duties, Theoctistus
was coming with papers in his hand for an audience with the
Regent, he discovered Bardas in the gallery of the Lausiacus,
which led to the Empress's apartments. Bardas did not rise
at his approach, but looked him up and down most insolently.
A little further on, Theoctistus met the Emperor, who forbade him to go to the Augusta, and ordered the Logothete to
make his daily report to him. As the minister hesitated in astonishment, the Basileus dismissed him roughly. But as he
was leaving, Michael cried out to the chamberlains in waiting: "Arrest that man!" Thereupon Bardas threw himself on
the Logothete, who fled; Bardas caught up with him,
knocked him down, and drew his sword to prevent anyone
from coming to the poor man's rescue. It does not seem,

however, as if the death of Theoctistus had been an essential part of the program; at first, the Emperor simply commanded that he should be taken under close guard to the vestibule of the Scyla, there to await his commands. Unfortunately for the Logothete, the noise had alarmed Theodora, who came running, in disordered attire, her hair disheveled, demanding the release of her favorite, inveighing against her son and her brother, and crying that she forbade anyone to put Theoctistus to death. It was perhaps her eagerness for his safety that cost him his life. Michael's companions feared, if he were allowed to live, that the Regent would restore him to power, and that he would then take cruel vengeance upon his enemies; for safety's sake they decided upon his death. In vain some of the guard officers who had remained faithful to him tried to defend him; in vain the poor wretch hid under the furniture, attempting to avoid his fate. A soldier bent down and with a thrust of his sword ran him through the belly. Bardas finished him off.

The assassination of the Prime Minister was a direct blow at Theodora, and she took it as such. In the midst of the tumult she had heard menacing voices crying out against her; people had shouted to her to beware, that it was the day of murders. Moreover, in her wrath she refused all excuses and all consolation. Savagely, tragically, she invoked the vengeance of Heaven upon the murderers, but chiefly upon her brother Bardas, and openly prayed for their death. By taking this unyielding stand she made herself irksome, and Bardas, whose ambitions she hindered, decided to get rid of her. First, her daughters were taken away and put into a convent, in the expectation that she would soon follow them there of her own free will. As she still hesitated, she was ordered to retire to the convent of Gastria. Not wishing to trouble the State by a useless resistance, she nobly resigned the power, after having delivered officially to the Senate the moneys which under her sound financial administration had been deposited in the Treasury. It was the end of her political career.

In the convent where she found refuge, Theodora lived piously with her daughters for many long years. She forgave her son, over whom she seems later to have regained some influence, but always remained bitterly opposed to Bardas, whom she justly held responsible for the death of Theoctistus. To such a pitch did she carry her hatred that she, the pious, Orthodox Empress, plotted against the brother she loathed, and tried, with the help of some of her friends at court, to have him assassinated. She failed in the attempt, and seems to have been rather severely punished for it. It was doubtless on this occasion that all her property was confiscated, and that she was deprived of the honors attached to her imperial rank. But to console her for her disgrace, fate was to raise up an avenger, destined to satisfy her hate even beyond her hopes. This was Basil, the illustrious founder of the Macedonian dynasty.

❧❧ VI ❧❧

THEOPHANO

In the series of Byzantine Empresses, Theophano is almost as celebrated as Theodora. Since M. Gustave Schlumberger in a charming work set himself to evoke her picturesque, fascinating personality, and to tell the story of her romantic life, this forgotten Princess has suddenly resumed her place in history and in fame. Writers of renown, like Maupassant, graceful writers like the Vicomte de Vogüé, have been carried away by the charm of this beautiful creature, "who disturbed the world as much as Helen, and even more." [1] Such novelists, indeed, as Hugues le Roux have described "this young woman of supernatural loveliness, containing in the delicate perfection of her harmony the power that troubles the world." We too, therefore, must find room in our portrait gallery for "this great sinner," as M. Schlumberger calls her, "whose charms had so fatal an influence, and who was destined to be loved by three successive Em-

[1] E. M. de Vogüé, *Regards historiques et littéraires*, p. 189.

114

perors." It must be admitted at once that many points in
connection with this mysterious, enigmatic Empress are still
obscure, and from the outset we must resign ourselves to a
large measure of ignorance. When the sources are silent,
imagination, however ingenious, has, I think, no right to sup-
plement them; in taking such liberties with the text we run
the risk of writing fiction rather than history. Now, Byzantium is in no sense what M. de Vogüé calls it—"a fairy-
land, a country virgin and unknowable." It is a very real
country, which one can and should endeavor to understand
in a scientific spirit. Studied thus, Theophano may appear to
some less picturesque than she is usually portrayed, but I
hope that she will at least be more convincing.

<h1 style="text-align:center">I</h1>

Whence came this famous Empress, who, toward the end
of the year 956, married the only son of the Basileus Constantine VII, Romanus, the young heir apparent? Little is
known. The court chroniclers, in their concern for the fair
name of the dynasty, assert that she sprang from a very old
and very noble family, and that the Emperor and his wife
were overcome with joy at finding so well-born a bride for
their son. But if the historians less favorable to the Macedonian house are to be believed, the parentage of the future
Basilissa was far more modest. Her father, Craterus, of La-
conian origin, was an obscure plebeian who kept a public
house in one of the slums of the capital. She herself, before
her marriage, was called Anastasia, or more familiarly, Ana-
staso; it was only on drawing near the throne that she received the more high-sounding name of Theophano, "to indicate," say her panegyrists, "that she was manifested and
chosen by God."

In one respect at least she was worthy of her name: her beauty was radiant, superhuman, divine. "By her beauty and her elegance," says a contemporary, "she surpassed all the women of her time." "Her beauty," says another chronicler, "was beyond compare, a miracle of nature." It was doubtless by means of it that she fascinated Romanus. But where did he meet her? how did he win her? We do not know. Did she owe her extraordinary good fortune to one of those beauty shows that were commonly held in Byzantium when a Prince was to be provided with a wife, and in which the fairest girls of the monarchy were inspected by the Emperor and his relatives? I think it not unlikely. Or had there been some love affair between the beautiful plebeian and the young heir to the throne, that ended in marriage? The adventures of Theodora prove that such things were possible, and Romanus's character as we know it does not exclude the possibility.

He was a big, handsome fellow, broad-shouldered, "straight as a cypress." He had beautiful eyes, a clear complexion, and an amiable countenance; his speech was soft and persuasive. He was made to please, and he loved amusement. Being a great hunter and fond of every kind of sport, he was always doing something; his vigorous constitution appreciated the pleasures of the table, and other pleasures as well. He was unfortunate in his companions and ill advised by them, thought only of larks and adventures, and rewarded ill the great pains his father had taken with his education. The old Emperor Constantine VII, who was so ceremonious and so pious, had tried his best to impart his qualities to his son. "He had taught him," says the chronicler, "how a Basileus should speak, walk, stand, smile, dress, sit down." And after these lessons he would say gravely to the young man: "If you follow these precepts, you will reign

many years over the Roman Empire." For the political and
diplomatic instruction of his heir, Constantine VII had, furthermore, composed very learned treatises—and most valuable they are to us—on the *Themes* and on the *Administration of the Empire*. But Romanus was eighteen years old and
not at all anxious to become a statesman. In any case, as his
father adored him, there were certainly no great difficulties
made about his marriage with Theophano, whatever her origin. Soon after the marriage, in 958, the young wife bore her
husband a son, the future Basil II, and thereby strengthened
her position at court and increased her influence in the Palace. When Constantine VII died in the month of October
959, Theophano, of course, ascended the throne with Romanus II. At that time she was eighteen years of age, and the
young Emperor twenty-one.

This young woman's character is by no means easy to ascertain. The court chronicler whom I have already quoted
says with unqualified praise: "She was fair of body, lovely of
face, and utterly pure of soul." Her most recent historian, on
the other hand, insists that she was "profoundly vicious and
profoundly corrupt," and that this fascinating enchantress,
this "crowned siren," was altogether "shameless and lascivi-
ous." These are hard words and ugly names, considering the
little we know of her. But it should be observed, however,
that among her contemporaries and even more among later
chroniclers, she had a well-established reputation as a sinister, ill-omened woman. One historian says that, in order the
quicker to ascend the throne, she and her husband poisoned
the Emperor her father-in-law. Other writers say that, when
her husband died, it was common talk in the capital that
Theophano had administered poison to him. If other reports
are to be believed, she rid herself thus of a Prince of the family of Romanus Lecapenus who seemed likely to become a

possible rival and pretender to the throne, and thus likewise she is said to have revenged herself upon her lover John
Tzimisces for having abandoned her. Armenian chroniclers
go so far as to say that the "infamous Empress" intended to
poison her own sons. But all these tales, told by people not
living at court, and dating for the most part from one or two
centuries after her time, are of small significance. Some of
these ugly rumors are flatly contradicted by the facts; others
seem really too incredible. Besides, we must not forget that
when Theophano actually made up her mind to commit a
crime—a thing which happened at least once in her life—it
was not by poison that she did the deed, but frankly and
openly by the sword.

This observation must not be taken as an attempt on my
part to rehabilitate Theophano. But there are plenty of
known facts to lay at her door without swelling the indict-
ment unnecessarily by the addition of vague epithets, and
assertions that cannot be proved. As I see her, she is above
all else ambitious, with a lust for power and influence, and
capable of anything, even crime, to hold the throne to which
she had attained. She is often intriguing, sometimes violent
and passionate, unscrupulous always; when her interests, dis-
likes, or fancies are involved, she is dissimulating and perfidious. On ascending the throne, she exercised great influence
over Romanus II, and would allow no one else to share it with
her. Not only were all the favorites of the preceding reign
dismissed and all the principal personnel of the administration changed: the young Empress's first act, when she had
become mistress in the Palace, was to send away her mother-
in-law, the Basilissa Helen, and her five sisters-in-law.

These were charming Princesses, who had been admirably educated by an adoring father. Under the government of
Constantine VII, they had even taken part from time to time

in affairs of State. One of them, Agatha, the old Emperor's favorite, often acted as his secretary, and the various departments and the officials were aware of her influence. This did not suit Theophano's book. She therefore extracted an order out of the feeble Romanus inviting them to enter a convent. In vain their mother pleaded for them; in vain the young girls, clinging closely to one another, begged with tears to be spared. All was to no purpose. The Basilissa Helen alone was allowed to dwell in the Palace, where she died in sorrow a few months later. Her daughters were obliged to bow to Theophano's inflexible will and enter the cloister, and, by a refinement of cruelty, were even separated from one another. The Princesses made a last vain resistance. When the Patriarch Polyeuctes had cut off their hair, and they had been clad in the religious habit, they protested, pulling off their sackcloth garments and insisting on eating meat every day. Romanus finally allowed them the same fare and the same state that they had enjoyed in the Sacred Palace. They were nonetheless forever dead to the world, and Theophano had won.

Must we believe that, because she acted thus to such near relatives, she next poisoned her husband? "Most people suspect," says Leo Diaconus, a contemporary, concerning the death of Romanus II, "that poison was administered to him in the Gynaeceum." This terrible accusation clearly demonstrates what the people of her time thought Theophano capable of; and it is certain that a woman who could have her second husband assassinated in order to marry a third, might just as well have had the first poisoned so as to marry the second. Nevertheless, the historian's accusation, grave as it is, seems in this case utterly absurd. In the first place, the chroniclers have given us a perfectly satisfactory explanation of the premature death of the young Emperor, exhausted in his youth by the love of pleasure and excesses of all kinds. And the very writer who brings poison into the affair mentions elsewhere that the Basileus died of internal complications resulting from a wild ride. But, above all, what object could Theophano have had in getting rid of her husband? She was Empress, she was all-powerful; she was, furthermore, on the best of terms with Romanus, to whom, in their six and a half years of married life, she had borne four children—only two days before his death she had given birth to her daughter Anna. Why should she have poisoned the Basileus, when his death, by leaving her alone with infant children, would expose her, more than any other conjuncture, to the sudden loss of the power she loved? Theophano was too intelligent to run such a risk groundlessly.

But it is worthy of special observation that in the facts just cited there is really nothing that can be characterized as vicious, wanton, or lewd. So long as Romanus II lived, there is every reason to believe that his young wife's conduct was irreproachable. After his death she married, chiefly for reasons of State, a man some thirty years her senior, but such an event is neither rare nor extraordinary in the lives of sovereigns or even of private citizens; and, without laying stress on the point that it was perhaps Theophano's only means of saving the throne for her sons, at least she can hardly be blamed for believing that supreme power was worth some sacrifice. The only serious accusation that one can make against her is not that five years later she deceived this old husband of hers with a younger lover—for, however deplorable, this is not an exceptional occurrence—but that when she wanted to marry her lover she did not hesitate to rid herself of the Basileus, her husband, by a horrible murder. It must be added, moreover, that she made bitter expiation for her crime.

II

At the time of Romanus II's sudden death, on the 15th of
March 963, Theophano was twenty-two years of age. She
was left alone with four children, two boys and two girls.
Without delay she assumed the regency in the name of the
two young Porphyrogeniti, Basil, aged five, and Constantine, aged two; but the situation was a singularly difficult
one for a woman, and even more so for an ambitious woman.
She found an all-powerful minister in office, the Parakoimomenos Joseph Bringas, who had governed despotically during Romanus's reign, and who might be tempted to get rid
of the Regent in order to have the power to himself during
the long minority of the young Basileis. And, on the other
hand, at the head of the Asiatic army, she found a victorious
general, whose ambitions she might well fear, the Domestic
of the Scholae, Nicephorus Phocas.

Nicephorus Phocas was at that time the best-known and
most popular man in the Empire. He belonged to a great
aristocratic family of Cappadocia, he was the descendant of
a long line of illustrious generals, and by splendid victories
he had still further enhanced his prestige and his fame.
Crete, which had fallen to the Arabs fifty years before, he
had reconquered; beyond Taurus, into Cilicia, he had carried
the imperial standards; the great city of Aleppo he had just
taken by storm, thus breaking the pride of the Hamdanid
Emirs of Syria. Being an admirable soldier, an able tacti-
cian, and an incomparable general, who knew the way to
talk to his men and make them follow him anywhere, he was
the idol of the soldiers, all of whose fatigues and dangers he
shared. "He lived for the army," one of his biographers says
of him. Nor was he less popular in Constantinople. When,

on returning from the Cretan expedition, he had celebrated a triumph in the Hippodrome, he had astonished the city by the splendors of the stately procession, "in the course of which all the wealth of the barbarians seemed to flow into the circus in an immense and never-ending flood." The recipient of as many honors "as in olden times the generals of Rome had received," immensely rich, maintaining in his Asiatic domains retinues of vassals passionately devoted to his person, he was loved and admired by all. He seemed the only leader capable of defending the Empire against the Saracens, and Romanus II on his deathbed had given explicit directions that he should be continued in undisturbed possession of his command.

Whereas to a statesman such a man might seem a formidable danger, it should be remarked that in the eyes of a young woman this victorious general had none of the attributes of a hero of romance. Nicephorus Phocas, in 963, was fifty-one years of age, and not beautiful to look at. He was a little man, rather fat, with a powerful body set on short legs, and he had, furthermore, a large head, a very dark, sunburned skin, and long black hair; his nose was aquiline, his beard short and grizzled, and his black eyes, under their heavy eyebrows, were thoughtful and sad. Liudprand, Bishop of Cremona, who came on an embassy to his court, says that he was of unusual ugliness, "as black of skin as a Negro, and terrifying to one who might chance upon him in the dark." Furthermore, he was hard and austere, melancholic in disposition and habitually taciturn. Since the loss of his wife, and the death of his only son in an unfortunate accident, he had become an ardent devotee of religion and mysticism. He had taken a vow of chastity, he no longer ate meat, he slept on the ground like an ascetic in the hair shirt of his uncle Malinus, a religious who had died in the odor of

sanctity, and he took pleasure in the society of monks. For
his spiritual director, he had chosen Athanasius, the future
founder of the oldest monastery on Mt. Athos, and, feeling
unable to do without his advice, kept him with him even in
camp. In the society of this holy man he conceived like him a
longing for the religious life, and thought very seriously of
retiring from the world. He was actually having a cell constructed for his own use in the monastery that Athanasius
was building on the Holy Mountain. Ascetic and warlike,
hard, sober, stern, money-loving but unworldly, capable both
of clemency and of perfidy, he, like many of his contemporaries, united in his complex personality the most unexpected contrasts, and under his cold exterior was profoundly
passionate.

It is very hard to tell whether or not he was ambitious.
With devoted and victorious troops at his command, Nicephorus Phocas was in a position to risk everything in the
crisis arising from the death of Romanus II; and the temptation to revolt was the stronger because his own personal
safety seemed to demand the step. The general knew that
Bringas hated him, and that he had everything to fear from
the all-powerful minister. At first, however, as a loyal and
pious soldier concerned chiefly with the war against the infidel, he made no move. And his final determination to
take sides was almost entirely due to Theophano.

One must beware of introducing too many romantic
touches into the story of the relations between Nicephorus
Phocas and the fair Empress. It is certain that during the
lifetime of Romanus II there was neither affection nor intrigue uniting the Basilissa and the Domestic of the Scholae.
But after her husband's death, the Regent soon understood
that, among the many perils threatening her, the general
was a real power, whom she could make use of to offset the

ambitions of Bringas. She saw that in order to retain the
throne she would have to win over Nicephorus to her side,
and, being an attractive woman, she doubtless felt that it
would not be a difficult task. In any case, it was due to the
Empress's initiative, and in spite of the Prime Minister's opposition, that Phocas was summoned to the capital, and it
seems that he was not long in falling a victim to her charms
and in espousing her cause. "It was well known in Byzantium," says M. Schlumberger, "that the exquisite sovereign's
intoxicating charm had made an ineradicable impression
upon the simple soul of the austere Domestic of the Scholae."
It may be imagined indeed, though contemporary evidence is
slight, that, while at first Nicephorus's relations with the
Regent had been confined to business and routine, he soon
gave evidence of his love and declared himself ready to do
anything to win her. There are no grounds for believing that
Theophano reciprocated his affection—indeed, she never
loved him; but she fully realized the great power that he
wielded and the use she could make of it to further her interests and her ambition. For political reasons she encouraged
his passion, just as later, for the same motives, she married
him.

It must also be observed that, during his stay in Constantinople, another and no less decisive reason was added to
that of Theophano's charms to overcome Nicephorus's hesitancy. This was the revelation which he had of Bringas's implacable hatred. Of course, the Prime Minister had been unable to refuse the general a new and splendid triumph. But
the increasing popularity of Phocas disturbed the statesman,
who is said, furthermore, to have suspected that a plot was
being hatched by the Domestic of the Scholae and the Regent. In vain Nicephorus, with the tortuous diplomacy so
dear to Byzantine hearts, tried to calm the apprehension of

the Parakoimomenos by announcing openly that his one desire was to embrace the religious life. Bringas was not deceived. Blinding seemed to him the surest way of getting rid
of his rival. Phocas, fortunately for himself, when he was
summoned to the Palace on some pretext, was either suspicious or else had received a friendly warning, for he took refuge in the Great Church and besought the Patriarch's protection. Polyeuctes had his faults; he was obstinate, unyielding,
narrow-minded, and shortsighted; but he was courageous
and outspoken, and he disliked the Prime Minister. He hurried off to the Sacred Palace, insisted that the Senate should
be convoked without delay, and expressed himself with such
energy and directness that Nicephorus was continued in his
command with extraordinary powers, in spite of Bringas's
ill will. The Domestic of the Scholae immediately left the
city and went to his headquarters at Caesarea: he was master of the situation.

In these intrigues and counter-intrigues Theophano did
not appear openly. It is, nevertheless, highly probable that
she helped her ally to the utmost of her ability, and backed
the intervention of the Patriarch Polyeuctes with all her
might. Similarly in the events that followed, when, in July
963, circumstances obliged Phocas to declare himself; when,
more and more threatened by Bringas's hatred, and fearing
for his life, the general unwillingly allowed himself to be
proclaimed Basileus by his troops, and in the camp at Caesarea put on the purple buskins; and when at last, in August
963, he appeared before Constantinople, and a popular
revolution, sweeping away Bringas and his friends, opened
the gates of the capital to the usurper, Theophano played no
visible part and seemed willing to let events take their course.
But, as a matter of fact, if Nicephorus Phocas had become
ambitious, and if then, in spite of his hesitations and scru-

ples, he had decided to assume the purple, the love that the beautiful Empress had inspired in his breast had figured largely in his resolve. And likewise, during the tragic days of August 963, when the mob "in a fury of madness" was charging the Minister's soldiers and destroying his palace, and when the Patriarch Polyeuctes and the former Parakoimomenos Basil were in apparent charge of the movement in favor of the pretender, we may well believe that, in the depths of the Gynaeceum, Theophano had come to a private understanding with the leaders of the revolt. Although her name is nowhere mentioned, this intriguing, ambitious woman was the very soul of the great events that had just taken place.

However it may have been, on the morning of the 16th of August 963, Nicephorus Phocas made his solemn entry into Constantinople. On horseback, in the imperial robes of state, he passed through the Golden Gate amid the acclamations of the entire city, hailed by the people as the savior of the Empire and of Christianity. "The State insists that Nicephorus be Basileus!" cried the enthusiastic mob as he went by. "The Palace awaits Nicephorus! The army calls for Nicephorus! The world looks to Nicephorus! Such are the wishes of the Palace, the Army, the Senate, and the People! Lord, hear our prayer! Long live Nicephorus!" Riding up the Mesé, he reached the Forum of Constantine, where, in the Church of the Theotokos, he devoutly said his prayers; thence he walked in procession, the Holy Cross in front, to St. Sophia, where he was received by the Patriarch, and there he went, holding lighted candles, to prostrate himself before the holy altars. Then, ascending the ambo with Polyeuctes, he was solemnly crowned Basileus of the Romans, as a colleague of the two young Emperors, Basil and Constantine. This done, he entered the Sacred Palace. To complete his happiness there remained only the sweetest recompense of his ambitions, the hope of which had armed him and led him forth: there remained only to wed Theophano.

Certain chroniclers say, however, that the Empress was at first obliged by the new master to leave the Palace. If that is true, it can have been nothing but a ruse, for the two allies had had an understanding for several months past. There is not the slightest doubt that Nicephorus was passionately in love with the young woman, and reasons of State, further-more, suggested such a marriage as a sort of legitimation of his assumption of the purple. Theophano, though, according to some writers, unenthusiastic over this new marriage, felt it to be her only means of retaining the power, and was there-fore quite willing. The two partners thus had little difficulty in persuading one another. On the 20th of September 963, in the New Church, the marriage was solemnly performed.

Nicephorus was at the pinnacle of joy. He took a new in-terest in life. He utterly forgot his austerities, his mystical dreams, and his promises, all in the happiness of possessing Theophano. But, unlike him, his friends the monks had not forgotten the past. When Athanasius, in his solitude on Athos, heard of the imperial marriage, he hurried off to Con-stantinople, frustrated in his hopes and deeply offended. On being received by the Emperor, he treated him with his usual freedom and reproached him harshly for having broken his word and for having caused a scandal. Phocas exerted him-self to calm the monk. He explained that it was not for his own pleasure that he had accepted the throne, and swore that he intended to live with Theophano as with a sister; he promised that as soon as affairs of State should permit he would join the brothers in the monastery. To these fair words he added splendid gifts, and Athanasius returned somewhat mollified to the Holy Mountain.

In Constantinople the astonishment caused by the marriage was no less, and the scandal greater. The Patriarch Polyeuctes was, as we have seen, a virtuous, austere man, uncompromising toward the things of this world, from which he was completely detached, concerned solely with the duties and interests of the Church, whose guardian he was, and endowed with unconquerable courage, inflexible obstinacy, and formidable frankness. His first act on becoming Patriarch had been severely to reprimand the Emperor Constantine VII, so pious a man and with such respect for sacred things. This time his ardent, unbending temperament showed itself more harshly still. It was not that he felt the slightest hostility toward Nicephorus, nor that he intended to oppose him as a usurper; in the revolution of 963 he had given evidence of his devotion to Phocas, and his attitude had helped not a little in the overthrow of Bringas and in the success of the Domestic of the Scholae. But, on the ground of canon law, he considered intolerable the marriage of the Basileus, a widower, with a Princess likewise widowed; and when Nicephorus, in accordance with his privilege as Emperor, attempted to pass through the iconostasis at St. Sophia to receive communion, the Patriarch stoutly forbade him to approach the altar and, as penance for his second marriage, laid this inhibition on him for the space of a year. The Emperor, despite his irritation, had to give way before the Patriarch's uncompromising firmness.

Soon another difficulty arose. Polyeuctes learned that Nicephorus had stood godfather to one of Theophano's children. Now, according to ecclesiastical law, a spiritual relationship of this kind was an absolute impediment to the marriage that had been contracted; and the Patriarch, without mincing words, gave the Basileus his choice between repudiating Theophano and the interdict. For so pious a man as Phocas such a threat was peculiarly serious. Nevertheless, the flesh was weak: Nicephorus refused to separate from Theophano, and thus did not pause at precipitating a grave quarrel between State and Church. At last, however, an arrangement was effected. A priest came forward and swore that the god-father of the imperial child had been Bardas, the Emperor's father, and not Nicephorus himself. Polyeuctes saw through the falsehood, but as he was abandoned by all, even by his clergy, he yielded to necessity and professed to believe what he was told. In his distress he did not even insist that the Emperor should carry out the penance which had been imposed on account of his second marriage. But the Basileus was none the less extremely irritated by this attack upon his prestige and upon his love. He never forgave Polyeuctes for his unseasonable interference, and Theophano was no less bitter toward the prelate. The Emperor and his wife never succeeded in living the matter down; a few years later Liudprand, echoing the stories that were current in Constantinople, declared outspokenly that Nicephorus's marriage was incestuous.

III

A marriage so ill assorted and so inauspiciously begun ran great risks of coming to grief. And this indeed was the swift result. Here again detailed information upon the private life of the imperial household during these six years is of the scantiest; and the part that Theophano, with her usual caution and cleverness, played in it must be rather inferred from hints than ascertained from direct testimony. We have to content ourselves with a general view of the situation and of the tragedy in which it ended.

Madly in love with Theophano and intoxicated with her radiant beauty, Nicephorus, to quote the reserved, laconic phrase of Leo Diaconus, did "more than was proper." This serious, austere, parsimonious man loaded the beautiful Princess with sumptuous gifts, marvelous garments, and splendid jewels; he surrounded her with all the refinements of the most dazzling luxury; he presented her with a fortune in estates and villas. "Nothing was too costly," says M. Schlumberger, "nothing too beautiful to give his beloved Empress." He was totally unable to tear himself away from her. When, in 964, he left to rejoin the army, he took Theophano along with him, and for the first time, perhaps, in the course of his long military career, interrupted a campaign to return the sooner to her.

But this old soldier had nothing of the courtier. After a brief interval of passion, war, his old love, reasserted her supremacy over him; every year he left for the frontier to fight Arabs, Bulgars, or Russians, and now he no longer took Theophano with him. Furthermore, he prided himself on being a conscientious Emperor, and so, little by little, the once-beloved Prince became more and more unpopular. The people, groaning under the weight of taxation; the clergy, whose privileges Nicephorus diminished; the monks, whose enormous landed property he tried to reduce, did not hide their discontent. The Patriarch was in open opposition to the Emperor. Rioting broke out in the capital. Nicephorus was insulted and stoned by the mob, and, in spite of the admirable composure which he displayed on this occasion, he would have lost his life if his friends had not dragged him away in the nick of time. Lastly, he became a prey to the same religious mysticism that had troubled him in the past; he became melancholy, and would no longer sleep in his imperial bed, but lay down in a corner on a panther-skin with a purple pillow on it, and he resumed wearing the hair shirt of his uncle Malinus. He was anxious, disturbed, and preoc-

cupied; he feared for his safety, and turned the Palace of the
Bucoleon into a fortress. Undoubtedly, he still adored Theophano, and was more subject to her soft, hidden influence
than was prudent or reasonable. But the contrast between
the rough soldier and the elegant Princess was too pronounced. He wearied her, and she was bored. The consequences were serious.

Nicephorus had a nephew, John Tzimisces. He was forty-
five years of age, short, but well built and very elegant. He
was white of skin, with blue eyes, a halo of light-golden hair,
a reddish beard, a delicate and beautiful nose, and a bold
look—a man who feared nothing and nobody. Being likewise
strong, clever, agile, open-handed, and magnificent, and a bit
of a rake into the bargain, he was very fascinating. Theophano in her boredom naturally found him pleasant; and it
was now that passion led her on to crime. Tzimisces was ambitious; he was vastly irritated, moreover, at the disgrace
which had befallen him: as the result of an incident of war,
the Emperor had degraded him from his post of Domestic of
the Oriental Scholae and had invited him to retire to his estates, and his one thought was to revenge himself for an outrage that he deemed unmerited. Theophano, for her part,
was utterly weary of Nicephorus; their former understanding had been succeeded by dislike and suspicion, and the
Empress even affected to fear that her husband intended to
make some attempt upon the lives of her sons. She was still
more impatient at being separated from her lover, for Tzimisces seems to have been the great and probably the only
real love of her life. In these circumstances, she surrendered
herself gradually to the contemplation of a most revolting
crime.

Nicephorus, since his return from Syria, at the beginning
of 969, had been a prey to dark forebodings. He had a feeling

that plots were being hatched against him in the dark. The death of his aged father, the Caesar Bardas Phocas, had increased his melancholy. However, he still loved Theophano. The latter perfidiously used her influence to have Tzimisces recalled to court. She pointed out to the Emperor how annoying it was to have to forego the services of such a man; and very cleverly, in order to prevent Nicephorus from becoming suspicious at too open an espousal of John's cause, talked of marrying him to one of her relatives. The Basileus, as usual, gave way to his wife's wishes. John returned to Constantinople; and, owing to channels of information skillfully contrived by Theophano in concert with some of her household, the two lovers met in the Palace itself, unknown to Nicephorus, and prepared their plot. No less was planned than the assassination of the Basileus. Among the discontented generals John readily found accomplices; many conferences were held between the conspirators and between Tzimisces and the Empress; at last, thanks to the many ramifications of the Gynaeceum, armed men were smuggled into the Palace and hidden in the Augusta's apartments.

Leo Diaconus, who has left us a very striking account of the drama, says that it was now early December. The murder had been set for the night between the 10th and the 11th. The day before, several of the conspirators, dressed as women, had, with Theophano's aid, entered the Sacred Palace. This time the Emperor was mysteriously warned, and he gave orders to one of his officers to search the women's quarters; but, whether the search was carelessly carried out, or whether by deliberate intention, no one was discovered. Meanwhile, night had fallen; they awaited only the coming of Tzimisces to strike the blow. The conspirators became apprehensive; if the Emperor were to lock himself in his room, if they had to break open the door and he were to

awake, would it not ruin everything? Theophano, with revolting composure, took upon herself to overcome this obstacle. At a late hour she went to see Nicephorus in his apartments and chatted pleasantly with him; then, on pretext of
having to visit some young Bulgarian women staying in the
Palace, she went out, saying that she would be back presently
and asking him to leave the door open: she would close it on
her return. Nicephorus agreed, and when he was left alone,
said his prayers and fell asleep.

It was about eleven o'clock at night. Outside, snow was
falling, and on the Bosphorus the wind was blowing a hur-
ricane. In a little boat John Tzimisces reached the deserted
strip of shore under the walls of the imperial castle of the
Bucoleon. By means of a basket fastened to a rope, he was
hoisted up to the Gynaeceum, and at the head of the conspirators went to the sovereign's bedchamber. They had a moment of fright, for the bed was empty. But a eunuch of the
Gynaeceum, who was acquainted with Nicephorus's habits,
pointed out the Basileus lying asleep in a corner on his
panther-skin. They rushed furiously at him, whereupon he
awoke and jumped up. One of the conspirators with his
sword split open the Emperor's head to the eyebrows. The
wretched man, drenched in blood, cried out: "Mother of
God, help me!" The murderers, paying no heed, dragged
him to the feet of Tzimisces, who abused him indecently
and tore out his beard. At this they all fell upon the poor
creature, who was now in the last throes. Finally John, with
a kick, turned him over and, drawing his sword, struck him
a great blow on the head; another of the assassins finished
him off. The Emperor fell dead, bathed in his blood.

At the noise of the struggle, the soldiers of the guard hurried to the scene, but arrived too late. They were shown by
torchlight at a window the severed, bleeding head of their

master. This tragic sight stifled at once all thought of resistance. The people followed the Empress's example and proclaimed Tzimisces Emperor.

IV

Theophano, who had arranged everything, who had, as it were, led the assassins by the hand, expected to profit greatly by the murder. But history contains some examples of poetic justice, as the Basilissa was shortly to learn.

Once more the Patriarch Polyeuctes gave evidence of his indomitable energy. He had been openly at odds with the dead sovereign. Nevertheless, when John appeared at the gates of St. Sophia to assume the imperial crown in the Great Church, the prelate inflexibly refused him admittance on the ground that he was stained with the blood of his relative and master, and gave him to understand that he would be denied access to the holy place until the murderers had been punished and Theophano driven from the Palace. As between the throne and his mistress, Tzimisces did not hesitate a moment. He impudently denied that he had had any share in the crime; and, the better to clear himself, complied with the orders of Polyeuctes, betraying his associates and sacrificing Theophano. She had dreamed of marrying the man she loved, and of sharing with him the power so dear to her; but it was her lover himself who decided her downfall. He exiled her to one of the convents of Proti, in the Princes' Islands.

But, with all her energy, and with the knowledge that she was still beautiful—she was scarcely twenty-nine—Theophano refused to resign herself to disgrace. A few months later she escaped from prison and took refuge in St. Sophia. Was it that she counted on her lover's affection? Was it that

she hoped that, after the initial difficulties had been sur-
mounted, Tzimisces in gratitude would take her back again?
Did she flatter herself that the very sight of her would win
him over? It is indeed probable. But the all-powerful minister who directed the policy of the new reign, the Parakoimomenos Basil, made short work of the fascinating Empress's
attempt. Disregarding the sanctity of the place, he had her
dragged away from the Great Church and decided to send
her to a more distant exile in Armenia. All that she could obtain was permission to see a last time before departing the
man for whom she had sacrificed everything, and who was
abandoning her. This final interview, at which the Parakoimomenos took the precaution of being present, seems to have
been extraordinarily violent. Theophano reviled Tzimisces
unmercifully, and then, in a paroxysm of rage, fell upon the
minister with her fists. She had to be dragged out of the audience chamber. Her life was over.

What became of her in her melancholy exile? What sufferings did she endure in the distant convent wherein she
dragged out her life, far from the splendors of the court, far
from the elegance of the Sacred Palace, with the bitterness of
her frustrated hopes and the regret of her lost power? No one
knows. At all events, if she had been guilty, she paid dearly
for her crime. Six years she languished in her solitude, until
Tzimisces's death. She was then, in 976, recalled to Constantinople by her sons, who had now become the actual rulers.
But, whether her pride was broken and her ambition burnt
out, or whether, as is more likely, the Parakoimomenos Basil,
who was still all-powerful, had made it a condition of her return, she seems never again to have taken any part in affairs
of State. She died in obscurity in the Palace, the date of her
death being unknown. And thus to the very end, this ambitious, fascinating, perverse Princess remains to some extent
an enigma and a mystery.

⚛ VII ⚛

ZOË THE
PORPHYROGENITA

I

In the month of November 1028, Constantine VIII, Emperor of Byzantium, realizing that he was very ill, and being moreover nearly seventy years of age, decided that it was time to settle the succession to the throne. One may, perhaps, be astonished that, as the last male representative of the Macedonian dynasty, he had not previously thought of arranging so important and necessary a matter. The truth is that all his life Constantine VIII had never thought of anything at all.

Having been from childhood the colleague of his brother Basil II, he had lived for fifty years in the shadow of this energetic and mighty sovereign, taking no interest in public matters and accepting only the advantages and pleasures of power. Then, when Basil's death had left him sole ruler of the Empire, he had been unable to abandon his old, accustomed habits, and had continued as before to lead his own life to the neglect of all else. He was a great spendthrift, and

had squandered with open hands his brother's patiently ac-
cumulated savings. A devotee of pleasure and of the table—
he excelled in ordering a dinner, and occasionally condescended to invent a sauce to suit himself—he had entered
with such fervor into these amusements that he had become
so gouty as hardly to be able to walk. In addition, he adored
the Hippodrome, was passionately interested in the circus
contests, and doted on animal fights and on spectacles. He
loved gambling, and when once he had the dice in his hands,
everything else, the reception of ambassadors, business that
needed his attention, was all forgotten. At such times he even
forgot his chief pleasure, the table, and spent whole nights in
play. One can understand that, between so many absorbing
occupations, it had slipped his mind that he was the last male
of his race, and that his sole heirs were his three unmarried
daughters.

Their names were Eudocia, Zoë, and Theodora. Concerning the eldest, Eudocia, history has little to say. She was a
woman of simple tastes, moderate intelligence, and equally
moderate looks: an illness in early childhood had ruined her
beauty for ever. While quite young she entered a convent,
and is heard of no more. Her two sisters were totally different and very much more interesting, but they had both, by a
curious chance, been left to grow old in the obscurity of the
Gynaeceum. Neither their uncle Basil, who nevertheless
liked them well enough, but who seems to have had a certain
contempt for women—he himself had never married—nor
their father Constantine, had ever bothered to find husbands
for them. In 1028 they were very old maids: Zoë was fifty,
and Theodora but little less.

It was upon these two somewhat ripe Princesses that,
after the death of Constantine VIII, the throne would devolve. But although, since the foundation of the Macedonian

house, the hereditary principle had made sufficient progress in Byzantium for no one to take umbrage at the Empire passing to women, the Basileus thought that in the circumstances a man would not be out of place in the Palace, and hastily sought a husband to play the part of Prince Consort for his favorite daughter Zoë, whom he considered the better suited to the throne. He hit upon an Armenian nobleman, Constantine Dalassenus, and had him sent for. But Constantine was far from the capital, on his estates, and time was short. Then, changing his mind, the Emperor turned to the Praefect of the City, Romanus Argyrus. He was a handsome man, of good family, over sixty years of age; unfortunately, he was married and loved his wife, who adored him. This did not deter Constantine VIII. When he wanted anything, he employed expeditious means and unanswerable arguments: he gave Romanus the choice between divorce and blinding, and to hasten his surrender and, above all, his wife's, pretended to be furiously angry and ordered the Praefect's immediate arrest. Thereupon Romanus's wife, in great distress, realized that, if she wished to save her husband, she had only to disappear; so she hastily entered a convent, and Romanus married Zoë. Three days later Constantine VIII died contented, and his two daughters and his son-in-law ascended the throne.

For nearly a quarter of a century Zoë the Porphyrogenita was destined to make the Imperial Palace hum with her scandalous behavior; and the story of her life is certainly one of the raciest in all Byzantine history, and one of the most familiar. Whereas we are so ill informed about the majority of the Empresses who reigned in the Sacred Palace that we can with difficulty form even the slightest notion of them, Zoë stands forth in the full light of day. She has had the good fortune—for us—to have as biographer one of the most intelligent and remarkable men that Byzantium ever produced, namely Michael Psellus.

Knowing the Empress well, and acquainted, in his capacity as Grand Chamberlain and minister, with all the court intrigues, interested in everything that took place, eager for every bit of gossip, and very indiscreet and loquacious into the bargain, Psellus has, with admirable complaisance and often with extraordinary freedom of language, revealed everything he saw or heard. There is no secret hidden from him, no detail, even the most intimate, that he has not in some way become acquainted with; and as he had a deep fund of wit, humor, and malice, the story he tells is one of the raciest and most pungent to be found anywhere. Doubtless, we must not take all he says literally: at times he makes a wide detour around the facts, when politics, in which he played a great part, are too directly involved. But with practically this one exception he is very trustworthy, and since his natural idle curiosity, always on the watch for the slightest event, impelled him early in life to be observant, he is usually perfectly informed. And then it is such good luck to find, among so many dry, boring chroniclers, one who can both use his eyes and write, a master of the difficult art of portraiture, an incomparable teller of spicy tales. It has been said, without too much exaggeration, that Psellus reminds one of Voltaire, and, as a matter of fact, he touched on everything and wrote of everything. Besides his history, we have hundreds of little treatises from his pen on the most diverse subjects: speeches and verses, letters and pamphlets, philosophical treatises, works on physics, on astronomy, on physiology, and even on demonology. And like Voltaire he touches everything with a caustic wit, a malicious humor, and a universal curiosity. By the boldness of his conceptions and the originality of his ideas, Psellus was one of the most eminent men of his time;

by his love of classical antiquity and of Platonic philosophy, he, living in the eleventh century, is a kind of forerunner of the Renaissance.

His character was, undoubtedly, not the equal of his intellect. His mediocrity of soul, his love of intrigue, his servile flatteries, his rapid and scandalous changes of side, and his childish, unhealthy vanity, show that Psellus is but too perfect a specimen of the court life and of the corrupt Byzantine society in which he lived. But, on the other hand, he helps us so well to understand it all that he is really invaluable. In our narrative we shall have constantly to return to his book; and to it I must often refer the reader when his anecdotes, though always amusing and witty, become much too embarrassing to translate.

II

At the time when Zoë, with her husband Romanus, ascended the throne of Byzantium, she was, we are told, still perfectly charming, despite her fifty summers. Psellus, who knew her well, has drawn a very interesting portrait of her. She seems to have resembled her uncle Basil: she had large eyes under heavy eyebrows, a slightly aquiline nose, and beautiful fair hair. Her complexion and her whole body were of dazzling whiteness; she was of incomparable grace and most harmoniously proportioned. "Anyone not knowing her age," says Psellus, "would have taken her for a young girl." She had not a single wrinkle: "Every part of her," says the historian, "was firm and in good condition." She was of medium height, but slender and well made, and she had a very elegant figure. And although later in life she grew somewhat fatter, her face remained to the end remarkably young. At the age of seventy-two, when her trembling hands and her bent back betrayed her age, "her face," says Psellus, "was radiant with youthful beauty." She had a regal manner and a bearing truly imperial. But she was not overfond of the troublesome demands of ceremonial. Being very careful of her beauty, she preferred simple dresses to the heavy, gold-embroidered gowns decreed by etiquette, the massive diadem and the splendid jewels. "She clothed her beautiful body," says her biographer, "in filmy garments." On the other hand, she was devoted to perfumes and cosmetics, and imported them from Ethiopia and India; and her apartments, in which great fires were kept burning all the year round for the preparation of the salves and lotions that her women made for her, had the appearance of a laboratory. And there it was that she preferred to spend her time; she did not care much for fresh air, for walking in the gardens, or for anything that might sully her borrowed loveliness and impair a beauty that she was already obliged to take great care of.

Zoë was moderately intelligent, absolutely ignorant, lively, enthusiastic, and irritable. Gaily and thoughtlessly she decided matters of life and death, quick to take sides and to change them; with but little logic or stability of mind, she treated affairs of State with the same frivolity as the amusements of the Gynaeceum. In spite of her beauty she made a sufficiently incapable sovereign, since she was rather silly, very vain, childish, capricious, volatile, and quite open to flattery. A compliment delighted her. She was enchanted when one spoke of the antiquity of her lineage or of the glories of her uncle Basil, and even more enchanted when one spoke of herself. And it became a game among the courtiers to make her believe that no one could look at her without being immediately struck dumb with amazement. She was extravagant with regard to herself, absurdly generous to others, and affected an insane prodigality; but on occasion she could be inexorable and cruel. Like all her contemporaries she was pious; but it was an exclusively external piety, of the kind that burns incense before icons, and lights candles on altars. Public matters bored her, nor did women's work interest her either. She did not care for embroidery, weaving, or spinning, but would sit idle for hours at a time, fatuously. One can thus understand that her active, untiring uncle Basil, though fond of her, must have rather despised her.

This blonde, soft, silly creature had, moreover, none too good blood in her veins. As the granddaughter of that Romanus II who died young from the results of fast living, and of the notorious Theophano, and daughter of such an idler as Constantine VIII, she had every right to the amorous temperament which she was soon to manifest. Very proud of her beauty, convinced that she was irresistible, furious at having had to waste the best years of her youth in the Gynaeceum, full of unsatisfied desires, and fascinated by the call of the unknown, she was now, at the age of fifty and more, to fill court and town with her scandalous behavior, and with such passion and with so little restraint that her contemporaries were often in doubt as to her entire sanity.

Romanus Argyrus, finding himself married to a woman so headstrong and so eager for new sensations, felt that he owed it to himself, to Zoë, to the late Emperor his father-in-law, and to the State, to produce an heir to the throne as soon as possible. And at this point already, I am obliged to refer the reader to Psellus to learn by what means—both magical and physiological—by what learned combinations of unguents, massage, and amulets, Romanus and Zoë set to work to realize their desire. But, whilst engaged in these exercises, the Emperor soon awoke to the fact that he was sixty, which was considerable, and that the Empress was fifty, which was excessive; and so, leaving his wife and considerations of State in the lurch, he devoted himself to the government of the Empire.

The lady had not reckoned on such treatment. Deeply wounded in her pride, to begin with, at being thus scorned, Zoë had other grounds for discontent, unconnected with either vanity or considerations of State; as a crowning misfortune, and as if to cap the climax, Romanus in forsaking her society had had the idea of putting an immediate stop to her ridiculous extravagance. Furiously angry, and feeling more keenly than ever a longing for adventures, Zoë cast about for consolation and found it without difficulty. She singled out Constantine, the High Steward, and after him another Constantine, of the great house of Monomachus, whose relationship to the Emperor had gained him admittance to the Palace. They both pleased her for a while on account of their good looks, their charm, and their youth; but their favor was not of long duration. Soon Zoë's choice settled upon another lover. Among the intimates of Romanus III was a eunuch named John, an astute, corrupt man and a great favorite of the Emperor. This John had a brother named Michael, a remarkably handsome fellow with sparkling eyes, a clear skin, and a fine figure, whom the poets of the time unanimously praise for his captivating charm. John presented him at court: he pleased the Emperor, who took him into his service; and he pleased the Empress even more, so that she suddenly developed an overwhelming passion for him. And, as Psellus says, "since she was incapable of controlling her desires, she knew no rest until the handsome Michael had reciprocated her affection."

There followed a thoroughly amusing little comedy in the Palace, which Psellus has maliciously related. Hitherto Zoë had heartily detested the eunuch John; but now, in order to have excuses to talk with the man she loved, she treated him with cordiality, and sent for him to inform his brother that he would always receive a warm welcome from his sovereign whenever he should appear in her presence. The young man, not in the least understanding this sudden and extraordinary kindness, came to Zoë in some embarrassment, worried and blushing, to bow and scrape. But the Princess encouraged him; she smiled at him pleasantly, relaxed the sternness of her awful brow, and even alluded in discreet terms to her sentiments. Schooled, however, by his brother, Michael finally understood. He grew audacious; from loving attitudes he passed to kisses; soon he became more daring still, "less fascinated perhaps," says the impertinent Psellus, "by the lady's overripe charms than flattered in his pride by the glory of an imperial adventure." Zoë was very seriously in love, and committed every kind of imprudence. She was to be seen kissing her lover in public and sitting with him on the same couch. Naturally, she delighted in decking her favorite like an idol; she covered him with jewels and fine clothes, and showered him with magnificent presents. She went even further; one day she conceived the idea of making him sit upon the Emperor's very throne, crowned and sceptered, and pressing him close to her, called him by the most loving names: "My idol, my flower of beauty, joy of my eyes, consolation of my soul." One of the inmates of the Palace, happening to enter the room, nearly swooned at the shock of this unexpected scene; but Zoë, unabashed, ordered him to prostrate himself at Michael's feet, saying: "He is henceforth Emperor; one day he will be so in very truth."

The entire court knew of their liaison. Romanus was, of course, the only one who perceived nothing. Some of his intimate friends and his sister Pulcheria, who hated the Empress, thought it their duty to enlighten him. But the Emperor refused to believe it, and being a good-natured Prince called Michael to his study, and asked him what truth there was in the tale. Michael protested that he was the innocent victim of odious calumnies, and the Basileus was convinced and liked him even better than before. As a mark of his confidence he went so far as to permit him to enter the imperial bedchamber itself; at night, when he was in bed alongside of Zoë, he used to call the young man to his bedside and ask him to rub his feet. "Is it conceivable," says a prudish chronicler, "that in doing so he never touched the Basilissa's feet?" Romanus did not bother about that, for he was not a jealous Emperor.

He could reassure himself, furthermore, if he so desired. The handsome Michael suffered from an unpleasant disease: he had attacks of epilepsy. "Such a man," remarked the Emperor, "really could neither love nor inspire love." In the long run, however, Romanus was unable to doubt his misfortune, but being a philosopher he preferred to pay no attention. He understood Zoë, and knew that, if he were to remove Michael, he would run the undoubted risk of seeing her plunge into fresh and more numerous adventures; and considering a single intrigue less injurious to the imperial dignity than a succession of blazing scandals, he systematically shut his eyes to the proof. "And the Empress's liaison," says Psellus, "was publicly established and acquired an almost legal status."

Romanus, meanwhile, was failing visibly in health. He ate little and slept badly, and his character was undergoing a change. He became violent, irritable, and disagreeable; he no longer laughed; he distrusted everyone and grew angry over nothing, and was in fact wasting away. He insisted on performing conscientiously his duties as Emperor; but under his splendid robes of state he looked a dying man; his face was sunken, his skin was yellow, his breath came short and panting, and his hair fell out by the handful. It appears that Michael and Zoë had been administering a slow poison to the unfortunate monarch—though he scarcely bothered them at all—in order to rid themselves of his troublesome presence. But the poison did not act quickly enough to satisfy the amorous Empress. Consequently, on the morning of Holy Thursday, when the Emperor was in his bath, at the moment of dipping his head under the water, as he always did, some servants, who had received orders, held him in that position rather longer than was necessary. He was taken out fainting and three-quarters suffocated, and laid on his bed, breathing with difficulty and unable to speak. When later he regained consciousness, he tried to convey his meaning by signs; but, seeing that no one understood him, he closed his eyes sadly and soon expired. At this occurrence Zoë did not even take the trouble to hide her feelings. On learning of the accident she hurried to the imperial bedchamber to see for herself what her husband's condition was, and did not consider it worth while to be present at the end. She had more important things to think of.

III

Zoë's sole aim was to secure the throne for Michael. In vain the courtiers and the old servants of Constantine VIII exhorted her to think it over, to give the crown only to the worthiest, and above all not to put herself too much into her new husband's power. She thought only of her lover. The eunuch John, astute politician that he was, pressed her to decide quickly. "We are all lost," thought he to himself, "if there is any delay." Without waiting, therefore, on the night between Holy Thursday and Good Friday, Zoë sent for Michael to come to the Palace. She made him don the imperial robes, and, putting the crown on his head, sat him on the throne beside herself and commanded all those present to recognize him as their lawful sovereign. The Patriarch, summoned at dead of night, came in haste. He expected to find Romanus, but instead discovered Zoë and Michael in robes of state in the great Golden Triclinium; and the Empress asked him to marry her without delay to the new Basileus. The prelate hesitated; so, in order to convince him, they made him a splendid present of fifty pounds' weight in gold, and promised him a like sum for his clergy. He yielded to these arguments and obeyed. On the morrow the Senate was convoked to render homage to the new master and to pay their last respects to the old. And while, with face uncovered, according to the custom, Romanus III was being carried away, unrecognizable and already decomposing—Psellus, who saw the procession pass, has left a striking account of it—in the Sacred Palace the great dignitaries were prostrating themselves humbly before Michael and kissing the upstart's hand. Zoë had not remained a widow twenty-four hours.

The soul of the new government was the Emperor's brother, the eunuch John. He was a man who thought and acted with rapidity, hard and haughty of mien, a remarkable politician, and a first-rate financier. He had an excellent knowledge of public affairs, and was in close touch with all that went on in the capital and in the State; and he pursued the realization of his ideas and ambitions even in the noise of feasts and the tumult of banquets. Amid the glow of festivities he kept close watch upon his companions, and had the valuable power of remembering precisely what those around him had said in their cups, even when he himself had been intoxicated. Thus he inspired a wholesome terror, and was feared more perhaps when drunk than when sober. He was absolutely devoted to his brother, whom he adored, ambitious for him alone, and put at his service his intelligence, his ability, and his deep knowledge of men. It was he who had previously thrown Michael into Zoë's arms; but now that, thanks to her, Michael had become Emperor, he considered gratitude to the Basilissa altogether superfluous. The Basileus after his coronation had been at first very friendly to Zoë, obeying her least wish and seeking every opportunity to please her. But under his brother's influence his attitude soon changed. "It is impossible for me," says Psellus, "either to praise him or blame him for it. I certainly do not approve of ingratitude toward one's benefactress; and yet I cannot blame him for fearing lest he should meet the fate of her first husband." Michael knew Zoë too well not to distrust her.

He began by exiling all on whom she had formerly bestowed her favors. Next, on his brother's advice, he took matters into his own hands and commanded the Empress to confine herself to the Gynaeceum, and to refrain in future from appearing in the official processions. At the same time, he took away her eunuchs and the most faithful of her women, and in their place put some ladies of his own family to spy upon her. An officer devoted to Michael was appointed Master of Ceremonies to the Empress, and soon she was kept under such strict surveillance that she was allowed to receive no one unless it were known in advance who he was and what he had to say to her. She was forbidden even to leave her apartments, to take a walk, or to go to the baths without the Emperor's express permission. Zoë was exasperated at such treatment, but had no means of resistance. So she put on the best face she could and simulated unalterable sweetness and perfect resignation; she bore without complaint the outrages and humiliations that were meted out to her, never reproaching Michael, inveighing against nobody, and gracious even to her very gaolers. But after all that she had done for her former lover, the blow was as hard as it was unexpected.

The most difficult thing for her to bear was the fact that Michael himself, whom formerly she had loved so well, now kept away from her in horror and refused even to see her. Apart from some embarrassment at having repaid her kindness with such ingratitude, he felt his illness to be gaining upon him; his epileptic fits became worse and more frequent, and he was in constant fear of a seizure in Zoë's presence. Furthermore, as he was not a bad man, he suffered from remorse and tried to make expiation for his sins. All his time was spent in the society of monks; in the Palace he surrounded himself with ascetics, clad in rags picked up in the streets, and as penance he slept humbly at their feet, stretched out on a board with his head upon a stone. He built hospitals and churches; and he had a special devotion for Demetrius, the great saint of Thessalonica, and for Cosmas and Damian, the physician-saints, who bore the reputation in Byzantium of being able to cure the most incurable diseases. But nothing served to allay his sufferings or his restlessness. Therefore his spiritual directors, to whom he had confessed his follies and his crimes, ordered him to refrain from all physical connection with his wife. And he piously followed their directions.

Zoë, cut off from all that she loved, finally revolted. She knew that she was popular in the capital both as a woman and the lawful heir to the monarchy, and also on account of her lavish munificence. She rebelled, therefore, against the treatment which she was receiving. Soon she went even further, and is said to have attempted to have the Prime Minister poisoned, hoping that, once removed from his baneful influence, Michael, whom she still loved, would submissively return to her. Her attempt was a failure, and its only result was to increase her troubles. This state of affairs lasted until the Emperor's death. Michael's health was steadily deteriorating, and was still further impaired by the reaction following the burst of energy with which he had overcome the revolted Bulgarians. He felt himself at the point of death. Overwhelmed with remorse and anxious at least to end his life piously, he had himself transported in the month of December 1041, to a monastery that he had founded, where in accordance with a widespread Byzantine custom he put on the black monastic habit in order to die in the odor of sanctity. When this news was brought to the Imperial Gynaeceum, Zoë, wild with grief, and anxious to see for the last time the husband and lover whom she could not forget, despite her dignity and in the face of all etiquette ran on foot to the monastery to bid him a final farewell. But Michael was eager to die in peace, and he coldly refused to receive the woman who had loved and lost him. Soon afterward he passed away.

IV

For some time past, the eunuch John had foreseen this event and had taken the necessary steps. The death of Michael IV, by necessarily restoring to Zoë the fullness and the free exercise of imperial power, would certainly be the ruin of all the hopes that this exceedingly ambitious man had formed for his relatives. He had therefore suggested that his brother should associate with him in his lifetime one of their nephews, likewise named Michael, and take advantage of Zoë's popularity to give the upstart a legal investiture and smooth his path to power. It had therefore been suggested to the aged Empress to adopt this young man; and, strangely enough, in spite of the insults to which she had been subjected, Zoë had been only too delighted to comply with her husband's wishes. In the Church of Blachernae, in the presence of the assembled people, she had solemnly declared before the holy altars that she took her husband's nephew to be her son, after which the new Prince Imperial had received the title of Caesar and the rank of heir apparent.

Like all his family, Michael V was of very humble origin. His father had even been a calker in the port, and that is why the inhabitants of the capital, always ready for a jest, soon gave the young Caesar the nickname of Michael Calaphates, or the Calker. He himself was an unpleasant sort of person, bad, ungrateful, untruthful, with a private grudge against all his benefactors. His uncle, the Emperor Michael, who knew him well, cared very little for him, and, notwithstanding that he had brought him to the steps of the throne, excluded him from affairs of state and from the court. His uncle, the eunuch John, though his nephew professed great respect for him, likewise regarded him with distrust. He was destined amply to justify all the misgivings that he inspired.

The power was transmitted peacefully, however, when Michael IV died. Zoë, weak of character and old, was "very easily led," as Psellus puts it, and did whatever she was asked. Her former enemy and persecutor, the eunuch John, had only to show her great respect; he threw himself at her feet and said that without her the State was powerless; he swore that, if her adopted son were to ascend the throne, he would be Emperor only in name, and that all the actual power would be in her hands. She was fascinated by this clever comedy and enchanted at the unexpected compliments and at the influence that she enjoyed once more, and, therefore, she characteristically consented to everything. Michael V was proclaimed Basileus.

The new Emperor repaid ill all who had helped him rise. He began by getting rid of his uncle John, and gave his place as Prime Minister, together with the title of Nobilissimus, to another of his uncles, Constantine. Then he decided that Zoë was in the way. Like Michael IV, he too at first had shown great respect to his adoptive mother. "She is my Empress," he used to say in speaking of her; "she is my sovereign. I am wholly devoted to her." But soon he thrust her aside; he diminished her allowance, refused her the honors due to her rank, and kept her in the Gynaeceum under strict guard, taking away her women and openly ridiculing her. His companions kept telling him that he had better dethrone the aged Princess if he did not wish to suffer the fate of his predecessors. Michael thought himself strong enough to carry out the scheme; he imagined that he was popular in the capital—had not the people at the recent Easter festivities welcomed him in the streets with such unbounded enthusiasm that the road beneath his horses' hoofs was spread with priceless rugs? Believing in his star, proud of what he was daring to undertake, scorning all advice, on the 18th of April 1042, he determined to turn his benefactress out.

On Sunday night, Zoë was arrested in her apartments on the pretext that she had tried to poison the Emperor, and notwithstanding her cries and protests, was put hastily, with only one servant, aboard a vessel and taken to the neighboring island of Prinkipo. Upon her arrival there, she was shut up by the Basileus's orders in a convent, and forced to wear the habit of a nun, and her long gray hair was cut off and carried to Michael as evidence that his wishes had been executed. Having thus got rid of the Empress and believing her forever dead to the world, the Emperor convoked the Senate and solemnly pronounced her dethroned. But he had not counted upon the traditional devotion of the people to the

Macedonian house. As soon as the news spread through the city, there was great disturbance; everywhere there were sorrowful faces, angry looks, anxious talk, and stormy gatherings, which the guard soldiers had great difficulty in dispersing. The women, in particular, showed intense excitement, and filled the streets with their cries. Moreover, when the Praefect of the City appeared in the Forum of Constantine to read the imperial proclamation announcing the event, he had hardly finished before a voice cried out, bluntly: "We don't want the Calker to be our Emperor! We want the lawful heiress, our mother Zoë!" At these words, there went up a great shout: "Death to the Calker!" The revolution had broken out.

The people armed themselves in haste with anything that came handy, and the mob went surging through the city. Prisons were broken open and houses burned or pillaged. Soon the Palace was attacked. On the advice of his uncle Constantine, who with the people of his household had bravely come to the aid of the Basileus and had organized the defense, Michael decided to make a concession to the rioters. Zoë was hurriedly brought from her convent to the Sacred Palace, in dire apprehension as to her fate. In the greatest haste, without giving her time even to remove her religious habit, she was taken to the imperial box in the Hippodrome, where she and Michael appeared before the rebellious mob. The excitement of the people on beholding the Empress despoiled of the imperial robes, far from diminishing, grew more intense. In vain the Emperor tried to address the rebels; he was answered by insults and stones, and, returning with the aged Princess to the Palace, the wretch thought only of flight, until his uncle Constantine inspired him with fresh courage and prevailed upon him to resist.

Meanwhile, in St. Sophia, an unexpected occurrence had infused new strength into the revolt.

Zoë, as we have seen, had a sister, Theodora. Although she had been associated in the Empire since the death of Constantine VIII, this Princess, in spite of occupying a somewhat less exalted position than her elder sister, soon became a nuisance to the latter, who detested her. She was at first kept in the Palace under secret surveillance; later she was accused of conspiring against established authority, and on this pretext was sent away from court and banished to the convent of the Petrion. Then, a few months afterward, on the ground that otherwise it would be impossible, as a chronicler says, to put an end "to intrigues and scandals," Zoë went in person to the convent and in her own presence had Theodora's hair cut off. The Princess's public life was to all appearances over. She seems to have accustomed herself without much difficulty to her lot, satisfied with the external honors that the Emperor Romanus, her brother-in-law, permitted her out of kindness to retain, and in her cloister she was gradually forgotten. Michael IV treated her as he had treated Zoë—that is to say, badly enough. As for Michael V, he does not seem even to have suspected that, apart from Zoë, there was left any lawful descendant of Constantine VIII, and he would have been put to it for an answer had he been asked whether Theodora was alive or dead.

The revolution of 1042 suddenly restored this forgotten nun to the highest rank. When Michael V overthrew his benefactress, the insurgents, in casting around for a legitimate heir with which to oppose the usurper, remembered Theodora. She had retained some friends, furthermore, among her father's former servants and even in the Senate. These politicians realized that the doting, volatile Zoë was quite capable, once restored to power, of receiving again into full favor the man who had dethroned her; and they felt it necessary, if the revolution were fully to accomplish its end, to associate a more energetic Empress with the old, indulgent Basilissa. They therefore hurried to the convent of the Petrion and offered the Empire to the nun, and, when she hesitated and resisted, the mob carried her off almost by force. The imperial mantle was thrown over her shoulders; she was lifted upon a horse, and, surrounded by drawn swords, amid the cheers of the populace, was taken across the city to St. Sophia. The Patriarch, who was devotedly attached to the Macedonian house, awaited her there in order to proclaim her. The rioters now had an Empress.

This was on Monday evening. The first act of the new government that had been formed in the Great Church was to proclaim the dethronement of Michael V and to appoint a new Praefect of the City. But so long as the Palace held out, all was still to win. During the whole of Tuesday, fighting went on around the imperial residence, and in the bloody assaults upon it more than three thousand were killed. But at evening, the besiegers managed to break in the doors, and, while the mob stopped to pillage, the Emperor with his uncle the Nobilissimus and some friends had time to jump into a boat and make their way by sea to the venerated monastery of the Studion. There the defeated Basileus and his minister assumed the monastic habit, hoping thus to save their lives.

The victorious populace were wild with joy. "Some," says Psellus in a curious passage, "made offerings to God, while others cheered the Empress; the people of the lower classes gathered in groups in the public squares, dancing, and singing ballads about the recent events." Zoë, whom Michael V before his flight had set at liberty, and who had immediately resumed the power in the Palace, was no less happy, and quite ready in consequence to grant free pardons. But, in St. Sophia, the people of Theodora's following were less inclined to leniency; and the multitude, who had already forced Zoë to recognize her sister as colleague, now clamored for the execution of the guilty ones. Zoë tried in vain to persuade the Senate to be merciful; in vain, from a balcony of the Palace, she addressed the people and thanked them. When she went on to speak of the overthrown Emperor, and asked what should be done to him, a universal cry went up: "Death to the scoundrel, the villain! Impale him! Crucify him! Blind him!"

While Zoë hesitated, Theodora, confident of her popularity, acted. By her orders the Praefect of the City dragged the dethroned Emperor and the Nobilissimus, amid the jeers of the mob, from the Studion, where they had sought sanctuary, and outside in the street, under the eyes of the spectators, who ravened "like wild beasts" against their victims, had them blinded. Afterward they were exiled. The revolution was over.

In this crisis it was Theodora who, by her intervention, her energy, and her decision, had really saved the situation, and, as Psellus says, "overthrown the tyranny." In spite of herself, therefore, Zoë had to share the fruits of victory with her sister. Indeed, rather than have this detested colleague, she would have preferred anyone else; she would sooner have seen, says Psellus energetically, a stableboy on the throne than Theodora; and that was why she had tried as hard to save Michael V as Theodora's followers to be revenged upon him. But Zoë had no choice. The Senate and people pronounced in favor of her sister, and she yielded. She had a reconciliation with Theodora, threw her arms around her, offered her half of the power, and had her brought in great state from St. Sophia to the Sacred Palace. Theodora, with her usual modesty, accepted the imperial dignity only on condition that her elder sister should have first place. And now was seen an extraordinary state of affairs, unknown hitherto in Byzantium: namely, the Gynaeceum becoming the official center of public affairs, and the Empire governed by two old women. And, what is even more extraordinary, these two old women made themselves obeyed.

Seldom, however, have two near relatives been more unlike, both physically and intellectually, than these sisters. Whereas Zoë was pretty, well-proportioned, and elegant, Theodora, though rather younger, was ill-favored; she was ugly, and her overlong body was wholly disproportionate to her very small head. Whereas Zoë was lively, violent, and flighty, Theodora was dignified, calm, and slow to decide. Zoë threw money away by the handful, was wasteful, extravagant, and ridiculously generous. Theodora kept track of expenditures; she was very economical—possibly because before coming to the throne she had never had much to spend —and loved to store up her wealth in great strongboxes; and, having no taste for luxuries, nor being of a generous disposition, she spent little on herself, and even less on others. Whereas Zoë was eager and passionate, Theodora was chaste, proper, and irreproachable, and had always energetically refused to marry. She was a worthy creature, on the whole, amiable, kindly disposed, reserved, unassertive, and modest, and seemed made to fill the minor parts which fitted her so well. One quality, however, she had: she was a good speaker and liked to exercise her gift; and she was also, as we have seen, capable of occasional bursts of energy. Taken all in all, she, like Zoë, was mediocre, without very much character, and incapable of sustained effort. But, in spite of their common mediocrity, the sisters were too dissimilar to care greatly for one another or to get on well together for long.

Psellus has drawn a very curious picture of the court at this period. Every day, in accordance with etiquette, the two Empresses came in state costume and took their places side by side on the throne of the Basileis. Near them stood their councilors, and around them in a double circle were ranged the ushers, the swordbearers, and the Varangians carrying the heavy double-edged ax, all with eyes lowered out of respect for the sex of their sovereigns. The two Princesses gave judgment, received ambassadors, and dealt with affairs of State, giving at times an order or an answer in low tones, and even venturing occasionally to express their own wishes. And civilians and soldiers gave obedience to these gentle, tactful women.

But since, on the whole, they were both rather incompetent, this régime could not be of long duration. The luxury of the court—for now, as by a swift change of scene, each vied with the other in magnificence—and Zoë's absurd prodigality, soon emptied the treasury. Money was scarce, loyalty grew slack, and the need of a strong man was imperatively felt. Furthermore, the close association of the hostile sisters was becoming embarrassing, and the court was divided into two parties. Zoë could think of but one way to end the situation; namely, by making a third marriage. She was at that time sixty-four years of age.

V

Having made up her mind—and, strange as it may seem, everyone encouraged her—the old Empress set about to find a husband. At first she considered Constantine Dalassenus, to whom Constantine VIII had once wished to marry her. But this great and ambitious noble, who had been suspected several times of revolutionary designs, did not evince the tact and deference proper in a Prince Consort. He spoke out frankly, stated his conditions, and announced sweeping reforms and strong and vigorous resolves. This was not the sort of Emperor that the Palace was seeking, and so he was sent back to his province. Zoë next thought of another of her former favorites, the High Steward Constantine, who had been driven by the jealousy of Michael IV from Constantinople. From the point of view of personality, he would have been just the man; but unfortunately, like Romanus Argyrus before him, he was married, and his wife was less accommodating than Romanus's. Rather than surrender her husband to another, she preferred to poison him.

At last, after several fruitless attempts, the Basilissa recalled to mind still another of her former friends, Constantine Monomachus. As a relative by marriage of Romanus III, he had, some twelve or thirteen years back, cut an important figure at court, and by his beauty, his elegance, his fair speech, and his talent for amusing the Empress, had so captivated Zoë that there had been much gossip about them. Michael IV indeed, immediately after his accession, had taken the precaution of exiling this compromising friend. But Zoë had never forgotten him. She had seized the opportunity afforded by the revolution of 1042 to end his disgrace, and had appointed him governor of Greece. She now proposed to exalt him still further, and, as her choice was very acceptable to the court, where everyone was most eager for her to marry, she decided on him.

One of the Augusta's chamberlains was selected to carry to the new favorite the imperial insignia, the symbol and pledge of his high destiny, and to bring him back without delay to Constantinople. On the 11th of June 1042, he made his solemn entry, amid the shouts of the enthusiastic multitude, after which the marriage took place with great splendor at the Palace. And although the Patriarch felt himself unable personally to solemnize a third marriage that the Greek Church condemned (Zoë, as we have seen, was twice a widow, and Constantine had also been married twice), a

Byzantine prelate was usually too much a courtier and too thorough a politician long to withstand the powers that be. "Yielding to circumstances," says Psellus maliciously, "or, rather, to the will of God," after the ceremony he cordially embraced the newly wedded pair. "Was that a truly canonical act?" inquires the writer, ironically; "or was it flattery pure and simple? How can I tell?" Whichever it was, Byzantium had an Emperor.

In appearance the new sovereign fully justified the Empress's choice. He was a very handsome man. "As handsome as Achilles," says Psellus. "He was a finished work of Nature." His face was attractive: he had a clear skin, delicate features, and a delightful smile, and his whole personality irradiated charm. He was admirably proportioned, with a fine and graceful figure and beautiful, delicate hands. But remarkable vigor lay hidden, nevertheless, under this somewhat effeminate exterior. Accustomed to every kind of bodily exercise, an accomplished horseman, an excellent runner, a good fighter, Constantine had large reserves of hidden force. Those whom it amused him to squeeze in his arms felt the effects for several days, and there was no object too hard for him to break with his slender, well-kept hands.

He was a man of great fascination and charm. His voice was soft and he was a good speaker. Of a naturally amiable disposition, he was always in good spirits, ever smiling and ready to seek enjoyment for himself and others. He was essentially a good fellow, neither haughty nor vain, unaffected, without rancor, and eager to please everyone. And he had other qualities as well. Although quick to anger, so that he reddened on the slightest provocation, he had learned to control himself perfectly, and, as he was always master of himself, he was just, humane, and benevolent, and granted pardon even to those who conspired against him. "I have never seen," says Psellus, "a more sympathetic person." He was generous to the point of prodigality, and said repeatedly, somewhat like Titus, that a day on which he had not performed a humane or generous act was a day lost. As a matter of fact, his indulgence to others bordered upon weakness, for in order to please his favorites, he was in the habit of distributing the highest offices of State among them in the most casual way. Owing to his great desire to make everyone happy and contented, his generosity often amounted to wastefulness. He was unable to refuse anything, whether to his wife or to his mistresses; he was always open-handed, and ever ready for amusement, and he often remarked that it was the duty of all loyal subjects to participate in the pleasures of the court.

Constantine, without being a particularly learned man, was intelligent. He was quick-witted and enjoyed the society of men of letters. Among his associates were such scholars as Constantine Lichudes, Xiphilin, John Mauropus, and Psellus; it was on their advice that he reopened the University of Constantinople and added to it a law school to insure the proper training of men for the government service. He went even further, and, instead of assigning office according to the birth of the candidates, instituted the merit system. In order to make this reform effective, he promoted his friends the scholars to high office—Lichudes became Prime Minister; Psellus, Lord Chamberlain and Secretary of State; Xiphilin, Chancellor; Mauropus, Privy Councilor. All this made Constantine very popular. Furthermore, he was brave. This virtue was, perhaps, in his case a result of the somewhat fatalistic indifference which he acknowledged openly and which induced him to dispense, even at nighttime, with a guard at the door of his private apartments. But from whatever source derived, his courage was undoubted, and was manifested on many occasions. And if we consider that on the whole during the reign of Constantine Monomachus the Byzantine Empire, more than once victorious and usually at peace, preserved all its former prestige, we may perhaps come to the conclusion that this monarch was by no means so bad a sovereign as his detractors later asserted.

Unfortunately, his undoubted qualities were balanced by grave defects. Monomachus loved pleasure, women, and an easy, luxurious life. Having attained the throne by a stroke of luck, he regarded his position as essentially a means of satisfying his fancies. "After escaping a violent storm," says Psellus prettily, "he had reached the pleasant coast and secure haven of royalty, and was not anxious to put out again to sea." He bothered himself but little about public affairs, and left them to his ministers. The throne was to him, as Psellus says, only "a rest after struggle and a realization of desire." In the words of a modern historian: "To a government of women, there succeeded the government of a high liver and a hedonist." [1]

Constantine was a man of very amorous temperament, and had always delighted in gallant adventures, several of which before his accession had been rather notorious. He had been twice married and twice widowed, and had found consolation in his love for a young girl, the niece of the second wife, a member of the illustrious house of Sclerus, and known as Sclerena. She was pretty and intelligent. Psellus, who knew her, has left a very attractive account of her: "It was not that she was a flawless beauty; but her conversation was pleasant because it was free from malice and slander. She was sweet and gracious enough to have melted a rock. She had a wonderful voice, and a melodious and almost oratorical manner of speaking; her tongue was endowed with a native charm,

[1] A. N. Rambaud, "Michel Psellos," *Revue historique,* tome iii, 1877.

and when she spoke, it was with indescribable grace. She loved," adds the man of letters, "to ask me questions about Greek mythology, and she introduced into her conversation what she had learned from scholars. To a greater degree than any other woman, she possessed the gift of listening." [2]

She pleased not only Psellus, but everybody. The first time that she took part in the imperial procession, a courtier, both witty and educated, greeted her with a neat and delicate compliment, quoting the two first words of the beautiful passage in Homer where the old men of Troy, seated on the walls, remark at the sight of Helen passing by in all her radiant beauty:

> *Nor Greeks nor Trojans one can rightly blame*
> *That, for a woman's sake so beautiful*
> *They have alike endured so many woes.*

The allusion was ingenious and flattering; everyone caught his meaning at once and applauded. And is not this proof of the singular refinement of Byzantine society in the eleventh century, a society which in some of its aspects seems to us so barbarous, yet which is shown by this anecdote to have been so impregnated with the great memories of classical Greece, so endowed with acute intelligence, with literary taste, and with graceful and delicate thoughts?

At the beginning of his liaison with Sclerena, Constantine Monomachus would gladly have married her. But the Greek Church, as we have seen, was very unbending in the matter of third marriages, particularly when the parties were mere private persons; Constantine did not dare to flout its prohibitions. So she became his mistress and was the great passion of his life. The lovers were inseparable, even in misfortune. When Monomachus was exiled, Sclerena followed him to

[2] This translation is taken from Rambaud's article previously cited.

Lesbos, putting her entire fortune at his disposal, consoling him in his disgrace, rekindling his courage, holding out to him the hope of future vengeance, and telling him that one day he would become Emperor and that then they would be married and never part. Without regret or hesitation, the lovely young woman spent seven years on that distant island, and naturally, when chance raised Constantine to the throne, he never forgot her who had loved him so well.

Even in Zoë's arms his thoughts were of Sclerena. He managed so cleverly that, in spite of the Empress's notorious jealousy and in spite of the prudent advice of his friends and of his sister Euprepia, he was able to recall his mistress to Constantinople. From the very evening of his marriage he had spoken of her to Zoë, skillfully, of course, and with discretion, as a person to be treated with consideration on account of her family; soon he persuaded his wife to write inviting Sclerena to come to the Palace, assuring her at the same time of her goodwill. The young woman, who strongly suspected that the Basilissa did not care for her in the least, was not wholly convinced that this invitation was all it purported to be; but she adored Constantine, and so she returned. The Emperor immediately had a splendid palace erected for his favorite, and every day, on pretense of watching the progress of the work, spent many hours with Sclerena. The people of his suite, who during these visits were given an abundance of food and drink, thoroughly approved of the meetings; and when, in the midst of the official ceremonies, the courtiers gathered from the sovereign's bored manner that he wanted to go to his mistress, they vied with one another to find ways for him to escape to his beloved.

Soon their connection was openly avowed. The Emperor provided Sclerena with a household and a guard and made her wonderful presents: he sent her, for example, on one occasion an enormous bronze cup, beautifully engraved and filled to the brim with jewels. Every day he made her a new present, for which he emptied the Treasury. At last he treated her as his recognized and lawful wife. In the Palace she had her apartments, to which Constantine resorted freely at any hour, and she received the title of *Sebaste*, which gave her rank immediately after the two aged Empresses.

Zoë, contrary to the general expectation, took the affair very philosophically. "She had reached an age," Psellus indiscreetly remarks, "at which one is no longer very sensitive to wrongs of this nature." She was growing old, and was changing considerably in the process. She cared no longer for dress, had ceased to be jealous, and in her old age was turning pious. She spent many hours now at the feet of the holy images, enfolding them in her arms, talking to them, calling them by the most endearing names; dissolved in tears, she rolled before the icons in an ecstasy of mystical passion, giving to God what remained of the love that she had so lavished upon others. Therefore she consented without much difficulty to the most extraordinary arrangements. She gave Constantine his liberty, authorizing him to cease all intimate relations with her, and an official document to this effect, called the Contract of Friendship, was signed by husband and wife and duly registered by the Senate of the Empire. Sclerena had a recognized position at court, figured in the official processions, and was addressed by the titles of Sovereign and Basilissa. Zoë looked on delighted and smiling; she kissed her rival affectionately, and between his two wives Constantine Monomachus was a happy man. For the convenience of the household, a delightful arrangement was arrived at. The imperial apartments were divided into three sections. The Emperor occupied the central part, while Zoë and Sclerena took those to right and left respectively. By tacit agreement Zoë in future never visited the Basileus except when Sclerena was not with him and she could be sure of finding him alone. And this tactful contrivance seemed to everyone a miracle of ingenuity.

The people of the capital alone looked unfavorably upon this curious association. One day, when Constantine was going to the Church of the Holy Apostles, a voice from the crowd called out as the Emperor was leaving the Palace: "We don't want Sclerena for Empress! We don't want our mothers Zoé and Theodora put to death on her account!" The multitude joined in and a tumult arose; and, had not the aged Porphyrogenitae showed themselves on a balcony of the Palace and calmed the people, Monomachus might well have lost his life.

To the day of her death, Constantine remained faithful to Sclerena. When a sudden illness carried her off, he was inconsolable. Weeping like a child, he made public manifestation of his grief, had her buried with great magnificence, and built her a splendid tomb. Then, being a man, he cast about for other mistresses. After several passing fancies, he fell in love with a little Alan Princess who was living as a hostage at the Byzantine court. She does not seem to have been very pretty, but she had what in Psellus's judgment were two great points, a very white skin and wonderful eyes. As soon as the Emperor became aware of the existence of this young barbarian, he gave up all his other conquests for her, and his passion grew so strong that, when Zoë died, after having publicly announced her as his mistress, he thought seriously of making her his lawful wife. However, he did not dare take the step for fear of the thunders of the Church and the reproaches of his sister-in-law, the strait-laced Theodora. But at least he bestowed on his favorite the title of Sebaste, as he had formerly done on Sclerena; he surrounded her with imperial pomp and circumstance, and showered her with jewels and gold. And the little Circassian might be seen, her head and throat covered with gold, golden serpents around her arms, great pearls in her ears, a girdle of gold and jewels about her small waist, presiding like a typical harem beauty over all the Palace festivities. For her and for her parents, who came every year from distant Alania to pay her a visit, the Basileus squandered whatever sums remained in the Treasury, and he presented her to everyone as his wife and the lawful Empress. She was destined, moreover, greatly to sadden the last days of the sovereign who was so infatuated with her charms.

VI

Thus, toward the middle of the eleventh century, during the reign of Constantine Monomachus and Zoë, the Byzantine court presented a very curious appearance.

In leading the life he loved, the Emperor soon exhausted his vitality. He was no longer the handsome, elegant, robust Monomachus of former days. He suffered much from stomach trouble, but chiefly from gout. The attacks were so violent that his twisted, deformed hands could not hold anything, and his tortured, swollen feet were unable to support him. Sometimes at audiences he was incapable of standing; on such occasions he received stretched upon a bed. But even this position soon became intolerable, and his servants had constantly to shift him from one side to another. Frequently, even talking caused him pain. But his appearance was particularly distressing when he was obliged to take part in official processions. He had himself lifted upon a horse, and he set forth between two sturdy attendants who kept him from falling off. All along the way stones were carefully removed to save him from sharp, painful shocks; and thus the Basileus proceeded, his face distorted, gasping for breath, letting drop the reins that he was no longer able to hold. It must be put to Constantine's credit that he bore his troubles bravely, always smiling, always jovial. He used to say in jest that God must have afflicted him thus in order to curb his too fiery passions, and he diverted himself with philosophical reflections upon his sufferings. Moreover, as soon as he felt better, he denied himself neither his pleasures nor his mistresses.

Close by the sovereign lived the two old Porphyrogenitae, whose intellects age had somewhat weakened. Zoë spent her time in making perfumes, shutting herself up summer and winter alike in her overheated rooms, and never tearing herself away from her favorite occupation except to burn incense before her beloved images and to question them about the future; while Theodora counted over and over again the money that she had stored away, taking little interest in other matters, a chaste and sanctimonious virgin. Around them revolved the acknowledged mistresses, Sclerena, the little Alan Princess, and others, courtiers and favorites—often people of low origin—with whom the Emperor was infatuated and whom he raised to the highest offices in the State. And all these gentry had an excessively good time and did their best to amuse the Basileus.

For Constantine loved gaiety. Anyone who wished to command his attention in some important matter found that the best and indeed the only way to get him to listen was to begin with an amusing remark. Serious looks frightened him, but a clown could win his favor in a minute. He was, in fact, diverted chiefly by broad jests, heavy practical jokes, and extravagant puns. Music, singing, and dancing, bored him; he preferred amusements of a different nature and often in questionable taste. Psellus relates some of these pleasantries, and

it must be admitted that, however entertaining they may
have been in the eleventh century, today they seem very feeble. For example, one of the Emperor's greatest delights was
to hear someone stammer and exhaust himself in vain attempts to enunciate distinctly. The story is told of a courtier
who achieved an enormous success in the Palace by imitating
perfectly an affliction of this kind and relapsing gradually
into inarticulate cries and distressing stutters. His pleasing
talent so enraptured Constantine that he became the sovereign's prime favorite, and was henceforth in the habit of visiting the Emperor without ceremony at any time, holding his
hands, kissing him on the mouth, sitting down laughing beside him on his bed, and sometimes going to him even at night
to wake him up and tell him some more or less amusing tale,
usually taking the opportunity of extracting from him some
favor or gift.

As he was free to go wherever he liked, the buffoon in-
truded even into the Imperial Gynaeceum, and amused the
court intensely with the stories that he told there. He invented tales about the virtuous Theodora herself, saying that
she had had children, relating the affair with many obscene
details, and ending by mimicking the Princess's imaginary
accouchements, imitating her groans and the wails of the
newborn child, and putting into the aged and respectable sovereign's mouth all sorts of improper remarks. Everyone was
convulsed with laughter, even Theodora herself, and this fellow became the hero of the Gynaeceum. Only the sober-
minded were somewhat pained, but like good courtiers followed where the others led. "We were obliged to laugh,"
says Psellus bitterly, "though there was better cause to weep."

Relying on the universal indulgence, this extraordinary
favorite became bolder. He fell in love with the young Alan
Princess, and, as he was an amusing fellow, seems to have

made a conquest of the little barbarian. But his head was turned by his good fortune, and, being really seriously infatuated, he conceived the idea, in a burst of jealousy, of assassinating the Emperor, his rival, and taking his place. One evening he was discovered, dagger in hand, at the door of Monomachus's bedchamber. He was promptly arrested, and the next day was brought to trial before a court of justice presided over by the Basileus. But now we come to the amusing part of the story. When Constantine beheld his dear friend in chains, his weak indulgence overcame him and his eyes filled with tears. "For goodness' sake, free the man," he exclaimed. "It distresses me to see him in that condition." Then he gently asked the prisoner to be frank, and say what had impelled him to crime. The fellow answered that it was owing to an overpowering desire to wear the imperial insignia and to sit upon the throne of the Basileis. At this, Constantine burst into laughter and immediately gave orders that his fancy should be indulged. Then, turning to his favorite he said: "Now I am going to put the diadem on your head and clothe you in the purple. I ask of you nothing in return but to be your own agreeable self for the future." At this all present, even the judges, were unable to retain their gravity, and a great banquet sealed the Emperor's reconciliation with his friend.

The man was encouraged by the indulgence shown him, and naturally continued his attempts upon the sovereign's mistress. In the presence of the entire court and even under the Emperor's very nose, he smiled and made signs to her. But Constantine merely laughed at such conduct. "Just look at the poor creature!" said he to Psellus. "He is still in love, and his past misfortunes have not taught him a lesson." He himself was a "poor creature" after Molière's heart.

Whilst the frivolous Emperor wasted his time in these idiocies—the expression is Psellus's—whilst he squandered the revenues of the State in absurd prodigality, in magnificent buildings, and in childish and ruinous caprices, neglecting the army, begrudging the men their pay, and reducing the strength, the most serious events were in preparation. Two storms were already looming over the horizon and were soon to burst upon the Empire—the Normans in the West and the Turks in the East. Within the monarchy, the discontent of the military party, weary of the weakness of the civil authority and irritated at the disgrace of its most illustrious generals, was manifesting itself in dangerous leanings toward revolutionary pronunciamentos. And, taking advantage of the heedlessness of Monomachus, an ambitious Patriarch, Michael Cerularius, was completing the separation between Byzantium and Rome.

VII

In 1050, at the age of seventy-two, the long and tumultuous life of Zoë the Porphyrogenita came to an end. Constantine Monomachus, her husband, who for eight years, as we have seen, had been sufficiently detached from her, felt that he had done his duty in mourning her conscientiously. He even tried to find a place for her among the saints, and did his best to detect the performance of all kinds of miracles at her tomb, so as to prove to everyone that her soul was with the angels. This was doing a great deal of honor to a sensual and passionate old woman who had so disturbed the court and the capital with her scandalous marriages and love affairs. Monomachus, however, did not insist very strongly upon this attempted beatification; he soon consoled himself, as we have seen, and found Zoë's death an auspicious occasion for announcing his most recent favorite. Furthermore, he died a

few years later, on the 11th of January 1055, in the monastery of St. George of Mangana which he had founded, and to
which he had retired toward the end of his life.

Now, for the last time, Theodora, Zoë's sister, appears
upon the scene. After Zoë's third marriage, Theodora had
lived at court, nominally associated in the Empire, but playing in fact a very unimportant part. At the most, since the
Empress's death, she had acquired a little more influence,
and her brother-in-law Monomachus seems to have stood in
terror of the old lady's lectures. But this last descendant of
the Macedonian dynasty appeared, nevertheless, to count
for so little that Monomachus, regardless of her undoubted
rights to the throne, had considered nominating another as
his successor. Then it was that once again there stirred in
Theodora's veins the fiery blood and the proud energy of the
great Emperors her ancestors. While Constantine Monomachus lay dying, she resolutely took possession of the Great
Palace, strong in her right of birth and in the prestige which
the sufferings of her long life had given her among the people. The guard regiments pronounced in her favor and the
Senate followed their lead. Thus, at the age of seventy, the
old Princess firmly seized the power.

Warned by her sister's example and knowing how little a
Basilissa could count on the gratitude of the men whom she
associated with her, Theodora, to the general amazement,
refused to take a husband. She insisted upon governing alone,
and, as she was sensible enough to allow herself to be guided
by a capable minister, she seems to have governed well. Her
green old age, furthermore, excited universal admiration.
Her figure was straight and her mind alert; she was able to
work seriously with her advisers and to make the long
speeches in which she delighted. She gladly let her friends

the monks persuade her that her days were destined to exceed the allotted span of human life.

But in the long run, everyone in the capital and in the Empire tired of this feminine government that had lasted now for more than twenty-five years. The Patriarch Cerularius, who had become since the schism the Pope, as it were, of the Eastern Church, said openly that it was a shame that a woman should govern the Roman Empire. The military party, discontented at the position that the bureaucracy occupied in the State, and exasperated at the insulting distrust with which the court regarded the generals, were growing restless. And many good citizens who, like Psellus, prided themselves on their patriotism, recalled the glorious days of Basil II and passed severe judgement on these Princesses whose ridiculous prodigality, childish vanity, fantastic caprices, and limited intelligence, had prepared the ruin of the monarchy and sown the germs of fatal decay in the healthy body of the Empire. Everyone wanted a man and a soldier. Theodora was fortunate enough to die before the storm burst. She passed away on the 31st of August 1056.

✺✺✺ VIII ✺✺✺

ANNA COMNENA

I

In the month of December 1083, the Empress Irene Ducas, wife of Alexius Comnenus, was awaiting the birth of her child in the apartment of the Sacred Palace known as the Purple Pavilion, designated by ancient tradition as the birth chamber of the imperial children, whose title of Porphyrogenitus derived from it. The Empress's time was near, but the Basileus, detained by the war against the Normans, was still absent from Constantinople, and the young woman, feeling the onset of her first pains, was moved to make a charming gesture. Tracing the sign of the cross over her belly, she said: "Not yet, little child, wait until your father comes home." Irene's mother, a wise and reasonable woman, was very angry when she heard this: "And how do you know when your husband will come home? Supposing he does not return for another month? How will you hold back your pains from now until then?" But the young woman was proved right in the event. Three days later, Alexius returned to his capital, just in time to receive his newborn daughter into his arms. And in this way, with something marvelous about her from the moment of her birth, came into the world Anna Comnena, one of the most celebrated, one of the most remarkable of all the Princesses who ever lived at the court of Byzantium.

The birth of this miraculous child was welcomed with extreme joy. Besides providing an heir to the Empire, the event set a radiant seal on the highly political and wholly unsentimental marriage that six years earlier had united Alexius and Irene, and strengthened the latter's influence at court, which up until then had been somewhat tenuous. Irene's parents, "wild with joy," were highly gratified. A display of unusual extravagance, both in the official ceremonies with which it was customary to celebrate the birth of the imperial children, and in the gifts made on this occasion to the army and to the Senate, testified to the general satisfaction of the populace. The imperial diadem was placed on the head of the little Princess while she was still in her cradle; her name figured in the ritual acclamations with which the Byzantine sovereigns were saluted; and at the same time she was affianced to the son of the dethroned Emperor Michael VII, young Constantine Ducas, whose eventual rights of succession Alexius Comnenus, in usurping the power, had been obliged to guarantee out of respect for legitimacy. So, from her earliest childhood, Anna Comnena, born to the purple, could dream of the day when she would sit as Empress on the glorious throne of the Caesars.

Her mother, Irene, and her future mother-in-law, the Basilissa Mary of Alania, both took a share in her upbringing. And all her life she kept the glowing memory of those early years, which later seemed the happiest of her whole life. She adored her mother, who for her part always showed a special predilection for her eldest daughter, and she had a profound admiration for Mary of Alania, that beautiful woman with the elegant figure, the snow-white skin, and the charming blue eyes. Many years later, she recalled with emotion the affection shown her by this exquisite Princess, worthy of Apelles' brush and Phidias' chisel, and so beautiful that all who beheld her were enraptured. "Never," writes Anna Comnena, "were such perfectly harmonious proportions seen in a human body. She was an animated statue, an object of admiration for everyone with a sense of beauty; or rather, she was Love embodied, and come down to Earth." The little girl loved her future husband, the young Constantine, no less tenderly. He was nine years older than she, and a charming little boy, fair-haired and rosy cheeked, with wonderful eyes "that shone beneath his brows like jewels set in gold." "His beauty," says Anna Comnena somewhere else, "seemed to be of Heaven and not of Earth." And indeed, he was destined to die prematurely, when he was barely twenty years old, before the marriage on which his little financée was building so many ambitious hopes could be realized. To the end of her life, Anna Comnena fondly treasured the memory of this young man to whom she had given her childish adoration, and whom the Emperor Alexius had loved as his own son. A great many years later, when she thought of this Constantine Ducas, "marvel of nature, masterpiece formed by the hand of God and resembling a scion of that golden age extolled by the Greeks," tears would come into the eyes of the old Princess and she would have difficulty in controlling her emotion.

In this atmosphere of tenderness and affection little Anna Comnena, cherished and beloved, was brought up. To comprehend what she was, it will perhaps be helpful to consider the education given a Byzantine Princess at the end of the eleventh century.

Seldom was the taste for literature, and above all for the literature of antiquity, more widespread than in the Byzantium of the Comneni. This was the period that produced scholars such as Tzetzes, who commented on the poems of Hesiod and Homer with stupendous erudition, and John Italus, who resumed Psellus's studies of Platonic philosophy —to the great scandal of the Orthodox Church; the period in which the best writers of the time, imbued with the antique forms, prided themselves on imitating in their works the most illustrious Greek authors, and in which even the language itself underwent a process of refinement in the effort to reproduce, by a slightly mannered purism, the sober Attic grace. In such a renascence of classical culture, an Imperial Princess, particularly one as remarkably intelligent as Anna Comnena, could no longer content herself with the rather summary education formerly given to Byzantine women. She had the best teachers and she took advantage of their instruction. She learned all there was to be learned in her day: rhetoric, philosophy, history, literature, geography, mythology, medicine, and the sciences. She read the great poets of antiquity, Homer and the lyricists, the tragic dramatists and Aristophanes, historians like Thucydides and Polybius, orators such as Isocrates and Demosthenes; she read the treatises of Aristotle and the dialogues of Plato, and from these famous writers she learned the art of eloquence and "the very essence of Hellenism." She was capable of quoting freely from Orpheus and Timotheus, Sappho and Pindar, Porphry and Proclus, the Porch and the Academy. The arts of the quadrivium held no mystery for her; she knew geometry, arithmetic, music, and astronomy. Her mind was familiar with the great pagan gods and the beautiful legends of classical Greece; Herakles and Athena, Cadmus and Niobe, came naturally to her pen. She was equally well instructed in the history of Byzantium and in geography, and she had some interest in the ancient monuments; moreover, she was able, when necessary, to discourse on military matters and to discuss with physicians the best methods of treating illnesses. Lastly, this Byzantine seems even to have known Latin, a rare enough accomplishment in the East of her day.

She was not only a well-educated woman: she was a learned woman. Her contemporaries agree in praising the elegance of her Attic style, the power of her mind and its capacity to solve the most obscure problems, the superiority of her natural genius and the diligence with which she cultivated her gifts, her taste for books and for learned discourse, the universality of her attainments. And indeed, one has only to glance through her book, *The Alexiade*, to find in it the marks of distinction. Despite a certain preciosity of style, a deliberately mannered purism in the language, an occasional pedantic and pretentious passage, the work bears the stamp of the superior woman and the writer of real talent that Anna Comnena unquestionably was. She had given promise of all this as a child. Like every Byzantine, she was an expert in matters of religion, and well versed in the Holy Scriptures. Yet hers was a scientific rather than a religious mind. She professed a high regard for literature and history, convinced that through them alone even the most illustrious names could be saved from oblivion. On the other hand, her reason rejected the supernatural, the idle calculations of astrologers, the false predictions of soothsayers. She had investigated their so-called science, partly because she wanted to delve into everything, but chiefly to prove its vanity and foolishness. And, pious though she was, she had little taste for theological discussions, whose subtleties and fine distinctions she considered rather otiose. She was attracted above all by history, by its gravity and importance, and by the magnitude of the historian's task.

Such was Anna Comnena's intellectual training. Her moral formation was no less carefully supervised. Several years earlier, under the influence of the strict Anna Dalassena, mother of the Emperor, the tone of the Byzantine court had undergone a great change. This serious-minded and rigidly moral Princess had resolutely put an end to the intrigues of the Gynaeceum, to the scandalous love affairs that in the past, in the time of Zoë the Porphyrogenita and of Constantine Monomachus, spread their corruption throughout the Sacred Palace. With a firm hand she had put things in order, and under her stern supervision the imperial residence had assumed a monastic air. It resounded with the chanting of pious hymns, and its inhabitants led an exemplary and methodically regulated life. Probably the Basileus Alexius, who did not love his wife, allowed himself some minor peccadilloes, but he was careful to keep up appearances, he would have blushed at the idea of installing an accredited mistress in the Palace, and the general tone of his court was one of unrivaled decorum. In such an environment, and under the influence of a grandmother whom she profoundly admired, Anna Comnena quite naturally developed into a young girl of perfect breeding, serious, chaste, mindful of all the proprieties, irreproachable in speech and behavior.

But to see in this Princess no more than a woman of intelligence, well educated and well bred, would be to have an incomplete idea of her. She was much too fully aware of what she was, of her high birth as well as her intellectual superiority, not to be a woman of great ambition. And in any case, she came of ambitious stock. Her grandmother, Anna Dalassena, who by sheer tenacity and force of will had placed her family on the throne; her father, the Emperor Alexius, so clever, so crafty, so persevering; her mother, Irene, whose spirit was at once masculine, courageous, and intriguing—all these were immensely ambitious. And Anna had too profound an admiration for them all not to follow blindly the examples offered by their lives to her youthful spirit. Moreover, very proud of having been born to the purple, very proud of being the eldest child of Alexius and Irene, very proud of the imperial title bestowed on her in her cradle, she deemed anything lower than her lofty dignity as a Porphyrogenita beneath her consideration. Her pride, personal, ancestral, and national, was immeasurable. In her eyes Byzantium was still the mistress of the world, of whom all the other nations should be the humble vassals, and her throne the finest of all the thrones of the world. One should see how scornfully this Byzantine Princess speaks of the Crusaders, of those ill-bred barbarians whose rough, outlandish names she apologizes for introducing into her history, offended in her literary vanity by feeling the rhythm of her prose disrupted by these alien vocables, and in her imperial pride by being constrained to waste time over men who bored and disgusted her. Anna Comnena was very much a Princess, and the ceremonious world in which she spent her life could only have served to strengthen her natural tendencies. But her self-willed, authoritative, and ambitious spirit was to be strangely warped by her sense of her worth and rank.

Hers was by no means an arid soul, however. One detects in this learned and ambitious woman a hint of sensibility, even of sentimentality, that is both touching and, on occasion, amusing. And I do not speak only of her great affection for

her parents. She herself recalls rather drolly, with reference
to the miracle attending her birth, that even in her mother's
womb she was a docile and obedient child. Elsewhere she
declares that for her beloved parents she unhesitatingly exposed herself to the greatest vexations, to the gravest dangers, "risking for their sakes her position, her fortune, and
even her life," and that many of her calamities owed their
origin to her unusually strong affection for her father,
Alexius. Here we have family sentiments that are worthy of
infinite respect, but Anna, as we shall see, did not think it
at all advisable to extend these sentiments to her relatives in
general. Yet—and this is more piquant—there was room in
her heart for other affections; this *précieuse*, this prude, this
pedant, was, like Molière's Arsinoé, attracted by the ele-
mental. She has told us how, in 1106—when she had been
married for several years—she was looking out of the Palace
windows one day with her sisters, when a procession passed
by leading a conspirator, Michael Anemas, to execution. At
the sight of this handsome soldier, so attractive and so unfortunate, she was so strongly moved that she did not rest
until she had wrung a pardon for him from her father, the
Emperor; and so fired was she by this wild idea that she
dared—she who was so respectful of etiquette and good manners—to disturb Alexius in his oratory, while he was saying
his prayers before the holy altar. Ten years earlier, when she
was still a young girl, only fourteen years old, she had experienced an emotion of the same kind, and yet more profound. This was when one of the leaders of the First Crusade,
the splendid Bohémond, Prince of Taranto, disembarked at
Byzantium in 1097. One should read in *The Alexiade* Anna
Comnena's enthusiastic description of this red-haired giant
with the broad shoulders and narrow waist, the sparkling
blue eyes, and the terrific, exploding laugh, this hero at once

formidable and seductive, so eloquent, so supple and adroit of mind, and physically so well made that he seemed to have been constructed according to the "canon" of Polyclitus. "In all the Roman Empire," she writes, "there was no man who could be compared with him, either Greek or barbarian. He seemed to be the embodiment of valor and love, and he was second only to my father, the Emperor, in eloquence and the other gifts that nature had showered upon him." Such are the terms used by this Byzantine Princess to describe the barbarian from the West more than forty years after Bohémond appeared before her, like a sunburst, for the first time. And in the entire *Alexiade* no man, other than the Basileus Alexius himself, has been honored by Anna Comnena with a more flattering or a more finished portrait.

It is only fair to add that if Anna Comnena liked and admired fine specimens of manhood, it was in all honor, as befitted the chaste and honest woman that she was. But in the depths of her being, there was a wealth of tenderness ready and waiting for opportunities to expend itself. She never ceased to grieve for the fiancé of her childhood, the young Constantine who vanished so prematurely, and whose death dealt, as we shall see, a cruel blow to her vast ambitions. Afterward, when she was married, in 1097, to that great nobleman Nicephorus Bryennius, her tender and sensitive heart knew how to transform a union that was purely a matter of politics into a union of love. And indeed Bryennius was the right husband for her. Like her, he was scholarly; like her, he loved literature: "he had read all the books, he was versed in all the sciences"; and like her, he took pleasure in writing, and wrote well. A magnificent soldier, a clever diplomat, an eloquent orator, he was also a handsome man with a graciousness that was something more than royal, "a bearing that was almost divine." Anna Comnena adored "her Caesar," and never got over losing him. When Bryennius returned to Constantinople in 1156, seriously ill, she nursed him with admirable devotion. At his death, not long afterward, she inherited the pious task of continuing the history that his faltering hand had been unable to finish; and since she was, in her old age, a little plaintive and given to lamenting, she could not pen the name of her adored husband without watering it with abundant tears. The death of Bryennius was, if she is to be believed, the great tragedy of her life, the constantly bleeding wound that slowly brought her to her grave. And it is true that, as long as her husband lived, the ambitious Princess used every means to push him, and herself with him, to the sovereignty, and that in losing him she lost her last remaining chance to take her revenge on destiny. But if the bitterness of her grief was not unmixed with the bitterness of disappointment, in other respects her tears were sincere. This Princess openly cultivated in her heart a little flower of sentimental tenderness that she managed to keep alive even in the desert of politics. And it is by no means an unimportant factor in her personality, that this learned and ambitious woman should also have been an honest woman who loved her husband very dearly.

If we try to piece together the scattered fragments of information that we possess concerning this Byzantine Princess, and picture her as she really was, this is more or less what we see. Physically she resembled her father, Alexius, and probably she was, like him, of medium height, very dark, with beautiful, lively eyes, sparkling and heroic. Mentally, she was remarkably intelligent, aware of her intellectual superiority and proud of it; she was admirably educated, she loved books, and scholars, she took pleasure in all mental activities, and when she took up writing, it was with unquestionable talent. But it was her ambitious and headstrong

spirit, her soul of a Porphyrogenita, haughty, proud of her
birth and eager for sovereignty, that was to sway her destiny.
She had, as she herself says somewhere, a soul of diamond
capable of surmounting any possible misfortune and incapable of renouncing any project, any cherished dream, once
they had taken form in her imagination. Accustomed to action very early in life—for she had not been brought up as a
little queen, in luxury and idleness—energetic, tenacious,
daring, she allowed no obstacle to deter her from pursuing
any goal she wanted to attain, and there were times when she
forgot, in the heat of the pursuit, to listen to the promptings
of that tender heart on which she prided herself. With all
this, she was honest, and a good and affectionate wife. But
before everything, born to the purple, Empress from her
cradle, she was regal. Ambition filled one half of her life;
literature consoled the rest, though rather inadequately,
for her disappointments and grievances made her profoundly
unhappy. But the originality and interest of Anna Comnena
lie precisely in this fact: namely, that she was at once a
political and a literary figure in the complex Byzantium of
her lifetime.

II

Anna Comnena has written: "I was only eight years old
when my misfortunes began." It was in 1091, and this is
what happened to her. Eldest daughter of the Emperor
Alexius, betrothed to Constantine Ducas, the heir apparent,
Anna Comnena thought herself sure of the throne, when, in
1088, the Empress Irene presented her husband with a son.
Alexius was overjoyed to have a male descendant at last, and,
of course, the line of succession was changed. The Basileus,
formerly so full of consideration for the mother of Constan-

tine Ducas, so anxious to please her in every way, grew cool toward her. A man of his word, he probably had no intention of making any change concerning the projected marriage between the princely children; but he saw fit to take the little Anna Comnena out of the hands of her future mother-in-law, and this separation was the child's first great sorrow. A few months later, a more serious event took place. Alexius's son John, aged three years, was formally proclaimed heir to the Empire. It was the end of whatever hopes his sister may have cherished. Anna Comnena did not lose her fiancé, but her fiancé lost his rights of succession, and was relegated to an inferior position until his death in 1094. And when the Princess married Nicephorus Bryennius in 1097, he too, despite the title of Caesar accorded to him, ranked below the heir apparent, and the same applied to her as his wife.

So for Anna Comnena, the birth of a brother was the great misfortune of her life. It was because of her dreams of sharing a throne with young Constantine Ducas that she so tenderly cherished his memory. It was because the "dark little boy with the big forehead and the thin cheeks," who was her detested brother, had suddenly come to ruin her ambitions that she hated him so savagely. It was because she hoped to regain the throne through, and with, Nicephorus Bryennius, that she loved him so much. And it was because she believed herself qualified to reign, by right of seniority, that as long as Alexius lived she plotted, agitated, and used all her influence to push forward her husband, Nicephorus, with the aim of recovering the power that she considered herself unjustly deprived of. This was the constant goal of her ambition, the justification for all her acts; this one, tenacious, dream filled her whole existence—and explains it—up until the day when, having finally failed to attain her goal, she understood that she had, at the same time, wrecked her life.

In this struggle for the crown that went on between Anna
and her brother, all the members of the imperial family took
sides. Andronicus, one of Alexius's sons, sided with his sister;
the other, Isaac, with his brother; as for their mother, Irene,
she had a strange dislike for her son John. She thought him
frivolous, unbalanced, and morally corrupt, in all of which
she did him an injustice. She had, on the contrary, a great
admiration for her eldest daughter's intelligence; she asked
Anna's advice in everything and treated her opinions as
oracles. Moreover—and this was unusual—she adored her
son-in-law. She thought him eloquent, scholarly, and endowed with all the qualities requisite for a statesman and a
sovereign. The two women resolved to oust the legitimate
heir; and as Irene exercised a strong influence over the Emperor now that he was older, and already ailing, they could
hope to see their plans realized. Soon, thanks to these intrigues, Bryennius was all-powerful at the Palace, and it was
rumored that nothing was done without his approval. The
shrewd courtiers were zealous in their efforts to please him;
at the betrothal of his eldest son, Alexius, to the daughter of a
Prince of Abasgie, the official orators extolled in pompous
epithalamiums the qualities of the young bridegroom, who
seemed destined to the Empire, and the glory of his parents.
Attention was obligingly drawn to the Prince's striking resemblance to his grandfather the Basileus, whose name he
bore. The education that he and his brother, John Ducas, had
received under the direction of the eminent mother given to
them by Heaven, was enthusiastically extolled. It seemed, in
short, that all was going as it should, and that Anna Comnena
was going to get what she wanted. But the Emperor still reserved his final decision, and this was where matters stood
when, in the course of the year 1118, Alexius became seri-

ously ill. Then began the tragic drama that was enacted
around him as he approached his death.

If one reads in *The Alexiade* the account of these August
days in 1118 when the Emperor was dying, one finds in
these very beautiful pages, vibrating with sincere emotion,
no trace of the unrestrained rivalries and burning passions
that clashed about his deathbed. One finds helpless physicians uselessly busying themselves with their patient and,
like Molière's physicians, talking only of purging and bleeding. We see the stricken women weeping and lamenting,
and vainly striving to ease the last hours of the dying man.
The Emperor's wife and daughters encircle the bed. Mary
tries to pour a little water down the swollen throat of the
patient, and when he grows faint, she revives him by making
him inhale essence of roses. Irene sobs, having lost all the
energy that sustained her at the beginning of the crisis;
anxious, despairing, she questions the doctors, she questions
her daughter Anna, and her state is such that one wonders
whether she will be able to survive the death of her husband.
Anna, given over to grief, "despising," as she writes, "philosophy and eloquence," holds her father's hand and sorrow-
fully notes the faltering of his pulse. And now comes the
moment of death. To hide the final spasms of agony from
Irene, Mary discreetly places herself between her mother
and the Emperor. Suddenly Anna feels that the pulse has
ceased to beat. She remains silent for a time, her head bowed,
then, covering her face with her hands, she bursts into sobs.
Irene, realizing what has happened, utters a long cry of
despair; she throws her imperial headdress on the ground
and, seizing a knife, she cuts off her hair almost to the roots;
she throws off her purple buskins and puts on boots of plain
black; from the wardrobe of her daughter Eudocia, recently

widowed, she borrows mourning garments and a black veil with which she covers her head. In relating the events of this tragic day many years later, Anna Comnena asks herself whether she is not the victim of a dreadful dream, and why she did not die at the same moment as her adored father, why she did not kill herself on that day when "the torch of the world," Alexius the Great, was extinguished, the day on which, as she expresses it, "his sun went down."

In all this beautiful account, there is not a word that could lead one even to suspect the intrigues and ambitions at work in that sickroom. Irene, in her despair, has no thought for the diadem or the power; Anna, at her side, despises all the glories of this world. There is not a word about the coveted succession, nor about the last desperate efforts made to over-throw the established order. There is a discreet allusion to the haste with which John Comnenus left his father's death-bed to go and take over the Great Palace; a casual passing mention of the disturbances in the capital; and that is all. One must consult the other chroniclers of the time to see what the lamentations of these women concealed; Irene's violent attempts to make the Emperor disinherit his son in favor of Bryennius, and her fury when John Comnenus, having wrested the imperial ring from the dying man—or, more likely, having simply received it from him—had him-self hurriedly proclaimed Emperor in St. Sophia and took possession of the Great Palace. This occasioned an outburst of wild rage on the part of these ambitious women. Irene urged Bryennius also to proclaim himself Emperor, and to take up arms against his brother-in-law. Then she threw herself on the Emperor's agonizing body, crying out to him that his son was stealing his throne while he still lived, and entreating him at last to recognize Bryennius's rights to the crown. But Alexius, without replying, smiled and lifted his hands to heaven in a vague gesture. Irene, exasperated, burst into reproaches: "All your life," she screamed, "you have been a deceiver, using your words to conceal your thoughts, and you are just the same even on your deathbed." Meanwhile, John Comnenus asked himself how he ought to act toward his mother, his sisters, and Bryennius, on whose part he feared an attempted *coup d'État*. And when, toward nightfall, Alexius's agony came to an end, in this turmoil of ambitions and anxieties no one had time to bother about the dead man. His body was left almost entirely unattended, and early on the following day it was hastily buried, without any of the customary funeral pomp.

Anna's plots had failed: her brother was Emperor. For the proud Princess this was a terrible and unexpected blow. For so many years she had lived in the hope of inheriting the Empire. She considered the throne legitimately and essentially hers, she thought herself so superior to her detested younger brother. Now, all her dreams had crumbled. The audacity of John Comnenus and the hesitancy of Bryennius had overturned at a single stroke the whole edifice of intricate schemes so cleverly constructed by Anna and Irene. The daughter of Alexius was inconsolable, and her frustrated ambition, obliterating all other sentiments, kindled in her heart the fury of Medea. The year had not run its course before she attempted to seize the power by means of a plot to assassinate her brother John. But Bryennius, whose character was rather weak and who, in any case, was not really ambitious, hesitated at the last moment. He seems to have doubted the legitimacy of his wife's claims, and he said flatly that he thought his brother-in-law had every right to the throne. His scruples and his weakness paralyzed the zeal of the other conspirators, and thanks to his procrastination the plot was discovered. The Emperor prided himself on his clemency. He would not hear of any executions, and contented himself with confiscating the property of the conspirators. Not very long afterward, on the advice of his Grand Domestic, Axouch, he restored Anna's fortune to her in its entirety. To be reminded by her brother in this way, with a slightly disdainful magnanimity, of the family ties and affections that in a moment of folly she had completely forgotten, was the supreme humiliation for this proud Princess.

An anecdote, related by the chronicler Nicetas, shows how furious Anna Comnena was over this last failure. When she saw her whole enterprise brought to nothing by the shilly-shallying of Bryennius, she, so chaste and proper, swore at her husband like a trooper. Cursing his cowardice, she declared that nature had made a pretty mess of things, clothing her masculine spirit with a woman's body and Bryennius's timid and indecisive soul with a man's. Decency obliges me to paraphrase the actual terms she used, which were very different, much coarser and more vigorous. But Anna Comnena must indeed have felt cruelly stricken, to have stooped, literary and well-bred as she was, to utter words of such crudity.

III

Anna Comnena was only thirty-six years old, but her life was over. She survived the collapse of her great ambitions by twenty-nine years, consecrating herself wholly, as she says somewhere, "to God and to books." This long last chapter of her existence was, for her, mortally sad. She was overwhelmed by loss after loss. After her father Alexius, whose death, as she well knew had meant for her the end of everything, she saw die, one after the other, her mother Irene, "the glory of the East and the West," her favorite brother

Andronicus, and finally, in 1136, her husband, Nicephorus
Bryennius; and for her, each one of these deaths meant one
more stage in her decline. In a state of semi-disgrace after
the failure of her final conspiracy, she lived a life of retirement far from the court, often in the convent founded by her
mother Irene, in honor of Our Lady of Grace. The former
intimates of her father, the courtiers who had danced attendance on her in the past, now avoided her for fear of displeas-
ing the new ruler. Sadly she enumerated the ingrates she
encountered. At the same time, she saw the brother she hated
securing his seat on the throne. All this embittered her soul.
During the lifetime of her husband, in whom the Emperor
had not lost confidence, and to whom he had given an important position in the State, Anna Comnena had still
counted for something. But after the death of Bryennius, and
particularly during the reign of her nephew Manuel, silence
closed around her, and she suffered terribly because of it.

Every day she became more gloomy and morose; she saw
herself more and more as the victim of an unjust fate. On
every page of her book, she speaks of the misfortunes with
which her life had been filled, almost from the day of her
birth in the Purple Pavilion. It was in vain that she affected
to strike a gallant pose, to repeat with the poet, at each fresh
blow from fate: "Bear this, my heart, thou hast already borne
worse ills." She could never achieve real resignation. When
the old Princess recalled the brilliant beginnings of her life,
the radiant years of her youth, and her imperial hopes; when
she evoked the phantom procession of all those who had
accompanied her happiness, her young fiancé Constantine
Ducas, the beautiful Empress Mary, the incomparable
Alexius her father, Irene her mother, her husband, and many
others; when she compared with these vanished glories her
present solitude, the ingrates who forgot her, the old friends

who neglected her, the near relatives who treated her badly and made everyone shun her, she could not restrain her tears. Her embittered soul, full of rancor, took pleasure in the enumeration of her misfortunes. "I swear by God and his divine mother," she writes, "that from my cradle sorrows and adversities have overwhelmed me one after another. I say nothing of my bodily ills, that I leave to the domestics of the Gynaeceum. But to enumerate all the troubles that have assailed me from the age of eight on, all the enemies who have earned me the malice of men, would take the facility of Isocrates, the eloquence of Pindar, the vehemence of Pole-mon, the muse of Homer, the lyre of Sappho. There is no misfortune, great or small, that has not befallen me. Always, today as in former days, the torrents of the storm have crushed me, and even as I write this book, I am overwhelmed by a sea of tribulations, wave following upon wave." Then come tart, and transparent, allusions to "the powers that be" who leave her to live "in her corner" and do not permit even the most obscure persons to visit her. "For thirty years, I swear it by the blessed souls of the dead Emperors, I have not seen or received any of my father's old friends; many are dead, many avoid me out of fear, following the changes in policy." Elsewhere she declares that her misfortunes could move not only all sensitive beings, but even stones; draping herself in her sorrow, posing as a great martyr, she is amazed that she herself has not been changed into an inanimate object by so great an accumulation of misfortunes, like the famous mourners of pagan mythology; and recalling the tragic figure of Niobe, she counts herself equally, if not more, deserving of being turned to stone.

It must be admitted that these tears are somewhat exces-sive, and that, no matter how sincere, they end by being rather irritating. Besides, there is every reason to believe that in the account of her misfortunes, as with everything else that concerned herself, Anna Comnena, whether consciously or not, exaggerates, and depicts events under a light that is more tragic than true. In the last years of her life, this aged Princess, this survival of a past era, with the name of her father Alexius always on her lips, may have been rather tiresome, and something of a nuisance to her young nephew Manuel and the brilliant courtiers surrounding him. But she could, perhaps, have lived on good terms with her brother, the Emperor John, had she made the effort. As we have seen, this gentle and merciful Prince harbored no resentment against his sister's husband for having been the instrument of her ambitious plans. He treated her sons with similar kindness. He had the marriages of these two young men celebrated even though their mother had been concocting plots against him on the eve of the wedding festivities. We know, too, how he forgave Anna for conspiring against his life, hoping by this chivalrous magnanimity to awaken some remorse in her troubled soul and revive in it some feelings of affection. At all events, even in her retirement, the Princess's life was less isolated than she wished to admit; her patronage was sought, which proves that she was not without influence. And no matter how sad, how melancholy may have been Anna Comnena's last years, it must not be forgotten that she herself was to blame, rather than destiny. But it must have been peculiarly hard for her to go on living with her defeat until the age of sixty-five; indeed, it must have been torture for this ambitious woman to see the triumph of her adversaries and to be aware, during these thirty years, that there was no further part for her to play. But she had brought this on herself.

Her supreme consolation in retirement was the literature beloved of her youth. She had a little court of scholars, grammarians, and monks; and she poured all her sorrows, all her regrets, all her bitterness, all her memories, into a fine book, *The Alexiade.*

Knowing all that we now know about the author, we can easily guess what manner of work this was. Of course, Anna Comnena loftily credits herself with the serene impartiality of the historian. She remarks somewhere, that "whoever undertakes to write history must free himself equally from passion and from hatred, must know how to praise his enemies when their conduct calls for it, and to blame his closest relatives when their faults make it necessary." She is no less boastful of her regard for truth. "It may perhaps be said by my readers," she writes, "that my language has been modified by my natural affections. But I swear by the dangers that my father the Emperor faced for the sake of the Romans, by the feats that he accomplished, by all that he suffered for Christ's people, that I do not write this book in order to flatter my father. Whenever I shall find him to have been in the wrong, I shall sternly reject my natural impulses and adhere to the truth." She has taken care to list meticulously the various sources from which she has drawn the content of her history. She consulted the memorandums of her father's old comrades in arms, dipping into the simple and truthful memoirs in which, without regard for art or rhetoric, they have related their exploits and those of their master, the Emperor. She then combined what they told with all that she herself had seen, with all that she had gathered from the talk of her father, her mother, and her uncles, and with everything reported by the Emperor's great generals, who witnessed the glories of his reign and played a part in them. She stresses the unanimity of all this testimony, and the obvious sincerity with which it was given, "now that all flattery, all lies, have disappeared with the death of

Alexius, and people, having nothing to gain by flattering the
vanished ruler, but only the one now in power, give us the
naked facts, and describe events exactly as they happened."
And it is true that Anna Comnena was genuinely concerned
with collecting accurate and circumstantial information. Besides the oral traditions, she consulted the archives of the
Empire and copied records of capital importance, she tran-
scribed in her book the authentic texts of certain diplomatic
documents, of certain private letters, and she carried her
concern for documentation so far that, to relate the story of
Robert Guiscard, she made use of a Latin source, which has
been lost.

But in spite of all this, *The Alexiade* arouses uneasiness
and suspicion in the reader. This so-called history is a mixture of satire and panegyric. And it is easy to understand
why. When, after the death of Bryennius, the Princess made
it her task to continue the historical work begun by her husband, and to record the reign of Alexius for posterity, she
felt the quite natural temptation to paint in rosy colors the
period in which she had been happy, in which her hopes had
been high, and the future smiling. In exalting the great figure
of Alexius, it did not entirely displease her to lower a little,
by inevitable comparison, the successors of this foremost of
the Comneni. She also noted, not without some secret satisfaction, what she believed to be the signs of a rapid and ir-
remediable decadence. "Today," this lettered woman writes
somewhere, "historians and poets and the lessons one can
learn from them are despised as being of no value. Dice and
other such amusements, that is the great interest." Things
were not at all like that in the old days at the court of Alexius,
the pious and illustrious Emperor whom his daughter does
not hesitate to proclaim greater than Constantine, and to
associate with the holy company of Christ's apostles. The

very excess of this praise is enough to indicate the tenor of
this book to which Anna Comnena has given the significant
title of *The Alexiade*, a title for an epic poem in honor of a
legendary hero.

We must not forget that Anna Comnena was very much
a Princess, very Byzantine, and therefore incapable of fully
understanding the events of her time or of judging her fellow
men with real impartiality—as witness her enduring prejudice against the Crusaders, her preconceived hostility toward
them, with the sole exception of Bohémond. Nor must we forget that she was a woman, and consequently had a liking for
the decorative, for exterior magnificence, which sometimes
concealed from her the true heart of things; that she was a
passionate woman, consumed by hatreds and resentments,
and lastly, a learned woman, a literary stylist in love with fine
phrases. All this, though it may diminish the strictly historical value of Anna Comnena's work, does not by any means
make it less interesting. As a psychological study, *The
Alexiade* is a document of the first importance; and from a
more general standpoint it is a wholly remarkable book. And
that the last ambition of this stateswoman who was also a
woman of letters should have been to live on, beyond the
tomb, by what she believed to be the best in herself, her mind
and her thought, is a characteristic touch not devoid of
grandeur.

Anna Comnena died in 1148, at the age of sixty-five. A
contemporary who knew her well has praised her large,
lively eyes which revealed the quickness of her thought,
the depth of her philosophical knowledge, and the truly imperial superiority of her mind, and he concludes, wittily, by
saying that had she been known to ancient Greece she would
have added "a fourth Grace to the Graces, a tenth Muse to
the Muses." She was, to say the least, an altogether remark-

able woman, one of the finest feminine intellects ever produced by Byzantium, and far superior to most of the men of
her time. And whatever one may think of her character, there
is something melancholy about the unfulfilled existence of
this Princess who had every right to be ambitious.

IX

IRENE DUCAS

oward the end of the year 1077, Alexius Comnenus, the
future Emperor, who at that time was merely an ambitious noble, realized that a brilliant marriage would do more
than anything else to help him attain the throne to which he
aspired. Among the great families of the Byzantine aristocracy, none was more illustrious than that of the Ducae. Their
lineage could, according to the genealogists, be traced back
to Constantine the Great, by whom, it was asserted, the first
of their line had been appointed "Duke" of Constantinople,
from which title the family name of his descendants derived.
Whether or not these claims were justified, there is no doubt
that in the latter part of the eleventh century the Ducas
family, wealthy, powerful, respected, was one of the most
celebrated in the monarchy. It had provided Byzantium with
several Emperors, and one of its scions, Michael VII, was
now on the throne. There was no love lost between the

Comneni and the Ducae; Isaac, the first Basileus from the Comneni family, had been succeeded by a Ducas, and the similarity of their ambitions, combined with their equal rights to the throne, had set the fires of dangerous hatreds burning between their two houses. It seemed, therefore, to all sensible people, genuinely interested in preserving the public peace, that it would be highly advantageous to unite through marriage the two rival families, thereby unifying their interests and their aims for the future. Moreover, the subtle politician in Alexius Comnenus was quick to recognize how powerfully such an alliance would support his ultimate ambition. This is why, at the end of the year 1077, he overcame his mother's opposition and married the young Irene Ducas, daughter of Andronicus, Grand Duke of the Anatolian Scholae, Protovestiarius, Protoproedros, and granddaughter of Caesar John Ducas. And for the same reason, when Alexius overthrew Nicephorus Botaniates in 1081, everyone agreed that the revolt of the nobles and of the army through which the new Emperor was set on the throne "departed from lawfulness only to reinstate the law"—to repeat a well-known phrase. Born a Comnenus, related by marriage to the Ducae, Alexius, in reclaiming the Imperial crown, even at the point of the sword, was actually restoring it to its rightful heirs, whose representative he was. In revolting against his sovereign, says a contemporary writer, "not only was he blameless, but he accomplished an act that all thoughtful people must commend."

From his purely political marriage Alexius had now derived the maximum advantage. He was Emperor. And he apparently saw no reason why he should prolong his gratitude to a Princess for whom he felt no love. Indeed, ill-advised by his mother, who savagely hated the Ducae, he had no sooner achieved his victory than he began to think of divorcing his wife; for he was infatuated, according to the chroniclers, with the beautiful Empress Mary of Alania, wife of his predecessor. To ensure that the name of Irene should be associated with that of Alexius in the imperial acclamations, it was necessary for the Admiral, George Paleologus, to declare with brutal directness: "It is not for you, a Comnenus, that I have worked, but for Irene," and to order his sailors to acclaim the young Princess. It took all the stubborn tenacity of the Patriarch, who was devoted to the house of Ducas, to bring Alexius to the point of having Irene solemnly crowned Empress—a week after he himself had been anointed. It is easy to guess what the imperial marriage must have been like under these circumstances; what strained and difficult relations must have existed between this hostile couple, associates drawn from two rival families, and both aware of the inimical ambitions they represented.

How, from this secret hostility, there sprang up little by little a friendship between Alexius and his wife; how the young Empress, at first disdained and kept at a distance, imperceptibly came to exert a decisive influence on her husband, is one of those psychological enigmas in history that invite an attempt at solution. Since Irene's life also affords us a glimpse of the religious and monastic life in remote twelfth century Byzantium, we may judge it worthwhile, and not without interest, to try to reconstruct the figure of this woman, apparently unassuming and discreet but in reality a schemer, clever, cunning, and consumed by ambition—until the day when she was to seek in the cloister, as her daughter Anna Comnena sought in literature, consolation for her frustrated hopes.

I

When Irene Ducas became Empress of Byzantium, in April 1081, she was not yet fifteen years old. She does not appear to have been pretty. Anna Comnena, who professes a lively admiration for her mother, has not succeeded in presenting her to us as a finished beauty, for all her efforts to paint her in flattering colors. She was tall, harmoniously proportioned, and graceful in all her movements; she had beautiful ivory-tinted arms, which she liked to show off, and charming sea-green eyes. But her complexion was a little too florid and the strong color in her cheeks was notice-able even from a distance. "Her face," says Anna Comnena, "which was radiant as the moon, was not round, like the faces of Assyrian women, nor long, like those of the Scythi-ans; it was an almost perfect oval." According to another of her panegyrists, her beauty was of the spirit, interior rather than exterior. And in view of the fact that Irene cared little for dress, that, in the words of a contemporary, "she pre-ferred to shine with the radiance of her virtues than to deck herself out in gorgeous, golden-fringed apparel," that she used no artifice to enhance her looks, "as ultra-feminine women do, thereby insulting their Divine Creator," and that the art of cosmetics, so dear to Cleopatra, seemed to her both useless and vain, one can well believe that Alexius Com-nenus, flighty by nature, had no particular inducement to stay faithful to his wife, and that notwithstanding the seven children, three boys and four girls, he had by her, he was more or less indifferent to her, and consoled himself in nu-merous love affairs that strongly aroused her jealousy.

Irene cared no more for society than she did for personal

adornment. She had a deep distaste for appearing in public arrayed in all the paraphernalia of the imperial ceremonies, and when her rank made such appearances obligatory, she displayed a blushing embarrassment. Naturally taciturn, she would drift through the court festivities in silence, cold and mysterious as a marble statue (the simile is Anna Comnena's). All told, she appears to us as a modest and discreet young woman, a little shy, a little secretive, crushed between an unloving husband and a hostile, domineering mother-in-law.

Simple in her tastes, Irene took no pleasure in surrounding herself with a large retinue; magnificence, pageantry, and pomp, repelled her profoundly. She lived by preference in her private apartments, where, withdrawn into her self, she spent her days in reading and meditation. Her panegyrists compare her now to Athena "descended from heaven, splendid and unapproachable," now to the perfect woman described by Solomon; and they add that she assiduously cultivated the wisdom "that Plato calls the only beauty of the soul." Her private life was in fact dedicated to essentials; she divided her time between works of charity and the study of the Scriptures. The writings of the Fathers of the Church held particular charm for her; it was not unusual for her to come to table still holding in her hand some pious book in which she was absorbed; and when her daughter, Anna Comnena, more inclined to science than to theology, expressed surprise at her great interest in such books, and asked what pleasure she could take in these abstract and subtle theories "which make one dizzy," Irene answered with a smile: "Sometimes, like you, I am intimidated by these books, nevertheless I am unable to tear myself away from them. Wait and see: when you have had your fill of other books, you will discover the charm of these." But the Empress, highly intelligent and remarkably well educated, did not limit her reading to religious works; she was equally interested in secular literature, and was a patroness of writers. Above all, however, her piety was great and her charity indefatigable. Very generous, especially with the religious in whom she took such delight, her hand was always open, that "munificent hand" lauded by one of her panegyrists. She gave liberally to all, to every beggar, to every miserable outcast she happened to see. And to these, the humble and downtrodden, this woman, ordinarily so distant and reserved, made herself easily accessible; with them she felt no embarrassment, her tongue was loosened; she even went so far as to preach to them on occasion, and point a moral. She liked to speak of regeneration through work; she counseled her protégés not to abandon themselves to indolence, "not to idle from door to door begging for alms." Kindly by nature, she increased the value of her gifts by the manner in which she bestowed them.

In this partly voluntary seclusion, Irene Ducas passed twenty years of her life, and she must have suffered at times from the subordinate position into which she had been maneuvered; for she loved the husband who neglected her, and she was aware that her natural qualities were great enough to fit her for a more distinguished role. Her daughter has said of her that she had a masculine spirit, courage, intelligence, presence of mind, and business ability. Another contemporary extols her capacity for reflective thought, her sense of justice, her wise counsels, her adroit and supple mind, and above all, her courage, "which surpassed that of any man, and was the one point on which she renounced her womanliness in favor of a more masculine virtue." Finally it must be said that she was exceedingly proud of her birth, of her family's renown, of the rights that were her due. It is not surprising that such a woman should, when the opportunity came, have suddenly revealed herself as an immensely ambitious politician.

In point of fact, the young Empress's position at the court was imperceptibly strengthening all the time. She had consolidated it to begin with by providing the Emperor with heirs to the throne; later, the marriages contracted by her daughters served to reinforce her influence, through the power she exercised over one, at least, of her sons-in-law. Then, the retirement of Anna Dalassena, in liberating the Basileus from the subjection in which his imperious mother had held him for so long, left the door open for other counsels. Little by little, as he advanced in age, Alexius turned to Irene of his own accord. His passions had calmed, his taste for adventure was almost extinct, and he suffered from gout, from cruel attacks of pain that only the Empress knew how to assuage with gentle and expert massage. At last the hour had come for which Irene had waited so patiently.

Very soon she became indispensable to Alexius. He formed the habit of taking her with him wherever he went, on his travels, even on his campaigns, and as much for the sake of the affectionate care she bestowed upon him as for the wise political advice that she was able to give him. Also, perhaps, mistrusting her passion for intrigue, he thought it wiser not to abandon her in his absence to the promptings of an ambition that she no longer tried to conceal. Although she sincerely loved the Emperor her husband, Irene, aware of her influential position, now aspired beyond it. Her immediate purpose was to share the actual governing power, to rule the Empire according to her own ideas. For the future, she wanted above all to settle the order of succession. Her plan was to pass over the legitimate heir, her son John, and transmit the throne to her favorite daughter, Anna Comnena, and

Anna's husband, Nicephorus Bryennius, whom she admired
for his intelligence, his eloquence, his cultivated mind, and
his literary gifts. It is likely that storms broke out in the imperial household over this subject, and that Irene complained
about having to accompany the Emperor everywhere and always. But Alexius refused to listen; and as, apart from everything else, the Empress's skillful supervision protected him
more effectively than any amount of precautions against the
plotting of his enemies, he would not consent at any price to
the absence from his side of "this unsleeping guardian, this
always open eye."

In vain did Irene's political enemies jeer at the Emperor's
newly developed attachment to his wife. In his own tent, even
on his table, Alexius would find abusive lampoons advising
him to send back to the Gynaeceum this Empress whose
presence encumbered the camps. Nothing had any effect.
Every day the Emperor became more subject to the influence
of Irene, because, as Anna Comnena says, "she was quick to
discern the essential in everything that happened, and
quicker still to uncover enemy intrigues." And so, adds the
imperial chronicler, "my mother was, for my father the Basileus, an open eye in the night, a vigilant guard by day, the
best antidote for the dangers of the table, the salutary cure
for the perils that may lurk in a repast." In this role Irene
maintained the delicate and discreet reserve of her young
womanhood. She was never seen or heard, yet her presence
was felt. To the army, it was revealed only by a litter, drawn
by two mules and flying the imperial flag. Her "divine body"
remained invisible, and more even than in the Sacred Palace
she deliberately shrouded her activities in mystery.

When necessary, however, she was not in the least afraid
to "brave the eyes of men." In danger, or in grave emergen-
cies, she could give good proof of her courage, her presence

of mind, her decisiveness. Early one morning, when the
army was encamped in Asia Minor, news came that the
Turks were near. But Alexius was still asleep. Irene ordered
the messenger not to disturb him, and as she had already
risen, she pretended to busy herself with her usual occupations, notwithstanding her anxiety. Soon, another messenger
announced that the barbarians were advancing. The Empress, mastering her fears, stayed calmly at the Emperor's
side. Disregarding the danger, the imperial couple were
about to take their places at table when suddenly a man
covered with blood came in and collapsed at the Emperor's
feet, demonstrating the imminent peril and the presence of
the enemy at the gate. Even then Irene remained impassive,
"like the prudent woman of the Scriptures." Her fears were
only for the Emperor. When, finally, she was persuaded to
consider her own safety and fly before the impending battle,
she went reluctantly, "continually turning to look back at her
husband." So it was not without reason that the Emperor
now called her, "his dear soul, the confidante of his plans,
the consoler of his ills." Thus, little by little, she became all
powerful.

We have seen earlier how the ambitious Empress tried to
take advantage of her influence, and what conspiratorial
webs were spun around the death bed of Alexius. We have
likewise seen with what solicitude she nursed the dying man
to the end, how, in the hope of wresting his recovery from
God, she spared neither prayers nor alms, what courage she
displayed during this unhappy time, "fighting like an Olym-
pian athlete against the sorrow that overwhelmed her," and
also with what tenacity she strove to gain her ends and how
great was her despair and anger when she saw that she had
been vanquished. Nevertheless, she was better able to resign
herself to the inevitable than was her daughter Anna Com-

nena. She took no part in the plot that the latter hatched against her brother John, and she remarked on this occasion, not without irony: "One should seek to make an Emperor only when the throne is vacant; once there is a sovereign, he should not be overthrown." Irene was happier than her daughter, in that she tasted the joys of supreme power for ten full years after her early self-effacement. And when, after the death of Alexius, she retired into a convent, when, in the words of a contemporary, "like an eagle with golden wings, she took flight for celestial spheres," she could tell herself that all said and done her life had not been unsuccessful.

II

At the time when she exercised an all-powerful influence over Alexius Comnenus, Irene and her husband were associated in a pious undertaking. In the western part of Constantinople, in the district of the Deuteron, not far from the present site of the castle of the Seven Towers, husband and wife built two adjoining monasteries, one for men, in the name of Christ "who loves humanity" (*Philanthropos*), and the other for women, under the protection of the Virgin "full of grace." The Empress had decided to construct this holy house for diverse reasons. First and foremost, she wanted to show in this way her gratitude to the Madonna, who had, she said, protected her and overwhelmed her with favors throughout her life, who had privileged her to be born of "a race naturally pious and inclined to virtue," who had given her the benefit of an admirable education, and elevated her to that "summit of human happiness" the throne, who had, indeed, extended her divine hand to all those whom Irene loved —her husband, her children, her grandchildren, granting to

208))   BYZANTINE EMPRESSES

the Basileus great and fruitful victories in his wars against the barbarians, to the members of the Royal family miraculous recoveries from sickness, and to the Empire constant support and unequaled prosperity. Moreover, like all Byzantines, Irene believed the prayers that go up to God from the lips of monks and nuns to be particularly efficacious, and consequently she expected the Foundation to procure all sorts of benefits for the good government of the monarchy and for the peace of Christendom.

But to these spiritual motives were added some more human considerations. One of the Empress's daughters, Eudocia, had made an unfortunate marriage. Her husband, lacking all respect for the imperial birth of his young wife, treated her with contempt, and was scarcely less insolent to his mother-in-law, the Empress, with the result that when, finally, Eudocia fell ill, it had been deemed necessary to break up this ill-assorted union. The husband had been turned out of the Palace, the wife had become a nun. Now the immediate purpose of the new convent was to provide for this imperial recluse an asylum worthy of her rank. But in this Byzantium so fertile in revolutions no one could ever be sure of the morrow; one day the Princesses of Irene's family might find themselves obliged to seek in a cloister refuge from the storms of life; and Irene had to consider what her own future would be in the event that the Emperor should die before her. So she had erected next to the monastery another dwelling, more comfortable and luxurious, for the use of the imperial women. This was known as "the Princes' Dwelling" or as "the House of the Rulers." Just outside the enclosure of the monastery and independent of the convent, these buildings were, however, in easy communication with the cloister and partook of its sacred character. Thus, while Alexius, in the monastery of Christ, was preparing a tomb for his mortal remains, Irene, next to the convent of the Virgin, was arranging a refuge for her old age.

It was to this refuge that she withdrew after her husband's death. At that time the dwelling reserved for the Empress was enlarged. It was a veritable palace, with vast courtyards, porticos, several baths, even a special church, dedicated to St. Demetrius. Accompanied by her women and a large retinue of servants, Irene installed herself there with her favorite daughter, Anna Comnena, who occupied an apartment looking out on the garden of the Monastery of Christ, and Anna's daughter, who had been widowed when quite young, and who, like the Empress, was named Irene Ducas. There, among her children, in the vicinity of the religious whom she had always loved, re-enfolded in the pious atmosphere of her youth, the old Empress lived until her death, which seems to have taken place in 1123. During this period, however, she was by no means entirely divorced from the world. She delighted in entertaining, and she maintained a little court of literary men who sang her praises or consoled her in loss and sorrow. She continued to take an interest in things of the mind, and in particular she encouraged her son-in-law, Nicephorus Bryennius, whose literary talent she had always appreciated, to write the history of her lamented husband, the great Alexius Comnenus. This work has come down to us. In his preface, Bryennius lauds "the very wise spirit" of her who imposed on him this heavy task, "the herculean force" that constrained him to accept it. Irene seems to have enjoyed this inspirational role, through which she satisfied her desire to extol at one and the same time the separate glories of the Ducae and the Comneni. Her contemporaries proclaimed her, even in her presence, as "the siren of Caesar," and there is reason to believe that the compliment did not displease her.

III

In the Bibliothèque Nationale in Paris is preserved the charter of foundation, the *typikon*, drawn up by the Empress for her convent. It is signed, in purple ink, by Irene herself, "Empress of the Romans, faithful in Christ our Lord." In it, she has enumerated, in lengthy detail, the buildings that she has had constructed, and the revenues with which she has endowed the convent; she has minutely defined the multifarious duties that she prescribes for her religious, the Rule they must follow, the rigid discipline to which they will be subject; and lastly, she has determined, with precision, and in a singularly authoritative manner, everything that has to do with the administration of the convent funds and properties and with the safeguarding of its independence. This curious document, which is no less than sixty pages long, is, therefore, extremely interesting, as much for what it tells us about the psychology of Irene Ducas, as for the light it sheds on the monastic life of her time.

One is struck, to begin with, by the peculiar mixture of pious phraseology and sound judgment, of mystical exaltation and executive precision, dry, detailed, dictatorial. It is the same contrast that we have already encountered in the personality of the Empress, passionately religious and inclined to sermonize, yet so lucid and so daring in the conduct of her life and the pursuit of her ambitions.

The Founder's first concern is to ensure a scrupulous respect for morality in her convent. In the early twelfth century, Byzantine monastic life was in great need of reform, and it is not without reason that Irene is afraid "that the serpent, the age-old seducer, may find in the pious congregation some new Eve, into whose ear he will murmur his deadly

sophisms, luring her down into the nets of Hell." Ardently,
therefore, she entreats the Virgin to guard the nuns against
temptation, "to endow these feminine souls with virile virtues." But prudently she takes every precaution to keep them
out of danger. The convent will be strictly closed against all
intrusion from without. No man will be given entry, no alien
eye will get a chance to surprise the nuns in the pious intimacy of their cloister. The Empress carefully prohibits the
construction anywhere near the convent of terraces from
which the curious could look down into its courts. Even
the eunuchs attendant on the great ladies permitted to visit
the convent must stay outside the cloister wall. Even choris-
ters are excluded from this model convent. At most, and only
out of necessity, the presence of two priests will be tolerated,
on condition that they are eunuchs; and both the confessor
and the almoner of the community must be in this reassuring
category of persons.

So much for the inside. Irene ordered no less strictly the
relations that her nuns were liable to have with the outside
world. On this point, the doctrine of the Church was singularly rigid. "The monk," said the Fathers of the Church,
"must no longer have any earthly family." In practice, however, a few concessions to "human weakness" had to be made.
Consequently, the mother, sister, and sister-in-law of a religious were authorized to come to the convent once or twice
a year to take a meal with her in the common refectory, and
should she happen to be sick, they might stay in the convent
for two whole days. As for the father, brother, and brother-
in-law, they might see their cloistered relative only at the
outer gate, to which, if she were sick, she would be carried in
a litter, since a man must not enter the cloister on any pretext
whatsoever. And in any event, these interviews must be brief,
and must take place in the presence of an aged and venerable

nun. Inversely, if one of the religious should have a relative in the town who was gravely ill, she might pay him a visit, but accompanied by two other nuns of an age and bearing that would command respect, and she must at all costs return to the convent before nightfall. To check the slightest inclination toward irregularity in the matter of comings and goings, the gate-sister, an old woman of proven virtue, kept constant watch at the gate, and every evening, to make things doubly sure, she delivered the keys into the hands of the Superior. Nothing could be done in the house without the authorization of the Superior, which does not mean, however, that she herself was exempt from the common Rule. When she had to discuss the business affairs of the convent, when she was obliged to see the managers or the farmers of the community estates, she betook herself to the inner entrance door of the convent, escorted by two or three old nuns who were witnesses to the interview. In short, every effort was made to keep strangers out of the enclosure. As a great concession, those women for whom the sanctity of the house could be an inspiration were allowed a visit. In this, the Founder relied on the wisdom of the Superior, but with the reminder that these visitors must always be women of unimpeachable morals, and that their visits should never extend beyond the two-day limit. Even the Princesses of the imperial family, even those among them who were the special patronesses of the convent, were not, as a general rule, permitted to remain for any length of time, nor did they have the right to enter whenever they pleased.

It was not Irene's intention to found a large community; she believed that numbers tend to hamper the strict application of a Rule. She specified that there should be only twenty-four religious and ten lay-sisters, and in no case must the total number go above forty. At the head of the community was placed a Superior, who was chosen in a curious fashion. The nuns agreed on the nomination of three candidates, of whom one was to be chosen. The three names were written on three identical pieces of paper, each with the formula: "O Lord Jesus Christ, Who knowest all hearts! Through the mediation of Our Lady, immaculate Virgin full of grace, show unto us, Thy humble servants, whether Thou judgest our sister, so and so, worthy of the office of Hegumen." The papers, carefully sealed, were placed upon the altar on Saturday evening; the community passed the night in prayer, and the next morning, after the liturgy, the priest took one of the papers from the altar, and thus God designated her whom He willed to direct the community. Once installed, the Superior exercised an absolute authority over material as well as spiritual matters, and it was within her jurisdiction to debar a religious from the community without explanation, if she saw fit. She herself was not accountable to anyone for her actions, and she could be deposed only for serious dereliction of duty. In this event, the imperial patroness of the convent, who had, *ex officio*, supervised the election of the Abbess, would intervene to expel her from office. But such cases were altogether exceptional.

The Abbess was aided in her administrative work by a whole series of assistants, whom she herself appointed, and dismissed, at will. There was the σκευοφυλάκισσα who had charge of the relics, ornaments, and archives, and the ἐκκλησιάρχισσα who had the care of the church, and whose duty it was to see that the candles were lighted and the sacred chants properly performed. One sister was assigned to take in the provisions, another had charge of the wine; the cellarer preserved the produce of the monastic estates; the τραπεζαρία kept order in the refectory; the function of the ἐπιστημονάρχισσα was to maintain the discipline of the community, and in particular to prohibit frivolous talk and to punish idleness, "which is the source of evil." Two ἐργοδοτρίαι were responsible for distributing the work; two δοχειαρίαι took care of the clothing and the cash; finally, there was the gate-sister, appointed guardian of the door. Each of these functionaries had her own special task, and the duties of each were outlined in minute detail by the Founder. Everywhere a concern for exactitude, for precise and accurate accounting, is to be found; the condition of things at the moment of assuming charge of them, the pattern of comings and goings, everything must be ascertained with meticulous attention. Finally, Irene enjoins everyone to practice the strictest economy, and there are passages that show to what a point she urged the zeal for thrift. Should it be necessary to buy cloth for the community, a time must be chosen when prices are low as a result of a glut on the market. And on feast days, when the candelabras are furnished with new candles, those already begun must be carefully kept, and burned to a finish on ordinary days.

Inherently practical, Irene was above all anxious to create a well-organized, well-directed house; everything else came second. We find a very interesting proof of this in the care she takes to calm the scruples of those among her nuns who might think the occupations prescribed for them in the Rule rather too down to earth, and might be apprehensive, lest in giving themselves up to these duties too continuously, and on that account neglecting the Offices, they should compromise their eternal salvation. "Prayer," she tells them, "is a beautiful thing, a very beautiful thing; for it allows us to talk with God, and it lifts us from Earth to Heaven. But charity is far superior, far better." Now, to labor for the material good of the community is to perform a work of charity. "We are fearful, you say, to neglect the Offices.

Have no fear. A sincere confession will always ensure you absolution for this fault, provided that your neglect was not caused by laziness. That is what you have to fear. That is what you must guard against. If you have in no way sinned through slothfulness, rejoice in consecrating yourselves to the duties with which you are entrusted."

Such being the Founder's attitude, it is not surprising that the Rule for reciting the Offices occupies a relatively small place in her dispositions. She concentrates her attention on details of a material order. To uphold the regimen of the cenobitic life, which is, and must always be, the Rule of the convent, the dormitory and the refectory will be common to all the religious, and manual work will be done in common, while one of the sisters reads aloud from a pious book "that will keep away frivolous, useless, and guilty thoughts." To ensure a rigorous discipline, nothing is left to chance. Irene settles the number and the form of the reverences to be made in the church, the order in which the sacred chants are to succeed each other at the signal of the ἐκκλησιάρχισσα. She ordains that in the refectory, which the community will enter singing psalms, no one may utter a word except in answer to a question from the Superior, and that all shall lend an attentive ear to the pious reading "which rejoices and nourishes the soul." The τραπεζαρία sees to it that no one fails in this respect, she is to reprimand severely any nun who fidgets or whispers, and if the offense is repeated, the culprit is to be sent away from the table. It is forbidden to ask a neighbor for anything at table, even for water. It is forbidden to claim any kind of precedence "for fear of vainglory." Everywhere we find the same rigidity. No private conversations, no idle strolling, no rivalries or quarrels, no intimate friendships either, no clandestine meetings. Irene has anticipated everything, provided for everything, forbidden everything.

Even the daily diet has been settled by her. The menus are hardly sumptuous. On Tuesdays, Thursdays, Saturdays, and Sundays, two dishes will be served to the nuns, fish and cheese. On Mondays they will eat dried vegetables cooked in oil and shellfish. On Wednesdays and Fridays they will be given dried vegetables boiled in water, and a few fresh vegetables. Meat never appears on the convent bill of fare. To make up for this, wine is apportioned quite liberally; it serves to sustain the sisters fatigued by the Lenten vigils, and to revive their exhausted bodies during the heat of summer. For this purpose even vintage wines are stored in the convent cellar. And from time to time pious people "who love Christ" may ameliorate the harsh diet of the convent with a few sweetmeats. The regimen of the three great fasts is, of course, more severe and prescribed with equal exactitude. One injunction is constantly repeated: it is forbidden to eat anything between meals. "It was forbidden food," writes Irene, "that originally made us subject to death and deprived us of Paradise, and it is the Devil, author of evil, who introduced it into the world."

Nevertheless, here too some concessions are made to human weakness. The Empress does not wish her nuns to wear themselves out by an excess of exhausting vigils. She prescribes a special regimen for the sick, who are to be given a private cell and better food. All the same, they are exhorted not to take advantage of their state of health to make injudicious demands and to ask for unusual dishes "of which, perhaps, they have not even heard tell, much less seen or eaten."

Rather than go into the minute details defining the ceremonial of the great feast days and determining the number of lamps, candelabras, and candles that shall enhance the splendor of these solemn occasions—one of which is celebrated with special pomp, that of the death, or, as the Byzantines say, the Falling Asleep of the Virgin—I prefer to mention some other, more characteristic, points, which do credit to the Founder's practicality. A physician is attached to the convent, despite the fear that every masculine presence awakened in the Empress; furthermore, the convent is provided with installations that will bring water there in abundance, and the nuns are required to take a bath at least once every month. In this concern for hygiene, rare enough in the Middle Ages, we recognize once again the practical, rather mystical, spirit that presided over the Foundation.

All told, however, a Rule so austere, involving so many obligations, could weigh too heavily on certain souls. And so the Empress has judged it necessary to exhort her nuns not to be discouraged or incensed by their burden, but rather to accept it joyfully, remembering that after all, thanks to the wise provision of their Founder, they are free from all material cares.

IV

When she was regulating the moral life of her nuns, the Empress was at the same time taking measures to assure the future of her work.

Byzantine monasteries, at the beginning of the twelfth century, were exposed to certain disagreeable eventualities. All too often, to the detriment of their material prosperity and their moral health, they were given by the secular authority as benefices to some powerful personage in recompense for political or military services. The beneficiary, installing himself in the monastery "as in his own home," squandering the revenues on himself, neglecting the sacred things, in no time ruined the fortune as well as the discipline of the house. With him, the worldly life entered the holy retreat; guests were entertained there, profane ditties were sung, and, especially in the nunneries, the presence of a lay beneficiary, constantly in conversation with the Abbess, and constantly concerned with worldly matters, was an ever present cause of demoralization.

Irene was aware of these dangers, Alexius, more than anyone, having been prodigal of such donations, and she was determined to protect her Foundation from them. She intended to preserve for its original purpose the fortune with which she had endowed the convent, and to safeguard its independence against all attempts to encroach upon it. Accordingly, she prohibited absolutely the gift, exchange, or sale, of any properties belonging to the convent; at most, in certain well-defined circumstances, certain movable objects might be parted with to raise money in case of need, but this clause was hedged around with a hundred and one restrictions, to prevent its abuse and to close every possible loophole. The Empress likewise urged a watchful supervision over all that had to do with the administration of the convent properties. A Steward was in charge of this, and his function was to tour the various properties, examine the accounts of the sub-managers and farmers, control the payments of revenue—whether in money or in kind, and draw up a report on everything for the Superior. In the last resort, it was she who ruled on the temporal as well as on the spiritual plane. She appointed and dismissed the employees who administered the domains, received them in person to hear their statements of administration, audited their accounts with the Steward and endorsed them. The convent was, in fact, wealthy. And it was even accumulating savings in a reserve fund. But, of course, new donations were well received and strongly encouraged, whether they came from religious, who, on mak-

ing their profession, brought with them a voluntary offering
to the convent, or whether they sprang from the munificence
of pious laymen. Irene foresaw these future bounties and
decided how they were to be used. They were not to be
wasted in futile spending, on, for example, the improvement
of the daily meals; they must serve, above all, to increase the
distributions of money and food that were made to the poor
every day at the convent gate. On this particular point, as on
every other, Irene has left nothing to chance. On ordinary
days, the beggars were to be given bread and leftovers from
the dinner table; on feast days, and especially on those days
when the memorial anniversaries, the μνημόσυνα, of the eminent patronesses of the convent were celebrated, the distribu-
tion was more lavish, and to the bread was added wine and
money.

The Empress took other measures to ensure the independence of her Foundation. She formally forbade the dona-
tion of her convent to a private beneficiary under any pretext
whatsoever, its annexation to another convent or charitable
institution, its subjection to any authority, ecclesiastical or
secular: it must remain in perpetuity "free and self-govern-
ing." "If," she writes, "at any time, or in any manner, anyone,
an Emperor, a Patriarch, or the Superior herself, ever attempts to appropriate this convent and place it in other hands,
may he be anathema." In this epoch, as we know, monasteries
were frequently misappropriated. To avert this danger, the
Empress specifies that the Abbess alone shall be qualified to
exercise authority over the community; and to guarantee
still more securely the autonomy of her convent, it is placed
under the special protection of a Princess of the imperial
family.

Originally, this protective duty was entrusted to Irene's
daughter Eudocia, the Princess who had entered religion.

But she died prematurely in 1120, whereupon Irene herself assumed the position and the rights of protectress, which, at her death, would devolve successively on her favorite daughter, Anna, her second daughter, Mary, and her granddaughter, Irene Ducas, and then be transmitted from generation to generation of the female descendants of Anna Comnena.

But while assuring her convent of this protection, the Empress also had every intention of defending it against the smallest tendency to encroachment on the part of the protectress, whose powers she was careful to restrict. Their limits are minutely defined in the *typikon*. The Princess protectress may not interfere, in any capacity, with the internal administration of the convent. She shall watch over the election of the Abbess, whom she may, if need be, depose. It is her function to deal with any scandals that may come to trouble the peace of the community, but above all, her duty is to uphold the privileges and prerogatives of the convent against the outside world. To spare her all temptation to meddle in what does not concern her, Irene rules that she may not by any means visit the convent at all hours, whenever she feels inclined. The Empress exempts from this ruling only her "beloved daughters, the Porphyrogenitae Anna and Mary, and her beloved granddaughter, the Lady Irene Ducas." These three may enter the convent whenever they please, they may even take their meals there, with the nuns, but at no time may they be accompanied by more than two or three of their women. Irene shows the same exceptional indulgence toward her sons and sons-in-law, who may, under certain circumstances, be admitted to the convent. In this case, they are to remain in the exterior narthex of the church during the Divine Liturgy. When the community shall have withdrawn, they may go inside, and even, in the presence of two or three old sisters, converse with the Superior and make their devotions to the Virgin full of grace. And this leads us to the curiously interesting information that the *typikon* furnishes with regard to the Empress herself and her attitude toward her family.

V

In founding her convent, Irene Ducas seems above all to have had in mind its eventual use to her and her family, and this gives to the Foundation a rather special character. The Empress has foreseen the possibility that some of the imperial Princesses would be led to the cloister, if not by vocation, then by revolution, and she has made certain provisions with regard to them. If, after the "more brilliant life" they have led in the world, the existence common to the other nuns should seem to them a little too hard and austere, they shall bring their case before the confessor of the community, and their way of life shall be modified to suit their rank. Instead of the common dormitory, they shall have a private apartment, larger and more comfortable; instead of the common table, they shall eat in their own rooms and their fare shall be more elaborate; they may also have two women to serve them. Further, they may receive their male relatives whenever they wish, on the sole condition that these interviews shall take place in the passage leading to the main door. They may, if it pleases them, go into the town, provided they are accompanied by a sister of mature age; they may even be authorized to spend one or two days outside the convent and, should one of them have a dying kinsman, to remain at his side until the end. The same indulgences apply in the case of noble ladies wishing to retire to the convent; they too may have private rooms and serving women. But if they should take advantage of this privilege to provoke any scandal, if, in particular, they should receive the nuns in their private apartments or disturb the community with gossip, these noble pensioners will be relentlessly expelled.

It is interesting to see how private reasons, the desire to reconcile the monastic life with the tastes of persons who would probably be ill suited to it, have led the Founder to relax the rigors of the Rule, and transform the convent into a sort of "noble chapter house," of a more or less private nature. This solicitude for her imperial relatives appears on every page of the document, and certain passages throw an interesting light on Irene's family affections.

The Princess's first thought is for herself. She requests that perpetual prayers be said for her intention, and the anniversary of her death celebrated. She is no less solicitous with regard to her husband, the Emperor Alexius, who was associated with her in this pious enterprise. She affectionately wishes him many long years of life, and glorious victories over his enemies. Her relationship with him is one of such confidence and intimacy, that she is at pains to have him participate in the government and patronage of the convent: "To an exceptional man," she writes, "should be accorded exceptional honors." Another passage offers even more interesting data concerning Irene's inmost feelings and the hierarchy of her affections.

It was the custom in the Greek Church to solemnize the death anniversaries of the patrons of a religious community with a commemorative ceremony, the μνημόσυνα. In the magnificently illuminated church, a special liturgy was recited, and prayers were offered for the dead, after which an unusually abundant and elaborate repast was served to the members of the community, and at the gate of the convent alms were distributed to the poor. Irene has meticulously indicated all the members of her family for whom this com-

memoration must be held. She has not only made provision
for those who have already died—her father and her mother,
her father-in-law and her mother-in-law—she has also set
forth what it will be fitting to do one day for her, and for
those of her relatives who, like her, were still in the world
at the time. For each case she has made precise dispositions,
graduating the honors and the expenditure according to the
individual, and one cannot help finding these variations in
treatment amusing as well as informative.

For herself and for Alexius, she wants things done in great
style. The distributions to the poor shall consist of bread
made with ten *modii* (four hundred pounds) of wheat, plus
eight measures of wine, and twelve *nomismata*, or silver
pennies. For her sons and daughters, Irene reduces the expenditure by half, though for her youngest daughter, Theodora, she reduces it almost by three quarters. This is because
Theodora made a rather foolish match. She married Constantine Angius, a handsome youth of rather mediocre birth,
whose face was his only fortune, and probably the Empress
had not quite forgiven her daughter for marrying beneath her so improvidently. Of Irene's sons-in-law, Anna
Comnena's husband, Nicephorus Bryennius, and Mary
Comnena's husband are treated like sons; but Theodora's
husband, like his wife, is accorded only second-class honors.
For him, as for her two daughters-in-law, the wife of the
Sebastocrator Andronicus, and the wife of Caesar Isaac,
Irene reduces the expenditure to one quarter of that allowed
for herself and Alexius. Eudocia's husband is, of course, left
out altogether. Of the Basilissa's grandchildren, only one
figures in this list of names: Irene Ducas, the daughter of
Anna Comnena, who was evidently her grandmother's favorite. Indeed, the Princess's obvious predilection for her eldest
daughter Anna, and for Anna's family, is everywhere appar-

ent. It is to Anna that she bequeathes the Palace next to the
monastery; it is Anna's daughter, Irene, who will inherit it at
her mother's death. And it is Anna and Irene who will succeed the Empress as Patronesses of the convent. The Basilissa failed in her attempt to place her favorite daughter on
the throne when Alexius died. Now she tries to console her by
these proofs of favor and special affection.

Thus, even in her retirement, Irene Ducas's willful spirit
asserted itself. There is further testimony to her imperious
turn of mind. She reserved for herself absolute authority in
all that concerned the foundation of her convent. She nomi-
nated the Abbess and the Steward; she assumed for her lifetime the patronage of the convent and the command of it. To
compensate herself for spending so much money on it, she
claims the right, as Founder, to dispose everything, for the
future as well as the present, according to her wishes. And
she uses her prerogative. She prohibits any changes, even
improvements, in the buildings put up by her. She prohibits
the renting or the transfer of the Palace that serves as a residence for the imperial Princesses. She forbids the modifica-
tion, in any respect, of the Rule she has established. The
typikon is to be respected by all "as much as the Divine
laws," and, so that no one shall be ignorant of it, she ordains
that it shall be read aloud once every month.

Her regulations drawn up, Irene addresses a long sermon
to her nuns, urging upon them the strict observance of the
Rule, piety, obedience, detachment from worldly possessions,
the perpetual effort toward good. "It is not," she says, "for
luxury and ease that you have left the world, but to gain, by
fighting with all your strength, the rewards promised in the
Gospels." After this, with seeming humility, she asks the
sisters to grant her the help of their prayers, so the Empress,
in return for her pious Foundation, may merit the mercy of

God and eternal salvation. But even in this request, Irene's spirit of domination emerges. "Even if we are no longer bodily present," she writes, "be mindful of our presence in spirit."

So we see that she was in her last days what she was all her life, on the throne and in retirement: pious, generous, fond of the nuns and having a special confidence in their prayers, but very much a Princess, authoritative and imperious, anxious to impose her will in spiritual as well as in temporal matters. And we are better able to understand why the apparently shy and self-effacing young woman that Alexius Comnenus married, ended by attaining the influence on the worldly scene that she deserved by right of her qualities, and that her ambition craved. She offers an interesting example of the Byzantine Princesses of the twelfth century, women at once lettered and political, rather grave and austere, but of impeccable moral behavior, and endowed with a solemn grace that is not without beauty.

X

BERTHA OF
SULZBACH

Since the First Crusade had brought the East and the West into more intimate relations with each other, Byzantium had become a great European power. The successive expeditions undertaken for the recovery of the Holy Sepulcher, the foundation of the Frankish States of Syria, had, in multiplying the contacts between Greeks and Latins, awakened the ambitions of the latter, kindled their desires, excited their animosity, and established for them new interests. The Greeks had been made to grasp the necessity of giving up their accustomed attitude of haughty disdain toward the "barbarians," and of making allowance for these new nations that were coming into existence. To be sure, no real sympathy was born of this reconciliation; a certain curiosity, however, an obscure awareness of their mutual need, drew together these two worlds that for so long had ignored each other. In the twelfth century, the great Eastern Empire, emerging more and more every day from its isolation, was

involved in all the important transactions of European politics. In fact, Constantinople was actually one of the centers
for these transactions, particularly during the reign of Manuel Comnenus.

In the first half of the twelfth century, the monarchy of
the Basileis was threatened by a grave danger. The powerful
kingdom that the Normans had founded in Southern Italy
and in Sicily was setting its ambitious sights beyond the
Adriatic; Roger II, like Robert Guiscard and Bohémond, had
dreams of aggrandizing himself at the expense of the Empire of Constantinople. To cope with an adversary of this
stature, the Byzantines needed an ally, and they looked for
one in the direction of Germany, whose persistent ambitions
with regard to Italy qualified it more than any other State to
neutralize the efforts of the enterprising Sicilian sovereign.
As early as 1135, and again two years later, in 1137, Greek
ambassadors were sent to Germany to pave the way to an understanding. In 1140, a new mission came to Conrad III,
bringing him more specific offers. To set a definite seal on
the projected alliance, the Byzantine court proposed to unite
the two dynasties by a marriage, and requested that a "young
girl of the blood royal" should be sent to Constantinople, there
to become the wife of the Sebastocrator Manuel, fourth son
of the Emperor John Comnenus.

Conrad III of Germany was an exceedingly proud man.
Aspiring to the title of Emperor, he considered himself an
equal of the Basileus and claimed equal honors. Moreover,
aware that the Greek Empire was of Roman origin, he
thought that the Byzantine monarchy owed to the Germanic
Holy Roman Empire the same respect that a daughter owes
to her mother. Infatuated with his own power, he boasted of
the submission in which he held the entire West. Such ideas
were so sharply wounding to Greek vanity that the conclu-

sion of an alliance seemed no easy matter. Fortunately, Conrad himself felt the need of support against the growing ambitions of Roger II. So he responded to the overtures made to him through the Byzantine envoys, and proposed to give his wife's sister, Countess Bertha of Sulzbach, in marriage to Prince Manuel. After lengthy negotiations, an agreement was finally reached, and toward the end of the year 1142, a Byzantine ambassador went to Germany to fetch the young fiancée.

She was given the most brilliant welcome in Constantinople. A contemporary writer, Theodore Prodromus, or one of the other numerous official versifiers at the court of the Comneni, has described in a poem written for the occasion, the splendors of the reception that greeted the newcomer. He has told of the grand procession that escorted the German Countess, the crowd that lined the way, decked out in festival attire, the magnificently decorated streets, the organs that played as she went by, the perfumes and aromatics that were scattered under her feet—all the refinements of luxurious ceremonial that Byzantium delighted in on such occasions. The imperial Princesses themselves took the trouble to meet this "flower of the West," as the poet puts it, "that the Emperor was planting in the imperial garden." And this seems to have given rise to a curious incident. Among the young women assembled to greet the German Countess, was the wife of the heir apparent, Alexius, eldest son of the Emperor. She was garbed in deep blue discreetly relieved by touches of purple and gold. Struck by this color, which stood out darkly against the more brilliant attire of the others, the foreigner asked the identity of this "religious" who spoke in such an imperious tone. Byzantine superstition was quick to interpret this as an evil omen; and the premature death of Prince Alexius shortly afterward justified the prognostic.

In 1143, Manuel's two older brothers, Andronicus and Alexius, were suddenly carried off, one after the other, within a few weeks. Thus, Manuel inherited the Empire, having been named heir to the throne by his dying father in place of his eldest son, Isaac. Now, for a Byzantine Basileus, lord of one of the most brilliant sovereignties of the time, an alliance with a simple German Countess was rather less than mediocre. In addition, Constantinople seems to have been a little shocked by the disdainful manners affected by Conrad III. In the poem we spoke of just now, Prodromus retaliated sharply to the German pretentiousness. He made it quite clear to the "glorious King" Conrad, that, for all his glory, the supreme honor for him was this alliance with the house of the Comneni. He proclaimed the new Rome incontestably superior to the old: "If the latter," he wrote, "produced the bride, it is the former that gives us the bridegroom, and as we all know that man is superior to woman, it follows that the same relationship should obtain between the two Empires." For these and other reasons, the Emperor Manuel was in no hurry to celebrate the marriage arranged for him. He made the young woman who was destined to be his wife wait almost four years for the nuptials.

As it happened, Byzantine policy was swerving toward Sicily just at this time. A marriage was being considered between a Greek Princess and one of Roger's sons, and relations with Germany were strained. Finally, however, Manuel decided to revive the Germanic alliance, and in 1145 an ambassador was sent to Conrad III to announce the Emperor's intention of solemnizing in the near future the marriage arranged in 1142. But the King of Germany was made to feel how greatly he was being honored, and the Greek envoy was so insufferably arrogant that the German sovereign had to turn him out, and demanded a public apology from him. Wounded to the quick by this kind of treatment, Conrad was not to be outdone in insolence. Writing to Constantinople, he arrogated to himself the title of Emperor of the Romans and disdainfully addressed his message to his "dear brother, Manuel Comnenus, illustrious and glorious King of the Greeks."

They ended, however, by coming to an agreement, since both parties had their own reasons for desiring it. A German ambassador went to Constantinople, and his chief, the Bishop of Wurzburg, arranged things to the general satisfaction of everyone. In January 1146, Bertha of Sulzbach married the Emperor Manuel Comnenus, and took, on ascending the throne, the Byzantine first name of Irene (the Greek word for *peace*), probably as a symbol of the reestablished peace between her new country and that of her birth.

What could have been this foreigner's impressions, at the time of her arrival in Constantinople, of the new world to which she was banished? An attempt to find out may prove rewarding, and, to help us, we have at our disposal a number of rather curious descriptions of the Byzantine capital as it was in the middle of the twelfth century. One of them is particularly worthy of our attention, since it is the work of a Westerner, Eudes de Deuil, who visited the city of the Basileis in 1147, just after the marriage of Irene and Manuel.

The imperial city had great prestige in the West, a prestige that seems to have been justified. On account of its delightful climate, its fertile soil, and its enormous wealth, Constantinople appeared to the Latins as a city beyond compare. "It is the glory of the Greeks," says Eudes de Deuil, "rich in repute, and even richer in reality." (*Graecorum*

gloria, fama dives et rebus ditior.) The chronicler never tires
of praising the splendor of the palaces, the magnificence of
the churches, and the host of precious relics preserved in
them. He is equally impressed by the picturesque view from
the city walls, at whose base large gardens extend far out
into the countryside, and by the viaducts that provide the
capital with a full and constant supply of fresh water. But
besides the public buildings, Eudes de Deuil—and herein
lies the great interest of his description—has managed to see
the city itself, and it strikes him as peculiarly dirty, malodor-
ous, and dark. It is an Oriental city, with covered, arcaded
streets. Above these low structures the magnificent dwellings
of the rich rear their towers into the open sky, but in the
depths, where the sun never penetrates, lives a wretched,
poverty-stricken populace, exposed by want to every temptation. There is no security whatsoever. Robbery and murder
are everyday occurrences. "In Constantinople," says the historian, "there are almost as many thieves as there are poor."
The police, impotent, never interfere; no one bothers to obey
or to enforce the law; the guilty go unpunished. To this
Western pilgrim, twelfth century Byzantium seems a mon-
strous city, overpopulated, seething and alarming, excessive
in everything, in its opulence as well as in its vices.

This is not, as one might think, the libel of a Latin unable
to see any good in the Greeks. A testimony of the same date,
and this time of Byzantine origin, shows us the imperial city
from the same point of view. The most frequented streets
are rendered impassable by pools of mud, which the rains
transform into quagmires. In this "Tartarus," in these "in-
fernal lakes," both people and beasts are bemired, and sometimes even drowned. Travelers who have crossed both moun-
tains and rivers without mishap, on arriving in port, are
"shipwrecked in the center of town." To extricate them from

their predicament, regular salvage operations have to be undertaken, it is necessary to wade waist deep into the mud to
unload the beasts of burden and then haul them out of the
swamp with the aid of ropes. And this is not all. By night,
other perils are added to those of the open sewers. The un-
lighted streets become the roving ground of thieves, and of
the stray dogs that pullulate in Constantinople to this day.
Respectable citizens shut themselves up in their houses. No
help is to be expected in case of accident or attack; no one an-
swers the cries of the victims, who can only let themselves
be plundered.

But an Empress had little opportunity to see these "sights
unfitting for a sovereign" ($\dot{\alpha}\beta\alpha\sigma\dot{\iota}\lambda\epsilon\upsilon\tau o\nu$). The Constantinople she knew was that of the imperial residences, and
in particular the Palace of Blachernae, which became in the
twelfth century the usual home of the Basileis. It was situ-
ated at the point of the Golden Horn, and its triple façade
commanded views of the sea, the city, and the countryside.
The exterior was magnificent, and the interior even more so.
On the walls of the great colonnaded galleries glittered mosaics set in gold and executed with "admirable artistry."
They represented in blazing colors the exploits of the Emperor Manuel, his wars against the barbarians, all that he
had done for the good of the Empire. The floors were richly
paved with mosaics. "I do not know," writes a contemporary,
"what contributes most to its beauty and its worth, the cleverness of the art or the value of the materials used." Everywhere was the same luxury, which it delighted the Emperors of the Comnenian dynasty to increase, and which
made of the Palace of Blachernae one of the marvels of
Constantinople. Foreigners who were permitted to visit it
have left us dazzling descriptions: "Its exterior beauty,"

writes Eudes de Deuil, "is almost beyond compare, and that of the interior far surpasses anything that I can say about it. On every side one sees gilding and paintings in variegated colors; the court is paved in marble with exquisite skill."

Benjamin de Tudele, who visited Constantinople some years later, expresses the same admiration. "In addition to the Palace inherited by Manuel from his ancestors, he has had built, beside the sea, another, called Blachernae, whose walls, and whose pillars too, are covered with gold and silver on which he has had depicted his own wars as well as those of his forefathers. In this Palace he has had made a throne of gold embellished with precious stones and ornamented with a crown of gold suspended by chains that are likewise of gold. The rim of this crown is studded with pearls and with priceless diamonds whose glittering fires almost suffice to illumine the dark without the help of any other light. An infinite number of other things are to be found there that would seem incredible if one were to describe them. To this Palace are brought the annual tributes, both in gold and in garments of purple and scarlet, with which the towers are filled to bursting. So for beauty of structure and abundance of riches, this Palace surpasses all the other palaces of the world."

An Empress also knew the exquisite residences to which the Basileis went to spend a cool summer. At the foot of the Palace of Blachernae was the beautiful park of Philopation, a vast, walled enclosure, where the air was kept perpetually cool by running waters, and where the great woods stocked with game provided the pleasures of the hunt. Here the Emperor had constructed a charming country seat, and the whole formed what Eudes de Deuil describes as "the Greeks' paradise." Elsewhere, by the sea of Marmora, there were splendid villas, where the Emperors had revived the oriental

luxury "of Susa and Ecbatana," and where Manuel, weary
from his wars, sought rest and relaxation in the refinements
of the table and in the pleasures of music.

Another aspect of Constantinople known to an Empress,
was the Hippodrome and its festivals, still one of the basic
pleasures of the Byzantine people in the twelfth century.
There, as in the time of Justinian, the horse races and the
athletic games took place, interspersed with all kinds of diversions, such as coursing with hares and dogs, and feats of
acrobatics and tightrope dancing, and fights with wild
beasts, bears, leopards, and lions. There too, according to
Benjamin de Tudele, were given "great pageants every year
on the birthday of Jesus of Nazareth. Figures representing all
the nations of the world, in their national dress, are brought
before the Emperor and the Empress. I do not believe," adds
the traveler, "that such magnificent games are given anywhere else on earth." They were very much appreciated at
Constantinople, and the court's delight in them was scarcely
less than that of the crowd, always "eager for novel sights."

Finally, an Empress knew the churches of the capital; the
splendor of the Divine Liturgy celebrated in St. Sophia,
"admirable and divine edifice," as the historian Nicetas Aco-
minates puts it, "miraculously erected by the hands of God
Himself, as His first and last work, inimitable church, ter-
restial image of the celestial dome." And no doubt the German Princess was moved, as were most foreigners, by the
beauty of the Greek liturgical chants, by the harmonious
mingling of the voices—the shrill tones of the sopranos and
the grave accents of the chanters—and by the no less harmoniously rhythmic gestures and genuflections. No doubt,
like most foreigners, she also appreciated the superb presen-
tation of the sumptuous dinners given at the Imperial Palace,
excellent meals, beautifully served, accompanied by all kinds

of entertainments, and, says a contemporary, "equally be-
guiling to the ears, the mouth, and the eyes." The magnificence of the costumes must have delighted her too, as well as
the pageantry of the ceremonial and all those refinements of
splendor that made the Byzantine court a unique marvel of
opulence and elegance.

One thing, however, disconcerted those who visited Constantinople for the first time. It was the indolence of the common people, of the "inert masses" accustomed to living on the
imperial bounty; and the Latins felt little affinity for this race
of "sly and crafty character and corrupted faith." Fortunately
the new Empress found in Constantinople many of her own
compatriots to console her for the failings of her subjects. In
twelfth century Byzantium there was quite a colony of
Germans. Merchants were established there, German soldiers served in the Imperial Army, and they were numerous enough to warrant a request from Conrad that a special church should be allocated to them. There were also
many customs, more or less recently introduced to Constantinople, to remind the foreigner of her far-off country. At the
time of the Comneni, the Greek Church celebrated in its
sanctuaries certain festivals that were curiously reminiscent
of those Western diversions of the same period, the Festivals
of the Fools, or of the Ass.

It must be admitted that the Emperor Manuel Comnenus
showed himself, at least in the early days of his marriage,
very anxious to please the young woman he had espoused.
This Byzantine Prince had, as we know, a lively admiration
for the Latins. He liked them for their chivalrous ways, their
fine swordsmanship, their magnificently reckless courage.
He delighted in their tournaments and enjoyed entering the

lists himself. He welcomed Westerners to his court, and placed so high a value on their services that Greek patriots were sometimes shocked by the degree to which he favored these semi-barbarian foreigners who "spat more expertly than they talked," and who, "completely uneducated, pronounced the words of the Greek language as roughly as the rocks and stones echo the flute songs of the shepherds." Through his association with these Westerners, Manuel had learned all that courtly custom imposed on the perfect knight. He knew, for instance, that it was a point of honor for a newly married Latin to distinguish himself by some great exploit; and emulating his Western models, he strove to merit the love of his lady by fine feats of swordsmanship. He seems to have succeeded. Irene greatly admired her husband's valor, and publicly declared that even in Germany, where they were experts in the matter of courage, she had never met with a better knight.

While Manuel was perfecting himself in Western manners to win his wife's admiration, she, on her side, was striving to acquaint herself with the beauties of Greek literature, and aspiring to play a role in which the majority of the Comneni women had delighted, that of Royal friend and patroness of letters. She made up her mind to study and to understand Homer, and she enlisted the help of one of the most illustrious grammarians of the day. It was for her that Tzetzes wrote his *Allegories on the Iliad*, in which he explained to his imperial pupil the subject of the poem, and the history of the principal personages in it, not omitting erudite notes on the life of the poet. And in his dedication of his book to the Empress, he admiringly described her as "a lady very much in love with Homer" (ὁμηρικωτάτη κυρία). This was in 1147. A little earlier, Tzetzes had likewise dedicated to Irene a first edition of his *Chiliades*, and it seemed that the German Princess, in her circle of grammarians and rhetoricians, had become wholly Byzantine.

Despite their reciprocal good intentions, however, the imperial couple soon became disunited. The fault seems to have been on both sides. Irene, for her part, wearied of her role of literary patroness, and quarreled with Tzetzes over a petty matter of money. The grammarian himself tells us that his promised remuneration was at the rate of twelve gold pieces for each notebook filled with his learned dissertations. To demonstrate his zeal, he chose paper of an unusually large format and covered the pages with unusually close script, so that, as he says, a single one of these notebooks was worth ten. He imagined that he would be recompensed proportionately. Not at all. The Empress's comptroller claimed that Tzetzes's work should be paid for according to the prearranged tariff, and when the unfortunate man of letters complained, the comptroller retaliated by refusing to pay him anything. Furious, Tzetzes appealed to the Empress herself. Irene, who did not understand these Byzantine subtleties, sent the unhappy scholar packing. He revenged himself by telling the whole story; further, he destroyed the first edition of his *Chiliades*, and, tired of working for nothing, he cut short his learned commentary on the *Iliad* at the fifteenth Book and went in search of another patroness. The Empress's venture into the world of the literati had not been very successful.

This would not have mattered much had Irene not failed in another direction as well; she could not adapt herself to the customs of her new country. The Empress was, it seems, an attractive woman. Archbishop Basil of Achrida, who gave her funeral oration, says that "by her tall figure with its harmonious proportions, and the bloom and beauty of her coloring, she could have evoked a sensation of pleasure even

in the insentient." Over and above all this, she was endowed
with manifold virtues, "whose fragrance," says her panegyrist, "rejoiced both God and man." Pious, gentle, absolutely
honest, and extremely charitable, always ready to console the
unfortunate and to "extend her beneficent hands to all the
world," she certainly had high moral qualities. But she totally lacked elegance. "She took less care," says Nicetas,
"over the beautifying of her person than over the perfecting
of her soul." She cared nothing for dress, she did not paint her
face or make up her eyes, and she was rather contemptuous
of those "foolish women" who preferred art to nature. "She
wished," says the chronicler, "to shine only with the radiance
of her virtues." She combined this with a certain German
stiffness, according to Nicetas ($\tau\grave{o}$ $\mu\grave{\eta}$ $\grave{\epsilon}\pi\iota\kappa\lambda\iota\nu\grave{\epsilon}s$ $\grave{\epsilon}\theta\nu\iota\kappa\acute{o}\nu$), and a
disposition predominantly serious and haughty. This was
hardly the way to hold a passionate young man like Manuel,
a young man greedy for pleasure, gay gatherings, and flirta-
tions, given to all the amusements natural to one of his age
and ready for any adventure that happened to take his fancy.

Besides, Irene did not give her husband any children. In
1147, when the Emperor deposed the Patriarch Cosmas, the
latter, in his fury, had cursed the womb of the Empress publicly in the synod, and declared that she would never give
birth to a male child. Facts seemed sadly to justify the pre-
diction. During six years, despite the prayers of the most illustrious monks on her behalf, despite the gifts and honors
with which she overwhelmed the Church in the hope of thus
ending her sterility, Irene gave no heir to the Empire. And
when, at last, a child was born to her in 1152, it was a girl,
Mary. Later, she had another child, but again it was a girl,
who died, moreover, at the age of four. Manuel was strongly
affected by all this, and, firmly convinced that it was the re-

sult of the Patriarch's curse, he was annoyed with his wife
for proving the prelate right.

So, for many reasons, Manuel tired rather quickly of his
wife. To be sure, he courteously allowed her to retain all the
outward honors of her rank, her court, her guard, all the
trappings of supreme power. But he broke with her completely. After numerous love affairs, he ended up by taking
an accredited mistress. This was his niece, Theodora, and he
was all the more attached to her because, luckier than Irene,
she gave him a son. After that there was nothing he would
not give her. Like his legitimate wife, she had a court and a
guard, and she shared, almost to the diadem, all the prerogatives of supreme power. The Emperor wantonly squandered
money on her; as Nicetas says, "seas of wealth were poured
out at her feet." Proud and arrogant, she accepted both the
homage and the money. Following their master's example,
the courtiers flocked around her, neglectful of the legitimate
Empress.

Irene does not seem to have made any attempt to break out
of her isolation. She lived her own, separate, life, and filled it
with good works, helping the widows, protecting the or-
phans, providing penniless young girls with husbands and
dowries, visiting the monasteries and enriching them. She
liked to help others, and her panegyrist had said of her charm-
ingly "that she counted it a grace to be asked for her aid and
gave the impression of entreating one to entreat her." Converted to Greek Orthodoxy at the time of her marriage, and
very pious, she enjoyed the society of priests and religious,
and showed them infinite respect. All the same, in this Eastern court, she remained very Western and very German.
Basil of Achrida, in the funeral oration he delivered in her
honor, could not resist bringing up the fact that she was "a

foreigner, born under other skies, ignorant of our civilization and our customs, the daughter of a proud, arrogant, and
stiff-necked people," and he felt obligated to sing the praises
of Germany, of this "powerful and dominant" nation that,
more than any other Western people, "commands but will
not be commanded." In speaking thus, the prelate showed
that he had penetrated into the depths of the Empress's soul.

Indeed, she never forgot her native country. When the
second Crusade brought her brother-in-law, King Conrad,
and a Latin army to Constantinople in 1147, she was delighted. While the Greeks watched with dismay the alarming cloud from the West break over the Empire, while the
gaping Byzantines marveled to see women in the Crusaders' ranks, clothed and armed like knights, modern Amazons
riding astride their horses like men, Irene was intent on preparing a good reception for her compatriots. When the pride
of the Greek Emperor threatened to clash with the pride of
the German King, she did her best to dissipate whatever
trouble had arisen between the rival Princes. And since the
pretentions of Conrad, irreconcilable with Byzantine etiquette, did not permit of a personal meeting between the
two sovereigns at this time, it was thanks to the influence of
the Empress that they maintained a tolerable relationship.
Manuel and Conrad bombarded each other with courtesies.
The Emperor sent to the Latin camp an abundance of provisions and valuable gifts, to which the King responded with
rich presents.

A little later, when the French army appeared below the
walls of Constantinople, Irene maintained the most pleasant
relations with the wife of Louis VII, Eleanor of Guyenne.
But it was particularly after the disasters experienced by the
Crusaders in Asia Minor that the Empress's good will toward her compatriots became apparent. After his defeat on

the Meander, Conrad III had retreated with the remnant of
his troops to Ephesus, where he fell ill. Irene went with Manuel to visit him. She brought him back to Constantinople on
the imperial dromond, and the Basileus, who was skilled in
medicine and in surgery, insisted on caring for him with his
own hands. When Conrad III, his vow to the Holy Sepulcher
finally fulfilled, again passed through Constantinople, he received the same warm welcome. The Byzantine court was
openly interested in an alliance with Germany, to counter-
balance the unconcealed hostility of the Normans in Sicily
and of the French in France. Marriages were in the making
between the two Royal houses, Henry of Austria, half brother
to the King of Germany, was marrying one of the Emperor's
nieces, and the poets of the imperial court were pompously
extolling this union. A little later it was proposed that Conrad's son should marry another of the Emperor's nieces;
this was a political move in which the hand of the Empress is
unmistakable, and an interesting letter written by Conrad III to Irene confirms this. He confides to her the task of
choosing a bride for his son from among the Princesses of the
imperial family, "the one who seems to you, who have
brought them up, to excel in character and in beauty." (*Quae
moribus et forma noscatur a te, quae eas educasti, precel-
lere.*) The marriage never took place, but the closest alliance
continued to exist between the two States. When, in 1150,
Roger II and Louis VII thought of forming a comprehen-
sive Western block against Byzantium, it was the categorical
opposition of the German King that defeated the project. In
remaining a good German, Irene had by no means rendered
a disservice to the country of her adoption.

With the death of Conrad III in 1152, the bond between
the two countries slackened. But the Empress never lost her
fond interest in all that concerned Germany. With uncon-

cealed sympathy she followed from afar the progress of her
nephew, Conrad's young son; she sent him gifts and made
sure that he was equipped as a knight. With the passing of
time she seems to have come closer to Manuel, and to have
given him valuable assistance in affairs of State. Basil of
Achrida speaks of the "conformity of feeling," the "spiritual
affinity" that existed between the spouses. In this he was no
doubt exaggerating in the usual manner of funeral orators.
But there is evidence that on more than one occasion Irene
successfully intervened with the Emperor to obtain the release of captives, or pardons for those condemned to death,
and that she willingly undertook to bring such appeals before the Basileus. In 1158 she rendered him a more signal
service, in saving him from a plot hatched against him; and
if what her panegyrist states is true, namely that the "Arch
Despots of Persia," who had experienced her beneficence,
wished to honor her tomb with magnificent oblations, we
may safely conclude that she exercised some influence on the
foreign relations of the monarchy.

Fair-minded, endowed with good sense, presence of mind,
and a very clear idea of what ought to be done in given circumstances, her advice must have been valuable indeed. And
we can well believe that when she died rather suddenly, in
1160, of a malignant fever, Manuel felt her loss keenly. But
we can also believe that Basil of Achrida's picture of the
grief-stricken Emperor filling the Palace with his moans,
incapable of pulling himself together, is a trifle over-
dramatized, and that Nicetas exaggerates when he writes
that the Emperor was driven to despair, as if one of his limbs
had been torn away from him, and that he passed his period
of mourning in a "state of collapse—half dead." Be that as it
may, he gave his wife, who seems to have been universally
regretted, magnificent obsequies. She was buried in the Mon-

astery of the Pantocrator, which was founded by John Com-
nenus to be the royal burial place of the dynasty, and where
Manuel had made ready his own sepulcher. Furthermore,
he commissioned a fine funeral oration in honor of the dead
Empress, which has come down to us, and in which Basil of
Achrida, Archbishop of Thessalonica, lauded in the traditional manner, and not without personal emotion, the qualities and virtues with which the Empress had been adorned.
Afterward, the Emperor lost no time in consoling himself.
Anxious, says Nicetas, to have a son to carry on his line, and
no doubt susceptible as always to feminine charm, he announced as early as 1161 his intention of remarrying. From
all the brides that were offered to him, from among the
daughters of all those Princes and Kings who desired him as
an ally, he chose "the most beautiful Princess of her time,"
Mary of Antioch, whom he married in 1161. Irene the German had been very quickly forgotten.

XI

AGNES OF FRANCE

All his life the Emperor Manuel Comnenus had a strong liking for the Latins, and twenty years after his death, the memory of this openly avowed predilection was found by the chronicler Robert de Clari to be still alive in Constantinople. He tells us, in his naïve phraseology, of the warm welcome and good treatment accorded to the Westerners by the Basileus, in spite of all the Greek reproaches. "I command you," he said to his courtiers, "that no one among you shall make so bold or be so rash as to complain of my liberality, or of my liking for the French. Because I do like them, and I trust in them more than in you, and I shall give them yet more than I have given them."

This natural sympathy was reinforced by serious reasons of policy. Manuel sensed the invincible strength of the young Western nations. He knew them to be arrogant, unmanageable, always ready for war. He also knew of the old hatreds they fostered, the grudges they nursed, against the Byzantines. He was always afraid that a coalition would unite them against the Empire, and "that their common accord," as he says, "would submerge the monarchy as a suddenly swollen torrent devastates farmlands." So he applied himself to circumventing this dangerous coalition by every possible means, encouraging division between the European powers, supporting Italy's resistance to Barbarossa, attracting with generous commercial concessions the merchants of Ancona, Genoa, Venice, and Pisa, ceaselessly striving to form an alliance with one of the great Western States. It was in this way that he came, early in his reign, to rely on Germany. Later, near the end of his life, he inclined toward an alliance with the French. At that time he was in open enmity with the Emperor Frederick Barbarossa, and looked in every direction for support against him. That of King Louis VII seemed particularly advantageous, and he assiduously sought a means of establishing friendly relations with this Prince. The idea, moreover, was already in the wind. As early as 1171 or 1172, Pope Alexander III, with whom Manuel was on exceedingly good terms, had perceived the value of a Franco-Byzantine alliance, and had advised Louis VII to unite the House of France with that of the Comneni by a marriage. So when the Greek Emperor decided to make definite proposals, he found the way prepared.

In 1178, Philippe of Alsace, Count of Flanders, returning from Palestine, broke his journey at Constantinople. The Basileus gave him the usual magnificent reception, and during the course of conversation with the Latin Prince, he disclosed his project. "The Emperor asked him," relates the chronicle of d'Ernoul, "if the King of France had no marriageable daughter, and the Count replied that he did have one, but small she was, and young. To which the Emperor Manuel replied that he had but one son, who was a young child, and that, if the King would send him his daughter, he would marry his son to her as soon as she should come, and he would permit both to wear the diadem: he should be Emperor and she Empress. Of this the Emperor spoke, and asked the Count to convey it to the King, for a nobler man he could not find or send. And he would send with him his most valiant men to bring the damsel back, if the King would confide her to them.

"The Count replied that he would gladly deliver the message and thought to obtain a favorable reply. So the Emperor had his emissaries make ready to go, gave them sufficient gold and silver for their spending, and sent them to France with the Count. When they came to France, the Count went to the King and delivered the Emperor's message.

"With which the King was pleased and joyful, seeing he could not marry his daughter better. He equipped her most nobly and most richly (as befitted the daughter of such an exalted man as the King of France) and handed her over to the emissaries, and they brought her to Constantinople, to the Emperor."

This child "small and young" was named Agnes of France. The second daughter of Louis VII and his third wife Alix de Champagne, she was the younger sister of Philippe-Auguste. When she left Paris in the spring of 1179 to embark on the Genoese vessel that was to take her to Constantinople, she was barely eight years old. Transplanted at such a tender age to a new country, quickly forgotten in distant Romania by an apparently indifferent family, she was obliged, more than others, to adjust herself to the country of her adoption. There she was destined to lead a remarkably strange and dramatic life, to witness important events, even,

at times, to play an important part in them; and for this reason her obscure figure merits the illumination of history.[1]

At the time of Agnes's arrival in the Imperial City, in
1179, the reign of Manuel Comnenus was nearing its end.
But despite the sorrows of his last years, the Emperor maintained his high confidence in himself, and his court its accustomed elegance and pomp. The betrothal of the heir to the
Caesars' throne and the daughter of King Louis VII was
celebrated on the 2nd of March 1180, amid pageantry and
feasting. As the young Alexius was only eleven years old, the
marriage was put off until later, but from the moment of her
betrothal, the little fiancée was treated as a future Empress,
and in accordance with custom she discarded her French
name of Agnes for the more Byzantine one of Anna.

A few months later, in September 1180, Manuel's death
cast all the burdens and responsibilities of supreme power on
the shoulders of the two children. The circumstances were
peculiarly difficult, and the future was pregnant with danger.
The Emperor had died without making any dispositions, so
the worst happened very quickly. A Basileus who was a
minor, "who still had need of a nurse and a tutor," and who,
for want of a proper education, was both incompetent and
unstable; a Regent, Mary of Antioch, surrounded by the
wrong people, mistrusted, loved too much by a few, detested
by many; a favorite, insolent and mediocre, whom his rivals
suspected of aspiring to the throne; such were the leaders

---

[1] Cf. L. du Sommerard, *Deux princesses d'Orient au XIIe siècle*, Paris,
1907. In this book there is a pleasing biography of Agnes of France, a
little too romantic at times for a historical work, but interesting, even
though the author has failed to make use of certain important texts concerning the psychology of his heroine.

of government. It was enough to unleash the ambitions of all concerned: those of Mary, the Emperor Manuel's daughter, a passionate, violent woman, whose hatred for her stepmother, combined with an almost masculine energy, carried her to the utmost limits of audacity; those of Alexius, Manuel's bastard son, who thought he had a claim to the throne; those, above all, of the formidable Andronicus Comnenus, whose adventures had so disturbed the previous reign. Against these dangers that threatened from every side, those in power were without support and without strength. Even the members of the imperial family, the greatest personages of the State, dissatisfied and worried, thought only of their own interests. "There was no longer any concern for the public welfare; the Councils of State were unattended." The outcome of this lamentable situation, and the tragedies that, one after another, covered the capital and the Palace in blood, are well known. Mary Comnena upholding the revolt against her brother and undergoing a regular siege in St. Sophia; Andronicus elevated in his turn, soon to be acclaimed by the populace as lord of Constantinople and associate of the young Basileus; the favorite overthrown, imprisoned, blinded; then, in the words of Nicetas, "the imperial garden despoiled of its trees," Mary Comnena and her husband poisoned, the Regent, Mary of Antioch, condemned for high treason and ruthlessly executed, the young Alexius finally deposed and strangled, and Andronicus Comnenus seizing the throne: such were the events of these tragic years. Events of which Agnes of France was the horrified witness.

The little Empress was twelve years old when the death of the young Emperor left her lonely and abandoned in a foreign city—the defenseless pawn of its new master. Andronicus could think of no better way of consolidating the power he had usurped than to marry the fiancée of his predecessor, and despite the gap between their ages (Andronicus was over sixty), their marriage was celebrated in St. Sophia at the end of 1182, and consummated. Even in this Byzantium accustomed to crimes, the affair caused a scandal. "This old man, nearing his end," wrote Nicetas, "was not in the least ashamed to unite himself with the young and beautiful bride intended for his nephew; this dawn was embraced by the twilight; this rosy-fingered maiden who exhaled the perfumes of love was possessed by the used and wrinkled man." Public opinion in Europe was no less outraged by the event. Agnes's family alone seemed not to care; there is no evidence that Philippe-Auguste felt any qualms regarding the fate of his sister.

What is even more surprising, the Princess herself seems to have accepted her fate with equanimity. The explanation of this singularity may lie in the fact that her marriage with the old sovereign was primarily a political union, and that Andronicus, engrossed with his innumerable mistresses, seldom inflicted himself on his wife. She had all the exterior gratifications of supreme power, the pleasure of figuring in the ceremonies, of having her likeness reproduced on monuments, in full imperial regalia, beside her husband. And it is not impossible that she, like so many others, succumbed to the charm of the great seducer that Andronicus undoubtedly was. In the final tragedy that brought death to the Basileus, she was with him, side by side with his favorite mistress, and the two women, arrested with the Prince when attempting to flee, made desperate efforts to save him from his fate. This was in 1185. During the two years that she was married to Andronicus, the young woman had seen some strange sights, in this court where the courtisans and the flute-players were in better standing with the ruler than his statesmen, and in those villas on the Bosphorus where, with his beautiful mistresses, Andronicus enjoyed in rural peace the delights of passionate and voluptuous living. It seems that Agnes of France was not too scandalized by all this. She was, perhaps, the final conquest of this Andronicus Comnenus, so intelligent, so persuasive, so witty, supple, and charming, on whose lips, as Nicetas puts it, Hermes had rubbed the "moly," the magical herb that seduces hearts.

It is not known what happened to the young woman during the turbulent days that followed the fall of Andronicus. But there is every reason to believe that as soon as order was established, Agnes, widow of two Emperors, regained, under the rule of Isaac Angius, all the prerogatives that Byzantium accorded to its sovereigns. Farther on, we shall see that she remained in possession of her marriage settlement, and it is probable that she lived in one of those Imperial Palaces that offered a retreat to Princesses fallen from power. It was there that a new adventure came to her.

Theodore Branas belonged to one of the greatest families of the Byzantine aristocracy. His father, Alexius, who was reputed to be the finest general of that epoch, had been one of Andronicus Comnenus's most faithful servants. His mother was a niece of the Emperor Manuel, who liked to proclaim her "the most beautiful of women" and was pleased to call her "the ornament of his family." Thus related to the fallen dynasty, the Branae could have no sympathy for the government of Isaac Angius. In 1186, Alexius Branas revolted against the Emperor and met his death, weapons in hand, under the walls of Constantinople. And although Theodore served in the imperial army, he could feel nothing but hate for his father's murderer. Was this what drew him to Agnes, who was, in a sense, heiress to the rights of the Comneni? We do not know. At all events, in 1190 the intimacy between Branas and the young woman, who was then nineteen years of age, began to be talked about in Constantinople. A little later, in 1194, the Western chronicler, Aubry de Trois-Fontaines, specifies things in these terms: "The Empress, sister of the King of France, was kept by Theodore Branas, and although she remained in possession of her marriage settlement, he considered her as his wife; but he had not solemnized the union with a nuptial ceremony, because, according to the custom of the country, such a marriage would have meant the forfeiture of her dowry." In any case, the liaison was openly admitted, and before long it was universally accepted, the more so because Theodore Branas, having done much to overthrow Isaac Angius in 1195, held a high position at the court of the new Emperor Alexius.[1]

Through this more or less morganatic union, whose bonds were further strengthened by the birth of a daughter, Agnes had become more Byzantine than ever. She had, as we shall see, completely forgotten her native tongue; she had lost all recollection of a family which had never shown the smallest interest in her. There is not even any evidence that she met with her sister Margaret, widow of the King of Hungary, when the former journeyed to the Holy Land. And in 1203, when the arrival of the Barons of the Fourth Crusade brought her suddenly face to face with her compatriots, there is every reason to believe that she was completely "deracinated."

We know how Irene Angia, the Byzantine Princess placed on the German throne by her marriage, persuaded her hus-

---

[1] Alexius III, brother of Isaac Angius. [Translator's note]

band Philipp of Swabia to take up the cause of her brother, the young Alexius,[2] whose power had been usurped; and how the German Caesar aroused the interest of the Venetians, and of the Crusaders then assembled in Venice, in the restoration of his brother-in-law's rights. But the expedition destined to deliver the Holy Land was not diverted to Constantinople for this reason alone. The economic interests of the Venetian Republic, the attraction of the Byzantine capital and its splendors, the prospect of plunder and pillage offered by such an enterprise to this band of adventurers, the old grudges still alive in Latin hearts, all these things contributed to the decision of the Doge and the Crusader Barons. Another consideration was the mass of holy relics possessed by Constantinople. We know what a prominent place such precious relics occupied in the public and the private life of the Middle Ages, and what a high value was set upon those of Western origin. Byzantium was full of these sacred treasures, which were somewhat ostentatiously offered to the dazzled view of visitors in the Palace, the Imperial Chapel, St. Sophia, and other churches. So the Latins saw the imperial city as a vast museum, an enormous reliquary, predestined to stock the sanctuaries of the Western world. And in view of the importance of relic-hunting to the conquerors, one may well believe that this bait had a lot to do with the grave decision that, despite the express prohibition of the Pope, turned in the direction of Constantinople so many pious people, so many churchmen, eager to reap these rich and holy rewards of victory.

This is not the place to tell of the Fourth Crusade. It will suffice to recall how the Latins, who reached Constantinople the 23rd of June 1203, saw that in order to put the young

[2] Alexius IV, son of Isaac Angius. [Translator's note]

Alexius [3] back on his throne they would have to use force. On
the 17th of July, the assault was made. The usurper, Alexius III, panic-stricken, fled precipitately, and the populace
reinstated Isaac Angius. The Emperor's first care was to
come to terms with the Crusaders. He ratified all the promises made to them by his son; he welcomed them as "the benefactors and the preservers of the Empire"; most important
of all, he poured the wealth of the capital into their hands,
and this first occupation of the city, which lasted no more
than a few days, served only to increase the covetousness of
the Westerners.

It is here that we rediscover Agnes of France, in a scene
that reveals the evolution effected in her. Among the great
Barons of the Latin army were several close relatives of the
young Empress. Count Louis of Blois was her nephew;
Count Baudouin of Flanders had married her niece. On the
other hand, Theodore Branas, her lover, had been a leader of
the defense, one of the last loyal supporters of the Basileus
Alexius III. Agnes seems to have shown without hesitation
where her sympathies lay. Robert de Clari relates that the
Crusaders, having some vague recollection that a French
Princess, a sister of their King, had been married a long time
ago in Constantinople, inquired, as soon as the pretender was
installed in the Palace, whether this lady, "whom they
called," says the chronicler, "the Empress of France," was
still alive. "And they were told that she was, and that she
was married; that a man of high position in the city—by the
name of Vernas (Branas)—had espoused her; and that she
was living in a palace close by. There, the Barons went to
see her, they saluted her, and made great promises to serve

[3] Alexius IV was reseated on the throne in 1203 with his father as co-
ruler. [Translator's note]

her well. Agnes showed much displeasure, and seemed greatly wroth that they had come there, and that they had crowned Alexius, nor would she speak to them. But she had an interpreter speak, and the interpreter said that she knew no French. With Count Louis, however, who was her nephew, she entered into communication."

In the course of the twenty-four years during which the little Princess exiled in Byzantium had been forgotten by her French relatives, she too had forgotten her birthplace. She was interested now only in Byzantine concerns, in the deep-seated hatred of the Branae for Isaac Angius, and like any Greek, she resented the untimely and fatal interference of these foreigners in the affairs of the monarchy. In view of this, Robert de Clari's anecdote is highly significant; it proves to what a point Agnes of France was alienated from her native land.

What followed was hardly calculated to reconcile her with her compatriots. We know that the Greeks and the Latins did not agree for long. We know how the apparently good relations between them broke down during the course of the winter spent by the Crusaders under the walls of Constantinople, and how, after a national revolution had overthrown the weak and contemptible occupants of the throne, the Westerners made up their minds to conquer Byzantium for themselves. We know the atrocities that were committed, over a period of several days, in the city taken by storm. At the time of the assault (the 12th of April 1204) Agnes of France, with other noble ladies, had sought refuge in the fortified Palace of the Buculeon. The Marquis Boniface de Montferrat arrived in time to save the Princess and her companions from any disagreeable experiences, but one can imagine how she felt on seeing her capital pillaged, the palaces ransacked, the churches devastated, St. Sophia defiled and profaned, the panic-stricken population fleeing in all directions, and the incomparable city of Constantinople delivered up to the brutalities of a licentious soldiery. Robert de Clari's ingenuous account reveals what the Latins gained from their deplorable undertaking. "Since the world was created," he says, "no possessions so great, so noble, so rich, were seen or won, neither in the time of Alexander, nor in the time of Charlemagne, nor before, nor after; and I do not believe that in all the forty richest cities of the world there was so much wealth as was found in the heart of Constantinople. And to this the Greeks bear witness, that two parts of the riches of the world were in Constantinople, and the third part scattered over the world." At the sight of all this satisfied cupidity, of the insolence of these bandits without respect for anyone or anything, Agnes, like Nicetas, must have wept bitterly over the ruin of the imperial city, and thought that the Saracens would have been more merciful than the Crusaders.

Nevertheless, when her kinsman, Count Baudouin of Flanders, was seated on the throne of the Caesars, when a Latin Empire had replaced the monarchy of the Basileis, the consciousness of her French origin seems to have reawakened in Agnes's heart. This final change in her was to have rather curious consequences.

Nicetas speaks somewhere, not without bitterness and sorrow, of those Greeks "who, for the sake of a few territories, made peace with the Italians, whereas they should have wished to be perpetually at war with them." Among "these servile spirits, whose ambition armed them against their own country," was the lover of Agnes of France, Theodore Branas, who probably joined the new régime at the instigation of his mistress. She had, in fact, reaped an unexpected benefit from the establishment of the Latin Empire. Aubry de Trois-Fontaines reports that it was brought to the attention of Branas "that he was depriving the Empress sister of the King of France of the nuptials to which she was entitled," and he was persuaded to regularize the situation by a wedding. We may well believe that Agnes, out of gratitude for this, reconciled her husband with those to whom she owed it.

In any case, Theodore Branas became, from that time on, one of the most faithful supporters of the new Empire. Villehardouin says of him: "He was a Greek who stood by them, and no other Greeks but he stood by them." This rare devotion was suitably rewarded. The Emperor conferred on Branas the Feudal Lordship of Apros, where, at the head of several Latin contingents, he served his new master as a loyal vassal. Then, in 1206, when his town of Apros had been taken by the Bulgarians and demolished, the great Greek lord had the opportunity to fill an even greater role. He was very popular in the province of Thrace, which he had governed in the past for the Basileus, and particularly in Adrianople, his place of origin. The people of this region, horrified by the Bulgarian excesses, offered him their submission, and proposed to constitute, under his authority, a vassal Principality of the Latin Emperor. "In this way," as Villehardouin says, "the Greeks and the Franks could be friends." Henry of Flanders, who was governing for his brother Baudouin, who had been taken prisoner by the Bulgarians, adroitly seized the opportunity. In 1206, he formally ceded in fief to Branas and to "the Empress his wife" Adrianople, Didymoticus, "and all the appurtenances thereof." The act of investiture was made out in the name of the "noble Caesar Theodore Branas Comnenus," a resounding title that heightened the new overlord's prestige with the Greeks. A detachment of Latin knights remained in Adrianople to help him defend his Principality. And so, says Villehardouin, "the pact was made and concluded, and a peace made and concluded between the Greeks and the Franks."

In reconciling the conquerors and the conquered, Agnes of France had done what she could to consolidate the establishment founded by the Latins. And no doubt she carried on in her Principality the work of reconciliation that she had initiated. Theodore Branas kept his promises. To the last day of his life he faithfully served the Emperor and the Empire. In his domain, moreover, he was almost a King, and in this wholly Greek environment, Agnes of France must have continued to live like a Byzantine Princess.

Very little is known about her last years. One detail, however, seems to indicate that she turned more and more back to France. It was to a Frankish Baron, Narjaud de Toucy, that she married her daughter in 1218 or 1219. Another Frenchman, Guillaume de Villehardouin, son of the Prince of Achaia, was later to marry her granddaughter, and her grandson Philippe de Toucy liked to boast of his French origin and his relationship to the French Royal Family. Joinville relates that he came to Palestine to visit Saint Louis, "and told the king that he was his cousin, being descended from one of King Philippe's sisters, who had been wife to the Emperor himself." And as late as the beginning of the fourteenth century, Marino Sanudo was speaking of "the daughter of the French King" who became Empress of Byzantium, and who had afterward married a Baron of the Greek Empire.

Thus, many years after her death, which took place in 1220, the West remembered Agnes of France, Empress of the East, whose destiny was assuredly one of the most remarkable among those of the many Latin Princesses married in Constantinople. More than any other, she had been "deracinated" by circumstance; more than any other, she had become a Byzantine, in language and in feeling. And yet, when circumstances brought her, a quarter of a century later, once more face to face with her compatriots, her affection turned back to her native land—after a moment of hesitation. The wife of a great Greek nobleman, she did not join with him the party of patriots who were tenaciously resisting the foreigners; she did not emigrate with him to Nicea, or anywhere else. On the contrary, she won her husband over to the side of the Franks, made of him a Feudal Lord of the new Empire, and proposed that he should reconcile, if possible, the two enemy races. Born a daughter of France, dying in a Greek Principality under the suzerainty of a Latin Emperor, after founding with Theodore Branas a family that was to be wholly French, she thus harmoniously united her deathbed and her cradle, despite the intervening storms of her adventurous life.

XII

CONSTANCE OF
HOHENSTAUFEN

At Valencia, in Spain, in the little church of St. John the Hospitaler, one may see in the chapel dedicated to St. Barbara a wooden chest on which is engraved this inscription in Spanish: "Here lies the Lady Constance, august Empress of Greece." Who is this little-known sovereign of the Byzantine Empire, and what strange destiny brought her so far from the East, to live and die beneath the Iberian sky? Hers is a story at once romantic and melancholy; a curious episode in the history of the twelfth century and the relations then existing between the East and the West.[1]

About the year 1238, great events were brewing in Europe. In the East, John Ducas Vatatzes, the Greek Emperor

---

[1] M. G. Schlumberger was the first to draw attention to this forgotten Princess, in an interesting article: "Le Tombeau d'une impératrice byzantine à Valence," *Revue des Deux Mondes*, 15 mars 1902. We are greatly indebted to this interesting memoir.

of Nicea, was contending more and more successfully against the weak Latin Empire of Constantinople; and in the West, Frederick II of Hohenstaufen, was resuming once again his relentless war against the Papacy. Now, Baudouin II, Emperor of Constantinople, protégé of the reigning pontiff and sustained solely by him, was, for this reason, automatically against the great Swabian Emperor, and the policy of Frederick II was, of course, to strive for ascendancy here too, and thus put his irreconcilable enemy the Pope in check. To this end he did not hesitate, although he was a Roman Catholic and a Latin, to enter into an alliance with the schismatic Greeks against a Catholic Latin State.

This is not surprising when one remembers the free and powerful mentality of this last of the Hohenstaufens. Initiated from his childhood in Sicily to the splendors of Greek and Arabian civilization, learned, and as devoted to science as any Renaissance humanist, and in addition extraordinarily attracted by the violent and voluptuous ways of the Moslems, this Prince with the cosmopolitan and secular soul had undertaken to tear the world from the grasp of the Church, not only by destroying the temporal power of the Papacy, but also by breaking down the spiritual ascendancy of Rome. To put an end forever to the useless folly of the Crusades, to make peace with Islam, to transfer the supreme rule of Christendom from the Pope to the Emperor, these were some of the dreams cherished by this almost modern ruler. His enemies affirmed that he no longer believed in God, that he denied the immortality of the soul, that he proclaimed the supremacy of reason over blind faith, saying that "man should believe only that which exists in the natural order, and can be proved by reason." It is understandable that such a man, his mind freed from outworn scruples, should have felt no embarrassment in allying himself with schismatics and infidels, if their support could help him against his great adversary the Papacy.

This was the source of his involvement with the Byzantine court at Nicea. Frederick II promised Vatatzes that he would clear the Latins out of Constantinople and restore it to its legitimate ruler. In return, the Greek Emperor promised to consider himself the vassal of the Western Emperor and to reunite the two Churches. It is hard to determine to what extent these promises were sincere. In the pact that was concluded, the Greeks saw chiefly a means of depriving the Pope of a strength that the latter was endeavoring to enlist on his side. Whatever the case, the two parties were in agreement. As early as 1238, the Basileus put Greek troops in Italy at the disposal of the Swabian Emperor. Very soon the relations between the two sovereigns became still closer. In 1244, a daughter of Frederick II was married to the Greek Emperor at Nicea.

In 1241, John Ducas Vatatzes had lost his first wife, Irene Lascaris. Before long, "weary of his solitude," as a contemporary puts it, he thought of remarrying, and he asked his great ally for the hand of his daughter. She was named Constance, and she was born of Frederick's liaison with Bianca Lancia, who was also the mother of the famous Manfred. The Emperor gladly consented to a union that strengthened his alliance with the Greeks; and notwithstanding a remarkable disparity in age between the prospective bride and bridegroom—in 1244 John was fifty-two and Constance a very young girl—the marriage was decided upon.

It caused a prodigious scandal in the West, especially in the Pontifical party. At the Council of Lyons, a little later, Pope Innocent IV did not hesitate to include among the reasons that seemed to him to justify his excommunication of Frederick II the fact that he had contracted a marriage with heretics. Before that, and for the same reason, the Pope had solemnly excommunicated the Emperor Vatatzes and all his subjects, "impudently treating as heretics," wrote Frederick II to his confederate, "these most orthodox Greeks, by whom the Christian faith has been spread throughout the world," and stigmatizing as "apostate and scandalous a nation that for centuries, from its very origin, has been rich in piety and has carried the gospel of peace to the Latin world governed by the Pope." Nothing could have been more effective in consolidating the interests of the two sovereigns than this common condemnation. "It is by no means," said Frederick II to another of his correspondents, "only our own rights that we are defending, but those of all friendly peoples united by the sincere love of Christ, and especially the Greeks, our allies and friends, whom the Pope, on account of the affection we bear them and despite the fact that they are truly Christian, has treated with the utmost insolence, describing as impious this most pious people and as heretic this most orthodox nation." Vatatzes, too, while sending a contingent of his troops to the Emperor, congratulated himself on the Swabian Prince's victories over their common enemy. The young Princess Constance was the pledge of this political accord, and she was to become its victim.

The marriage between the Basileus and the daughter of Frederick II was celebrated at Broussa. According to the text, as yet unpublished, of Theodore Lascaris's funeral oration for his father, the Emperor Vatatzes, the Greek sovereign traveled in full military state from his capital city of Nicea to the town of Broussa, where his young fiancée awaited him. It seems that the journey was upsetting to the old Prince, and that he felt far from well. But the wedding was celebrated with no less pomp on that account. The Greeks felt extremely flattered by this match, "of which," writes Theodore Lascaris, "only the foolish and ignorant can fail to see the brilliance and the glory and the many other advantages." The court poets, therefore, vied with each other in extolling this fine and profitable union, and all the magnificence of Byzantine pageantry was unfurled around the young sovereign, splendor competing with splendor. According to custom, she changed her first name for the more Greek appellation of Anna, and she was given a warm welcome in the city of Nicea, a city that in the last forty years had taken on all the aspects of a great capital, and that was particularly dear to the Greeks, says Theodore Lascaris, "because its name held a presage of victory." But even this superficial happiness was of short duration; the harmonious relations between the imperial pair were soon disturbed by a peculiar intrigue.

As the Empress was little more than a child, her father had given her, when she left Italy, a large retinue of women of her own race. Among them, in the capacity of her "guardian and teacher" was an extremely attractive woman whom the Byzantine chroniclers style "the Marchesa." The Marchesa was beautiful; particularly remarkable were her glorious eyes and her exquisite grace. The Emperor had always been a man of highly amorous disposition, and his little Western wife, married for political motives, did not interest him much. It was not at all difficult for the Marchesa to interest him more, and, as she lent herself eagerly to the game, and, to quote a contemporary chronicler, "bewitched the Basileus with her amorous charms and her philters," it was not long before she became the declared favorite and the rival of her young mistress. Vatatzes refused her nothing. She was authorized to put on the imperial insignia, to wear the purple buskins; when she rode on horseback, the saddle cloth of her mount, and the reins, were purple, as for a Basilissa. She had a brilliant suite to escort her, and wherever she went she was accorded the same honors as the Empress, whose subjects, in the city as in the Palace, showed as much respect to the Marchesa as they showed to the legitimate sovereign, and even a little more. The Basileus, completely seduced, gave in to his mistress's every whim. Anna was openly relegated to second place.

The affair caused a certain amount of scandal at the court of Nicea. Among the Emperor's intimates, one of the most esteemed at that time was the celebrated writer Nicephorus Blemmydes. Charged by Vatatzes with the education of the heir apparent, he had, in this trusted position, won the friendship of his pupil and the favor of his sovereign. He was a man of harsh and inflexible nature, very pious, very disdainful of everything unconnected with religion, who had drawn attention to himself by his hostility to the Latins. He prided himself, moreover, on his outspokenness, and although his free speech had earned him frequent attacks, he had always managed to maintain his high standing. Blemmydes resolutely ranged himself against the favorite. He detested her not only because she was a foreigner, but also because she was a woman. In the past, when he was a young man of twenty, he had had a romantic love affair that ended badly and left him with an implacable grudge against the entire female sex. So he daringly set himself to attack the Marchesa. He composed satires against her, and, as this defender of morals had by no means a light hand, he spared his enemy no insults. "Queen of shamelessness, disgrace of the world, wanton,

Maenad, courtesan," such were some of the compliments he paid her.

The Emperor, a discreet man, was embarrassed by all this fuss; also, he felt occasional twinges of remorse over this love affair in which he had involved himself. But he was infatuated, and he calmed his scruples by telling himself that God would let him know when the hour for repentance had come. In the meantime he gave himself up to his passion. As for the Marchesa, she was brazen. More imperious, more insolent than ever, she put on airs with everyone, and openly set herself up as the Empress's rival, considering herself, as a chronicler says, "true Queen and more than Queen." Things had been going on like this for three or four years, when a dramatic incident brought the Italian Marchesa face to face with her enemy.

In 1248, Blemmydes was Abbé of the monastery of St. Gregory the Thaumaturge, near Ephesus. The favorite conceived the idea of going there to defy him. In full imperial dress, accompanied by a stately retinue, she invaded the monastery, since no one had the courage to shut the door against her, and she entered the church while the community was celebrating Mass. With a gesture to the priest at the altar, Blemmydes immediately brought the Divine Liturgy to a stop. Then, turning to the Marchesa, he ordered her to leave the sacred precincts that she doubly profaned in that she was unworthy, on account of her conduct, to participate in the communion of the faithful, and that by her presence she was publicly insulting the sacred laws of religion. Before this violent invective, the woman recoiled, then, bursting into tears, she begged the monk not to forbid her the holy place; finally, gripped by superstitious terror, she decided to give in, and left the church. But the men at arms who accompanied her were indignant at the humiliation inflicted on their mistress. Their chief, a certain Drimys, declared that after such an outrage the Abbé was unworthy to live, and, suiting the action to the word, he tried to draw his sword. But, O miracle! the sword stuck in the scabbard, and despite all his efforts the officer could not pull it out. Wild with rage, Drimys insulted, threatened, stormed. Blemmydes, impassive, declared that he would rather die than violate the law of Christ. Finally, their respect involuntarily aroused by so much courage in the face of danger, the assailants withdrew, but complaints were immediately brought to the Emperor against the insolent monk who had dared to stand up to the favorite. Incited by her friends, the Marchesa demanded vengeance, affirming that in her person imperial majesty itself had been affronted. Drimys, for his part, declared that there was sorcery in the whole affair, that only a spell could have kept his sword in its scabbard, and he demanded the punishment of the magician. Blemmydes began to feel anxious regarding the outcome of his audacity.

There is in existence a kind of circular addressed by him at this time to all the monks in the Empire, in order to ascertain, as far as possible, what the general opinion was concerning this incident. In it he recounted every detail of the affair, justified the stand he had taken, and, inveighing against the favorite in very violent terms, defined the attitude incumbent upon a man of God in such circumstances and with regard to such a woman. "He who tries to please men," he wrote, "is not a true servant of God," and he concluded his message thus: "For these reasons we did not hesitate to turn the impious one out of the holy place, unable to take it upon ourselves to give Holy Communion to the impure and immodest woman, nor to consent to cast the shining and splendid words of the Sacred Liturgy before one who wallows in the mud of corruption."

The Emperor Vatatzes refused, it seems, to fall in with his mistress's vengeful plans, despite the ardor of his passion. He merely said, with a sigh, and with tears in his eyes, "Why would you have me punish this just man? If I had been able to live without shame and disgrace, I would have kept the Imperial Majesty above the reach of attack. But I have laid myself open to the insults heaped upon my person and my dignity. So I am only reaping what I have sown."

Nevertheless, despite the Emperor's will for clemency, the monk was made to pay in other ways for his daring indiscretion. In the interesting autobiography he left behind him, he notes: "There were many troubles and vexations." This is rather vague, but there is no question that in 1250 the Abbé Blemmydes was somewhat in disgrace. Just then, very luckily for him, the Papal ambassadors arrived in the East, and the need for the eloquent dialectic and theological erudition of the learned Greek in discussions at the conference of Nymphaeon, served to restore his credit. So on the whole, Blemmydes managed to escape the disagreeable consequences to which he had laid himself open by contending with the powerful favorite, "whose name alone," he wrote, "inspires terror."

What did the Empress Anna, so openly neglected, think of all these explosive happenings? We do not know. In any case, her father, Frederick II, does not seem to have paid any attention to the affair—if the rumors of it so much as reached his ears. We still have several very interesting letters, written in the year 1250, in Greek, by the Emperor Frederick to his "very dear son-in-law." He expresses to Vatatzes his "complete sympathy and his sincere affections"; he tells him of the victories won by his armies in Italy, "because we know," he says, "that Your Majesty rejoices with us in all our successes and advances." Full of confidence in himself and in the future, he adds: "We inform you that, guided and upheld by Divine Providence, we are in good health, that we defeat our enemies every day, and that we are bringing all our concerns to the desired outcome." He goes on to congratulate the Greek Emperor on his triumphs over the Latins, and to put him on guard against the political intrigues of the Papacy.

One should see with what bitter violence Frederick II inveighs against "these pastors of Israel, who have nothing to do with the Bishops of the Church of Christ," and against their head the Pope, whom he calls "the father of lies." All this because Innocent IV had just sent a diplomatic mission to Nicea, in the hope of breaking up the alliance between the two Emperors and re-establishing the union between the two Churches. Although Frederick II affected great satisfaction in the "strong and unshakable love" cherished by Vatatzes for "his father," he was not without apprehension concerning the result of these proceedings. So he carefully warned the Greek sovereign that it was not at all "in the interests of the Faith" that this mission was coming to him, but solely "to sow dissension between father and son." And as Vatatzes, momentarily seduced by the Papal propositions, had decided to enter into negotiations with Rome and was sending ambassadors to Italy, Frederick II added: "Our Majesty wishes, very paternally, to censure the conduct of his son" who, "without the consent of his father," has made such a grave decision; and, with the reminder that he had some experience in Western matters, he remarked ironically that he would never permit himself to make a decision in matters pertaining to the East without first consulting Vatatzes, whose knowledge of them was far superior to his. Therefore, he said that he intended to receive the envoys of the Basileus before they went any further. This he did. When they disembarked in the West, he detained them in the South of Italy until further orders.

In these wholly political letters, there is nothing about the Empress Anna. At most, Frederick mentions her briefly in recalling his excommunication by the Pope on account of the marriage, however "legal and canonical," that had united the Basileus to "our very gentle daughter." So despite the infidelities of Vatatzes, despite, even, the Papal intrigues, cordial relations existed between the two sovereigns, and the Emperor's strong insistence on the close bond of kinship that united a father-in-law with his son-in-law was obviously designed to consolidate it. In point of fact, however, from this moment on the bond began to weaken, perhaps because the Princess Anna failed to interest her husband. And it was to dissolve altogether very soon after the death of the great Swabian Emperor in December 1250.

Having regained their liberty through this event, the Greek ambassadors joined Innocent IV and negotiations were begun, which culminated into a definite agreement in 1254. By this covenant, the Pope gave carte blanche to the Basileus with regard to the Latin Empire of Constantinople; in return, the Greek Emperor promised to effect the union of the Churches. To reunite Christendom, Innocent IV did not hesitate to sacrifice the policy established by the Fourth Crusade. To reconquer the capital of the Empire, Vatatzes did not hesitate to sacrifice the independence of the Greek Church. Each of the two parties completely abandoned a traditional policy, thereby making the issue one of singular importance. In any case, it marked the end of the Greco-German alliance that the marriage of 1244 had prepared and consecrated.

A little earlier, however, in 1253, perhaps because the Marchesa had disappeared, perhaps because in growing up the young Empress Anna had gained some influence over her husband, a curious thing happened at the court of Nicea. After the death of Frederick II, one of the first acts of Conrad IV, his legitimate son, was to banish the Lancia, the maternal relatives of Anna and Manfred, and it was at Nicea that the exiles sought refuge. John Vatatzes offered a warm welcome to his wife's uncle, Galvano Lancia, and to her other relatives; in fact, he extended his protection to them so unequivocally that Conrad took it as a personal offense, and complained strongly of the Basileus's attitude. On this count he sent a special ambassador to the East, Marquis Berthold of Hohenburg, whose mission, and whose haughty attitude, was remembered by the people of Nicea for a very long time afterward. The Greek Emperor ended by giving in to his demands. But we can assume that Vatatzes's displeasure over this put the finishing touch to his break with the Hohenstaufens, and threw him into the arms of the Pope.

The rupture, once achieved, was definitive. Contrary to what one might have supposed, Conrad's successor, Manfred, when he ascended the throne in 1254, made no attempt at reconciliation with his sister's husband. Indeed, he showed himself very ill disposed toward the Emperor of Nicea. So much so, that when the time came for John Vatatzes to die, on the 30th of October 1254, the alliance dreamed of by Frederick II was no more than a memory.

We can well believe that under the circumstances the widowed Anna would have liked to return to her native land. Her position at the court of Nicea had, in fact, become very difficult since the death of her husband. Theodore II Lascaris, who succeeded him, was extremely hostile to Latins in general, and, as the son of his father's first wife, he particularly disliked his stepmother, and treated her badly. Further, as the policy of Manfred became more and more hostile to the Greeks, the new Basileus, seeing in the sister of the Sicilian King a valuable hostage, thought it wise to keep her in his hands, and took the extra precaution of holding her in semi-captivity. Thus, although she was isolated and out of favor in a distant country, she was yet unable to leave it. And matters were the same after the death of Theodore Lascaris, when Michael Paleologus had usurped the throne and reconquered Constantinople in 1261. The only change in Anna's situation was that, though still virtually a captive, she left Nicea with the court and returned to Byzantium. It was there that a last love came to the daughter of Frederick II.

The young sovereign had of course kept up, in conformity with Byzantine etiquette, the rank and way of life proper for an Empress. She made only very modest use of her privileges. "She adorned her existence," says a chronicler, "with the beauty of her virtues, and the purity of her morals gave an added radiance to the grace of her countenance." But despite this voluntary self-effacement, she did not go unnoticed. At that time she must have been about thirty years old, and she was very pretty. The new Emperor, Michael Paleologus, became aware of it, and fell madly in love with the forlorn young woman. As we know, it was the custom for a Byzantine usurper to appropriate the widow of his predecessor, considering it a good way of legalizing the usurpation. But when Michael Paleologus decided to declare himself, he found that he had met his match. Anna rejected his overtures with haughty disdain, declaring that never could she, widow of an Emperor and daughter of Frederick II, lower herself by becoming the mistress of a man whom she had counted among her subjects in the past. The suitor was not at all discouraged by this contemptuous dismissal. When after further entreaties, Paleologus saw all his attempts rebuffed, he told himself that there was only one way to satisfy the tyrannical passion that was burning him up, and aggravating the Princess's contempt. Since she would not become his mistress, he proposed that she should become his wife.

As a matter of fact, Michael was already married, and his wife Theodora was a charming person of good family and irreproachable morals. Moreover, she adored her husband, to whom she had given three sons. It was difficult to find a pretext for divorcing such a woman, and she was not likely to be complacent. The subtle Emperor then called politics to his aid. He explained to his Council the grave dangers that were threatening the Empire, the preparations the Latins were making to retake Constantinople, the notorious inferiority of the Byzantine forces compared with those of their adversaries. Already the Bulgarians were on the verge of joining the coalition, and further, it was greatly to be feared that Manfred of Sicily would also associate himself with the league in order to avenge his sister. So there was good reason for drawing closer to him through a marriage; in this way he could be detached from the enemy side, and the Greek Emperor would be remarkably strengthened by the support of this powerful Prince who could not but be the friend and ally of his sister's husband. And Michael concluded that for the good of the State he should divorce his wife and marry Anna.

It is certain that at this time the Pope, Venice, and the Prince of Achaia, were forming an alliance against the Greek Empire, that Manfred, renewing the great Eastern ambitions of the Hohenstaufens, was frankly hostile to the Byzantines, and that policy as well as love dictated to Michael

Paleologus a marriage that would have allied him with the son of Frederick II. Besides, ever since 1259, he had realized the advantage of such an alliance and had tried in vain to get into the good graces of the King of Sicily. He failed this time, too, but for different reasons. Theodora, his legitimate wife, put up a desperate opposition to the Emperor's plans. She interested the Patriarch in her cause, and he, indignant, threatened Michael with the lightning of the Church if he should persist in his plans, and "tore his fine pretexts apart like spider webs." Faced with excommunication, the Basileus gave in; he realized that he was up against something stronger than himself. In any case, since he really did see the value of conciliating Manfred, he made use of the Princess Anna to do so, but not in the way he had planned. He gave her her liberty and sent her back to her brother.

In 1262, a Byzantine general, the Caesar Alexius Stratopoulos who had retaken Constantinople from the Latins, had fallen into the hands of the Despot of Epirus, father-in-law and ally of the Sicilian King, and had been sent to the latter in the West as a trophy. In 1262, or 1263, it was proposed to release him in exchange for the Princess Anna. Michael agreed with alacrity, to please Manfred. But it did not lead, as he hoped, to an alliance with the Hohenstaufens.

In this way, after an absence of almost twenty years, Anna Constance returned to her native country, only to be involved in further disasters. In 1266, Urban IV sent Charles of Anjou against Manfred, and soon the catastrophe of Benevento put the Empress and all her family at the mercy of the victor. But whereas Manfred's wife and sons were thrown into prison, Anna had the good luck to seem less dangerous. They let her go free, and in 1269, she retired to Spain, to live with her niece Constance, wife of the Infante Don Pedro of Aragon. It was there that she finally found peace after her many adventures. She finished her life piously, as a religious in the convent of St. Barbara in Valencia; and as a token of her gratitude to this austere community, she left to them in her will a miraculous picture of their patron saint, and a remarkable relic, a fragment of the rock from which sprang the water used to baptize St. Barbara. This seems to have been all that she brought back from her long sojourn in the East.

However, in that far-off time when she married John Vatatzes, the Greek Emperor had assigned her a dowry; he had given her three towns and numerous castles, with a revenue amounting to three thousand bezants. She bequeathed all her rights over these domains in the East to her nephew Don Jaime II, who was later to avail himself of them. As for her, she died in obscurity in the year 1313, at more than eighty years of age.

In the fate of these Western Princesses, Bertha of Sulzbach, Agnes of France, Constance of Hohenstaufen, who went in the twelfth and thirteenth centuries to reign over the Byzantine Empire, there is something melancholy that imparts a pathetic charm to their indistinct, their almost obliterated figures. Banished far from their native land by the game of politics, almost always remaining foreigners in the new world to which fate had consigned them, these exiled Princesses sadly proved the impossibility of a mutual understanding between the Greeks and the Latins of their day. Though they were involved in important historical events, it was chiefly as victims. But the fact that their lives were linked with those of the Comneni, Manuel and Andronicus, the Emperors of Nicea, and the last of the Hohenstaufens, is enough to make them interesting still. They witnessed great things, even if they but rarely controlled them. The splendors of twelfth century Byzantium, the tragedies of palace revolutions, the Fourth Crusade and the founding of a Latin Empire in Constantinople, the Eastern policy of Frederick II light up with a magical radiance the wavering outlines of these forgotten Princesses. But more than anything else, their history shows what a gulf the Crusades succeeded in creating between the East and the West. Never, perhaps, did these two worlds make more frequent and honest efforts to impress each other, to understand each other, to unite. And never, despite their reciprocal good will, did they fail so utterly in their attempts.

❧❧❧ XIII ❧❧❧

YOLANDA OF
MONTFERRAT

Yolanda of Montferrat was a descendant of the Marquis Boniface, and she was eleven years old at the time of her marriage to Andronicus II, in 1284. This would seem to have been a somewhat mediocre alliance for a Basileus. But a Basileus was no longer the brilliant match of earlier times. What with the Pope's disapproval of any union with a schismatic, and the undeniable decadence of the Greek monarchy, a Byzantine marriage seemed to the Latins of that day infinitely less of an honor than it had to their fathers. And in this particular case there was an added drawback. Andronicus was a widower and had two sons from his first marriage, the elder of whom, Michael, was already designated to the throne. So the children of a second marriage would, in accordance with Byzantine custom, be relegated to the status of private individuals. Under these circumstances, most of the great European rulers would have hesitated to marry a daughter to the Emperor. Aware of this, the court of Constantinople restrained its ambitions and made the best of Yolanda. Moreover, this alliance, modest though it was, offered an important advantage. The young wife had rights over the Latin Kingdom of Thessalonica, and her marriage, in transferring these rights to the imperial family, established legitimate grounds for opposing the claims of the West. For similar motives, Andronicus II tried, a little later, to marry his eldest son, Michael, to Catherine of Courtenay, heiress of the Latin Emperors of Constantinople. In this manner, by gathering into their own hands the various rights that could have been invoked against them by their rivals, the Paleologi strove to secure their power.

The little Italian girl, who took the Greek name of Irene on becoming Empress, was pretty, elegant, and slender. She fascinated Andronicus, who was barely twenty-three, and very soon he loved her to distraction. She gave him three sons one after the other, John, Theodore, Demetrius, and a daughter, Simone, not counting several children who died at birth. And the older they grew the more acutely she suffered over her inability to secure for them the exalted position of which she dreamed. Very proud of her race, very ambitious for herself and her family, Irene could not admit that her sons should be sacrificed for the children of the first marriage, whom she detested. Imbued with Western ideas, she demanded the equal division of the imperial inheritance between all the Emperor's descendants; or at least, that her own sons should be compensated with vast endowments. And being of a violent and imperious temper, as greedy for power as she was for money, she exercised no caution in her methods of solicitation. She was aware of her husband's great passion for her, and she exploited it in the hope of bringing Andronicus round to her point of view. To obtain the succession for her sons, or at least a share of the inheritance,

she pestered him day and night with complaints, recrimina-
tions, objections; and as the Emperor would not give in, the
young woman made use of all the means at her disposal;
now tears, declaring that if he refused her she could not live,
now coquetry, playing an artful game of "bedroom politics."
The Emperor finally wearied of these perpetual scenes; his
great love lessened, and he ended by partially forsaking this
wife who was too tiresome by far.

Furious, Irene then left the court and fled to Thessalonica,
and from there she vociferated against the Emperor, telling
all comers, "without respect for God, without fear of men,"
the details of her married life, in terms, says a chronicler,
"that would have caused the most shameless courtesan to
blush." She recounted these trumped up tales to the women
who surrounded her, to the nuns who came to visit her, and
she wrote them in letters to her son-in-law, insulting and ridiculing poor Andronicus, who was too dumbfounded to protest. "Nothing," sententiously remarks a contemporary, "is
so excitable and so prone to calumny as the imagination of a
woman." With her tongue "more clangorous than a bell,"
she disturbed everything, confused everything, "and God
Himself and all the waters of the sea," writes Pachymerus,
"would not have sufficed to wash clean of her insults and her
calumnies the unfortunate man against whom she had vent
her anger." The Emperor was understandably annoyed by
all these stories. But he was a good-natured man, so he did
all he could think of to appease his wife's fury. He loaded her
with money, he offered her an exaggerated share in the governing power, he strove, in the hope of hushing up the scandal, to satisfy her smallest whims. But she stubbornly refused to be placated, harshly demanding that first of all the
future of her sons should be assured. All the same, knowing
very well that she would not have the last word on this sub-

ject, she worked on her own to establish them brilliantly, through arranging advantageous marriages for them. This became a source of new difficulties in the imperial family.

Andronicus had a minister, Nicephorus Choumnus, of whom he was very fond. He thought of marrying his son John to the daughter of his favorite, who was, moreover, extremely wealthy. The idea that one of her sons should take a wife who was not of a princely family infuriated Irene. She had very different dreams for his future; she was planning to unite him with the widow of the Prince of Achaia, Isabella de Villehardouin, which would have the advantage of bringing the whole of Latin Morea back into the hands of the Paleologi; and she thought of establishing for him, with Aetolia, Arcanania, and Epirus, an independent State. There were heated disputes over this between the imperial pair. The Basileus declared that he was the father, and that his authority in the home should supersede that of the mother. Irene protested, insisted. Finally, however, Andronicus lost his temper. In 1304 he married John as he wished and gave him Thessalonica to live in and govern as a sort of Viceroy. The young man did not enjoy it for long: he died four years later, leaving no children.

For her second son, Theodore, Irene took no less trouble. She dreamed of marrying him to the daughter of the French Duke of Athens, and of giving him the means of forming a Principality for himself. The project failed. But just at the right moment another opportunity came along. In 1305, the Empress's brother, John of Montferrat, died, bequeathing his States to his sister. Irene transferred the rights to her son, who was thus enabled to fulfill his mother's wish and attain the status of a sovereign Prince. In his Piedmontese Marquisate, Theodore quickly transformed himself. He became completely Italian. He married an Italian girl, the daughter of the Genoese Spinola, he adopted the religion of the Latins, their habits, their dress. He cut off his Byzantine beard and kept his face clean-shaven like the Westerners. Thus meta-morphosed, he reappeared from time to time in Constanti-nople, usually when he had debts that he knew his parents would be weak enough to pay. And occasionally, remember-ing that he was the son of the Basileus, he advanced some claims to the imperial succession. But he was so fully expatri-ated that his accession would have caused a scandal in the East, and Andronicus rightly considered such a hope com-pletely unrealizable.

Irene was equally solicitous for her third son, Demetrius, and even for her son-in-law, the Kral of Serbia, Stephen Mi-loutin. About 1298, a purely political marriage had united this sovereign with the young Princess Simone. This Slav, who had already been married three times, had repudiated his first two wives one after the other, and was now beginning to get tired of the third. The Byzantine court decided then that it would be profitable to annex him by a marriage with a Greek, and Andronicus proposed his sister Eudocia, the re-cent widow of a "Prince of the Lazes"—which was the dis-dainful title given by the Byzantines to the Emperors of Trebizond. The Serbian could not have been more delighted. The canonists had in fact shown him that as long as his first wife was living his other marriages had been invalid, and that, his first wife having just died, most conveniently, he was now absolutely free. It was Eudocia who would not hear of it. She was, it seems, an inconsolable widow, and, besides, she was a trifle suspicious of the Slav's versatility. Failing her, Simone was chosen, though she was only six years old. The betrothal was celebrated, and the child, following the usual custom, was sent to Serbia, there to be brought up and to await her marriage in the house of her future husband. But this passionate Slav, who had forty odd years and deplorable morals (he had successively had relations with two of his sisters-in-law) lacked the patience to wait as long as he should have, with the result that his young wife lost all hope of ever becoming a mother.

Irene, however, held no grudge against her son-in-law. She loaded him with gifts and silver, and was pleased to receive him at Thessalonica, her usual place of residence. Since her maternal pride craved above all that her daughter should cut a fine figure in the world, and have the air of an Empress, she saw to it that the Byzantine chancellery accorded the Serbian Prince the right to wear a cap studded with precious stones, almost the same as that worn by the Basileus. Every year she sent him one of these badges of honor, each a little more magnificently ornamented than the last. Then there were gifts of gorgeous raiment for him and for her daughter. She emptied the imperial coffers for this foreign Prince. At this time she still hoped that Simone would have children, who might one day reign over Byzantium. When she was obliged to renounce this hope, her perpetually active imagination immediately started forming other plans. As the Serb could not have a son, she persuaded him to adopt one of his brothers-in-law as his heir. First, she sent him Demetrius, armed with plenty of money to facilitate his welcome. But the young man did not feel at home among the Slavs, and he returned to Constantinople. Then Theodore was sent. But he, even more than his brother, felt out of his element, and he went back to Italy.

For that matter, Simone herself was not very happy in her wild Kingdom. True, her husband adored her, but with a barbarian's love, violent, jealous, suspicious. Whenever she would leave to spend a few weeks in Constantinople, he would be in a state of constant anxiety, and no sooner would

she depart, than he would demand that she be sent back to
him without delay. And it was not without real terror that the
young woman would return, knowing him to be uncontrol-
lable in his moments of anger, and capable of anything. Indeed, on one occasion her fear was too much for her, and,
instead of leaving, she fled to a cloister, to the great embarrassment of those whose duty it was to take her home. They
had to reason with her, and compel her, almost brutally, to
relinquish her nun's habit and to go back to her terrible
spouse. She was delivered from him only by his death, after
which she hastened back to live in Constantinople, where we
will rediscover her a little later.

The last of Irene's children, Demetrius, was not much happier than his brothers and his sister. His mother had succeeded in obtaining for him the governorship of Thessalonica, with the title of Despot. There he was to be involved in
all the strife that was soon to trouble the imperial family. As
a good son, he sided with his father against his nephew,
Prince Andronicus, whose victory could have cost him dear.
Accused of *lèse-majesté*, he escaped the death penalty only
thanks to the affection of his sister Simone, who intervened
on his behalf with the judges. From then on he disappears
from history.

One sees with what intrigues Irene's ambitious and restless spirit kept the court of Andronicus II constantly seething. The Emperor, amiable, educated, and a fine orator, was,
despite his proud bearing, incorrigibly weak, and he let
everything go to pieces. Moreover, he was surrounded by the
most incredible dissension, which was fostered and aug-
mented by the children of his first marriage.

The youngest was named Constantine, and he held the

title of Despot. His first wife, whom he lost after a short time, was a daughter of the Protovestiarius George Muzalonicus. Left a widower without children, he took for mistress a chambermaid, by whom he had a son. But he left her before very long. Then, at Thessalonica, where he had been appointed Governor, he met a charming woman named Eudocia. Beautiful, elegant, well read, she was, say her contemporaries, "another Theano, another Hypatia." Unfortunately for the Despot, she was married to Constantine Paleologus, and she had every intention of remaining virtuous. Her resistance merely served to inflame the Prince's passion. To please her, he parted with his son, whose presence annoyed her, and sent the boy back to his mother. Wasted effort: Eudocia did not give way. At last, however, she became a widow; whereupon Constantine married her, and thereafter lived only for her. As for his bastard son, old Andronicus happened to take a liking to the abandoned child, whom he removed from the mother's care, brought up, initiated into the management of public affairs, and adored. Although the young man was utterly mediocre, without intelligence, without education—not even a good soldier; although, in the vigorous words of Cantacuzene, he was "good for nothing," the Emperor could not get along without him. He called him into the Council at every opportunity—apparently with the intention of giving him governmental experience, and, it seems, actually entertained the idea of making him Emperor. This was to have quite serious consequences.

The eldest son of the first marriage, Michael, had early been designated to the throne by Andronicus II. From his union with an Armenian Princess several children were born, of whom the eldest was named Andronicus, like his grandfather. This Andronicus the young, as he was called, was an active, restless man, fond of hunting, racing, and revelry. He found it hard to endure the sedentary life of the Byzantine court, and was bored to death by its complicated ceremonial. Carefree and frivolous, he thought of nothing but dogs, horses, and women. His favor could best be won by a gift of a fine hunting dog or some valuable bird. But more than anything else, he loved pleasure, reckless spending, and amorous adventures, being a great libertine and almost wholly without scruples. In spite of all that, he had at first been the favorite of his grandfather, who preferred him to all his other children and grandchildren, and had sacrificed them all to him. The result of this excessive affection had been that the child, very badly brought up by the Emperor, had become the young man we know, whose ways now frequently provoked and perturbed the Basileus. "If ever that boy comes to anything," he said to one of his cronies, "may I be stoned, and after I am dead, let them disinter my corpse and throw it into the flames."

While he was deeply humiliated by his grandfather's reproaches, Andronicus the young did not mend his ways. He made out bills of exchange in the name of the Basileus, which the Genoese bankers of Galata took upon themselves to accept; he demanded money and endowments; above all, he scandalized the capital by exploits worthy, in some cases, of a Cesare Borgia at his worst. The Prince had a mistress. Aware that she deceived him, he posted armed men along the road to waylay his rival. But the man who was murdered by the assassins was his own brother Manuel, who was walking by chance along the street of the ambush. Andronicus's father, Michael, suffered so mortal an anguish over this horrible crime that he died; and his grandfather, Andronicus II, was strangely troubled by it. The fact was that Andronicus the young would stop at nothing when a woman was at stake. Neither kinship nor religion prevented him from casting a covetous eye on his young aunt, Simone, who had entered a convent after the death of her Serbian husband, and from trying to seduce her. Neither friendship nor policy stopped him when he succumbed to the charms of the wife of Styrgiannes, his partisan. But it is only fair to add that, with all his faults and vices, he was intelligent, that he possessed the qualities of a statesman, and that he had great ambition, all of which made him very popular. So much so, that he was potentially dangerous to the public peace, and capable of shaking the Empire to its foundations—which, in fact, he did.

Meanwhile, the old Emperor, instead of making Andronicus heir to the throne after the death of his father, punished him by passing him over in favor of his uncle Constantine, the Despot, and reducing him to the status of a private individual, to his great dissatisfaction. Later, when circumstances forced the reluctant Basileus to give his grandson a share in the government, he spared his young associate no humiliation. When he came to the Palace, the old Emperor scarcely looked at him, and would go for months without speaking to him, except to say: "Go away, and hereafter remain at home." In Council, the Emperor would invite all the other dignitaries to be seated, but would leave him standing. And so, little by little, between the grandfather and his grandson the chasm was formed from which was to emerge the civil war that ended in 1328 with the fall of Andronicus II.

The Empress did not see the young Emperor's triumph, which would have been singularly painful to her. Since her quarrel with her husband, she lived for the most part in Thessalonica, and, as she was frequently bored, she amused herself by going to stay at one country residence after another. In the course of one of these moves she fell ill, and shortly thereafter, in Drama, died of a fever. This was in 1317. Her body was brought back to Constantinople and entombed in the church of the monastery of the Pantocrator. Toward the end of her life some of the tenderness she felt for her husband during the early days of their marriage seems to have revived; at any rate, it was to him that she willed her entire enormous fortune. Andronicus divided it into two equal parts; one he gave up, as a good father, to her children, and the other he piously used to repair St. Sophia.

It was for her children's welfare that Yolanda of Montferrat had striven throughout her life; and this is what gives to this Latin Princess, transformed by maternal love into a politician and a true Byzantine, her distinctive quality. We can believe that this Princess, who had fought so fiercely for her own, who had struggled so hard to establish them, doing all in her power to overthrow their half brother Michael who stood between them and the throne, would have worked no less valiantly in their interests when, after Michael's death, the final crisis arose that locked the old and the young Andronicus in combat. And perhaps, energetic as she was, she would have saved the throne for the old Emperor and realized her ambitious dream for her posterity. Death did not allow this to happen. After she had gone, her children lost interest in aspirations that seemed to them either unattainable or unfounded. But at all events, Yolanda of Montferrat had, for the first time, shown Byzantium a Western Princess interested in action and in making a place for herself in the new world to which her marriage had transplanted her. She would have liked to fill an important role, to take her part in the sovereignty, and to some extent she had succeeded. Her example was not to be wasted.

❦❦❦ XIV ❦❦❦

ANNA OF SAVOY

At the beginning of the year 1325, the young Emperor
Andronicus, to whose coronation in St. Sophia his
grandfather had reluctantly resigned himself, was looking
for a wife. He was twenty-eight years old and a widower. A
few months earlier, his first wife, Irene of Brunswick, had
died, leaving no children, and it was vital to the interests of
the dynasty that he should remarry without delay. Great efforts were made, therefore, to console him, to make him see
the necessity of a second marriage, and to find him a bride.
The Byzantine court finally chose a daughter of the Count of
Savoy, Amadeus V. She was an orphan, and lived with her
brother. An ambassador was sent to Italy to ask for her hand,
and although, at this time, a proposal had been made on the
part of a great Western sovereign (the Byzantines report
that it was the King of France), the Count of Savoy decided
in favor of the Emperor Andronicus. Highly honored by this
alliance, the Italian Prince wanted to do things very well. He

equipped the future Empress sumptuously for her trip to
Constantinople, and although he was her senior and her sovereign lord, he displayed the highest regard for her from the
day she was affianced to the Basileus. This was infinitely flattering to Greek pride; the writers of the day noted with delight that not only the barbarians, but the Italians and other
heads of State still considered the Roman Empire greater and
more illustrious than all the other powers.

In February 1326, the young fiancée disembarked at Constantinople with a large and brilliant retinue of women,
knights, and grooms. "Never until now," writes Cantacuzene, "have Empresses arriving in Romania from abroad displayed so much magnificence." But whether as a result of the
sea voyage or of the change in climate, the young woman had
no sooner arrived than she fell ill. The wedding celebrations
had then to be postponed until the month of October. They
were suitably splendid. According to custom, the Basileus
placed the imperial diadem on his wife's head, and, again
according to custom, the Empress changed her first name.
From then on she was called Anna instead of Jeanne, and under this name she was to play a considerable role in the history of Byzantium, and to have a baneful influence on the
destiny of her new country.

Anna of Savoy is a personage very difficult to judge, or
even to know. What information we have about her comes
almost entirely from her political adversaries, from men
who detested her both as the woman who opposed their ideas
and stood in the way of their ambitions, and as the foreigner
who, on the throne of Byzantium, remained passionately
Latin.

Indeed, it seems that Anna of Savoy was less Hellenized

than any other of the Princesses from the West, in an era
when this factor was of prime importance. She surrounded
herself with a little court composed exclusively of Italians,
and she confided in one of her own countrywomen, Isabella.
Even the Greeks admit that Isabella was a highly intelligent
woman, very well educated, and endowed with all the qualities that make for success in Royal circles; and, indeed, she
exercised an all-powerful influence over the Empress. This
Isabella had two sons, who were also great favorites, not only
of the Basilissa, but of the Emperor himself, to whom one,
Artaud, was particularly pleasing on account of his splendid
courage. Still other Italians flocked to the imperial city, and
were invariably well received and kindly treated by the sovereigns. "The young Emperor always had some men from
Savoy staying with him," says John Cantacuzene, not without resentment. They were such a success that under their
influence even the customs began to change. To the usual
pleasures of the court were added diversions dear to the Latins, such as jousts and tourneys, which these foreigners made
fashionable, and these exercises were so popular that the
most noble among the Greeks wanted to try their skill at
them, and the Emperor, in particular, acquired a skill in
them comparable to that of the finest knights of Burgundy,
France, and Germany. Of course, Byzantine nationalism was
very shocked by these novelties, and even more so by the high
positions given to these people from abroad when so many
persons thoroughly capable of holding public office were to
be found in the country itself.

The religious question was another cause of prejudice
against Anna. When she ascended the throne, the Empress
was converted to the Orthodox faith; but the sincerity of her
conversion was strongly doubted. She was suspected of still
adhering to the Roman dogma, of having a great respect for

the Pope, and she was believed capable of returning to Rome
one day and of secretly preparing for the submission of the
Greek Church to the Papacy. Moreover, she was on friendly
terms with the Genoese established at Galata. From this it
was easy to conclude that Anna heartily disliked the Greeks
—an inference no one failed to draw. And the Greeks rendered her hate for hate. To these reservations, which explain
in part the animosities that Anna encountered, it must be
added that she seems to have been a woman of very mediocre
caliber. Neither well educated nor intelligent, she was incon-
sistent, and incapable of any serious thought or of making
mature decisions. And too, she was violent, impulsive, jealous, and spiteful. Superstitious, she believed in the soothsayers, but what was worse, her weak and credulous mind rendered her accessible to every influence, amenable to anyone
who knew how to flatter her. And all her life she was surrounded by a *camarilla* of favorites and women. "At that time,
the center of power was in the Gynaeceum," says a contemporary. The Empress, understanding nothing of State affairs,
was guided only by her passions. There were people for
whom she nourished savage hatreds, and others for whom
she had inexplicable weaknesses. Very hardhearted, once her
anger had been aroused, she was capable of the most atro-
cious cruelties, the most dastardly murders. She took, says
Gregoras, "an extreme delight, an unspeakable pleasure, in
cruelties and blood; her heart rejoiced in them." When she
was enraged, no one found favor in her eyes; even her confessor was not immune from her attacks. At such times she
would utter the vilest insults, the most terrible threats. Then,
all at once she would grow calm, and, docile again, she would
blindly follow the lead of anyone who knew how to manage
her. But she was fundamentally unforgiving. Against those
who had once displeased her, she harbored a lasting resent-

ment that was increased by her sense of her own mediocrity and by the natural jealousy that all superiority aroused in her.

It must be said, in Anna of Savoy's defense, that she felt out of her element in this foreign world which she did not understand and with which she was not intelligent enough to integrate herself. She preferred to live in a perpetual dream, deluding herself about the significance of events and of the significance of her own actions. "She behaved," says a contemporary, "as if the misfortunes that threatened were taking place beyond the pillars of Hercules." Even her enemies, while drawing attention to her "jealous and evil disposition" and asserting that "because of it she became the ruin of the Empire," grant her some extenuating circumstances. Gregoras observes that she had been brought up in a completely different environment, that she was a foreigner, that she was, above all, a woman, and a passionate woman without much intelligence, "incapable," he says, "of distinguishing good from evil"; and he puts the blame for what happened less on her than on the Patriarch and the many other great personages who unprotestingly "obeyed this demented authority as if they were slaves."

Anna of Savoy's disagreeable character did not, however, do much harm during the lifetime of Andronicus III, of whom she was very fond, because while her husband lived, she took little or no part in the government. But when he died, in June 1341, things changed abruptly. The throne devolved on two minor children, John, who was nine, and Michael, who was four; and during their minority their mother was, by the explicit order of the late Basileus, to be Regent. Now, the circumstances under which Anna of Savoy assumed the power were well calculated to trouble a mother anxious about the future of her sons, and to alarm a woman who was, herself, very attracted by the idea of supreme power.

Around the throne a thousand and one different ambitions were at work. In the first rank of court personages at that time, was the Grand Domestic, John Cantacuzene. He had been the dearest and most intimate friend of Andronicus III. In the past he had done more than anyone to secure the crown for the young Emperor, and he had been rewarded by the unshakable trust of his master. During the whole reign he had been the Emperor's most devoted adviser, and the confidant of all his thoughts. "Such," he said later, "was the union of our two souls that it surpassed even the friendship of an Orestes and a Pylades." Anna of Savoy declared that the Emperor loved his favorite more than his wife and his children, more than anyone in the world.

Even during his lifetime, the Emperor had delegated a lot of authority to Cantacuzene, who was later to say of himself: "There was nothing imperial in the outward appearance, or in the apparel of the Grand Domestic; but in fact, there was scarcely any difference between him and the Basileus." Like the sovereign, he signed his name in red ink, and his orders were obeyed as punctiliously as those of Andronicus. Like the sovereign, he governed all public affairs, and so highly was he favored that in the field he and the Emperor occupied the same tent, and often the same bed, a privilege that etiquette forbade even to the imperial children. Andronicus shared everything with him, his table, his clothing, his boots, and rejoiced to see him behaving "imperially." He would even have liked to proclaim this intimacy publicly, by sharing the throne with Cantacuzene. In any case, he trusted him absolutely. During an illness that he suffered in 1329, he designated Cantacuzene as guardian of the throne in the event of his death, and solemnly confided his wife and his subjects to his favorite's care. Likewise, on his deathbed, his last words had been a recommendation to the Empress always to keep in agreement with Cantacuzene. "My end is approaching," he told her, "so take good care, when I have gone, not to let yourself be induced by lies and false arguments on the part of certain people to separate yourself from such a man in order to follow other counsels. If that should happen, the result could only be ruin for you, for your children, and for the Empire itself."

In these reports that we owe principally to Cantacuzene himself, there is probably an element of exaggeration; it was obviously in the interest of the Grand Domestic to brag about the favor with which his late master had honored him and to exaggerate the evidence. Nonetheless, his eminent qualities justified this favor. The old Emperor, Andronicus II, had already noticed how quick Cantacuzene was to find the right solution when a decision had to be made, how clever in presenting it, and how active in executing it: "If I have to die without leaving heirs," he would say, "that is the man I would advise the Romans to put at their head." Very intelligent, immensely able, the Grand Domestic was truly a superior man. Gregoras, who has no liking for him, declares that he could have been "a very great Emperor, capable of bringing the Empire to unparalleled prosperity." Unfortunately, he had great failings. He was inordinately ambitious, completely unscrupulous, and therefore extremely disquieting. Despite his affectation of modesty, he had been preparing his way for a long time. On the strength of his credit with the Emperor, he strove to ingratiate himself with the Empress, and thanks to his mother, Theodora Paleologus, an altogether remarkable woman, he came to exert a real influence over Anna. At the same time he endeavored to keep away from her all those who might have thwarted his designs, while he himself displayed deep devotion to her at all times, confident that in this way he could dominate her completely. And in point of fact, Anna declared that she loved him as much as, and even more than, her own brother, and on the surface a perfect understanding reigned between the wife of Andronicus III and his favorite.

So, in the confusion that followed after the death of the Prince, it was to Cantacuzene that the mourning Empress unhesitatingly confided her sons and the power. And the Grand Domestic was to be seen acting as a real ruler. While Anna, plunged in grief, remained in the monastery where her husband lay dead, Cantacuzene resolutely installed himself in the Palace with the imperial children and took the necessary measures to prevent a revolution. He corresponded with the provincial Governors, and with the financiers, sending out more than five hundred letters a day, "and thus he maintained order and obedience throughout the Empire, so well that it seemed as if no change had taken place and that the Basileus continued to live and rule." It is said that he conceived vast projects. He thought of reorganizing the army, of putting the finances in order, of inaugurating a vigorous foreign policy against the enemies of the Empire, of restoring the ancient splendor of the monarchy. Before this vigorous assumption of power, all bowed down, saluting in the Regent of today the Emperor of tomorrow. It is understandable that such a personage and such an attitude should have aroused in the Empress Anna justifiable misgivings, which were assiduously fostered by the enemies of the Grand Domestic. The foremost of these was the Patriarch John, an ambitious prelate, who, according to Gregoras, had no more of the priest about him than the pastoral crook and the habit. He had always aspired to control the State, affirming the necessity of uniting the Church and the Empire, the latter, of course, to be under the sway of the former. He was shortly to accept the privilege of ornamenting his Patriarchal tiara with silk and gold, and of signing his letters and decrees with red ink, and even to contemplate wearing purple boots, like the Emperor. For the moment, however, he aspired to share the Regency, and as he flattered the Empress, he soon obtained a great and unfortunate ascendancy over her.

The Parakoimomenos Alexius Apokaukos played a similar role. Having no loyalties, but supple, adroit, and scheming, this personage had risen very quickly to the highest positions, largely thanks to the support of Cantacuzene, who laughingly called him "my doctor," having been extricated by him from a number of awkward situations; and he had also become enormously wealthy. Extremely clever in taking advantage of circumstances, he was intelligent, active, and naturally eloquent. "If he had applied these outstanding qualities to the cause of justice and truth," says Gregoras, "he would have been the glory of the Roman Empire." But intoxicated by his rapid rise to fortune, he thought he was a law unto himself. One after another he had served and betrayed all sides, and always to his own advantage. Now he dreamed of governing the Empire, of disposing of the Crown, perhaps of sitting on the throne of the Caesars himself. But he did not allow ambition to prevail over prudence. At the gates of the capital, beside the sea, he had a castle built, well provided with water and stocked with food and money. He took refuge there when he felt himself in danger, and from this impregnable citadel he braved all his enemies. While flattering Cantacuzene, he detested him as a rival, and did not hesitate to ally himself with the Patriarch against him.

Many other persons were hostile to the Grand Domestic, and especially the Empress's Italian favorites, who, at the instigation of Apokaukos, set their mistress against Cantacuzene. These conspiring influences gained an easy hold on the Empress's weak, vacillating mind, and quickly destroyed the concord established between her and her Counselor.

In the beginning, loyal to the wishes of Andronicus, she had, as she said with her usual exaggeration, been convinced that her husband's ghost had returned to her in the person of the Grand Domestic. "Certain as I was that the Basileus was dead," she declared, "when you paid me a visit, it seemed to me that it was he who entered my apartments, just as he used to, and when you spoke to me, it was he whom I thought to hear." She was soon made to change her ideas. Playing on her "feminine credulity," Apokaukos and the Patriarch vied with each other in giving her proofs of the Grand Domestic's ambitions and demonstrating the danger in which she and her sons stood of losing their power and even their lives. "To-morrow," they told her, "he will kill you all and proclaim himself Emperor." They succeeded so well that the horrified Anna cut short the Novena that she had begun in the monastery where her husband was buried, and, three days later, thought it wiser to seek a more secure refuge in the Palace.

Then the intriguers brought all their secret forces into play, to induce her to take the reins of government out of the hands of Cantacuzene. It was explained to her that she had no need of him, that with the co-operation of the Patriarch she herself could govern the Empire admirably. The Regent, flattered, listened willingly to all these suggestions. At the bottom of her heart, Anna had always disliked the Grand Domestic, whose superiority she sensed. Also, she was extremely jealous of his wife, Irene Asan, a quite remarkable person who, says a contemporary, "triumphed over all other women by the power of her mind and the happy harmony of her disposition." The second-rate soul of the Empress suffered by comparison, and many people of the time thought, not without reason, that the secret envy and spite that this aroused in Anna was the primary cause of a rupture that was to unleash a civil war and precipitate the decline of the monarchy.

Upon discovering the Regent's true feelings, the adversaries of Cantacuzene grew more daring. There were some lively scenes in the Imperial Council, and the Grand Domestic was openly insulted. One of the functionaries of the Palace audaciously took the floor, and declared that, if the lowest of the dignitaries had something worth saying, he had the right to speak before the highest. "What does this mean!" exclaimed the friends of Cantacuzene. "Why! If the first comer has the right to express his opinion and impose it on those who know better the Roman Empire will be transformed into a democracy!" They almost came to blows. What was more serious, neither the Empress nor the Patriarch, who presided, intervened to stop or to censure an insolence that was obviously aimed at the Grand Domestic. The latter understood, and tendered his resignation.

But then the Basilissa and the Patriarch, afraid of the consequences of such a decision, did all they could to calm down Cantacuzene; and on both sides the adversaries pledged themselves by the most solemn oaths not to conspire against one another. In spite of that, suspicion remained. "I am convinced," said the Grand Domestic, "that the Empress meant what she said. But I am worried because I know her feminine weakness, and how, through cowardice, she lets her mind be easily changed, and I am very much afraid that, when I have to go to fight the barbarians, the sycophants who stay behind will lead her to change it." On the other hand, manifestations

in favor of Cantacuzene were increasing. The rumored resignation of the Grand Domestic brought demonstrations of loyalty from the soldiers for the chief they worshipped. They
even invaded the Palace courtyard to acclaim their favorite
and to hurl invectives at the Patriarch. The Empress was terrified, and, to pacify her and bring his tumultuous partisans
to reason, the Minister had to go out and speak to them himself. "As soon as he appeared," relates Gregoras, "the disturbances subsided, the waves abated, the tempest changed
to a calm." So much popularity with the troops did nothing to
diminish Anna's fears.

The break between her and Cantacuzene was inevitable.
Apokaukos, whose influence at the court was growing, multi-
plied his intrigues. "Like a serpent," says Cantacuzene, "he
hissed into the ear of the Empress and turned her from the
straight path." No means were too low for him; flattery, bribery, lies, he made use of them all. The Patriarch gave him his
cues; day and night he was at the Palace stirring up the Empress against the Grand Domestic, praising the devotion and
loyalty of Apokaukos. By judicious liberality, he won the
intimates of the Regent over to his side, and in this way, says
Gregoras, "he ruled the Empress *as if she were a slave*, and
also the Patriarch, who was not so much taken in by his flattery as frightened by his energy." The absence of Cantacuzene, who was making war in Thrace, facilitated these intrigues. Each of the two associates did his best for their
common goal. The prelate, "as if he held in his hands the
keys of the Kingdom of Heaven," promised Paradise to anyone who, by poison, sorcery, or incantation, should rid the
Empire of Cantacuzene. As for Apokaukos, certain of success, he now aspired to an even higher destiny. He was thinking of kidnapping the young Emperor, spiriting him away

to his fortress, and marrying him off to one of his daughters; and of forcing the Empress to give up to him, Apokaukos, and his relatives and friends, the highest Offices of State and the administration of the whole Empire. And Cantacuzene was notified, in the name of the Basileus, that he must resign from the government, disband his troops, and retire to Didymoticus in a state of semi-captivity.

For a long time the mother of Cantacuzene had been extremely anxious on her son's account. In common with most people of her time, this woman, in other ways so intelligent, was superstitious; she believed in omens. And it happened that she had seen one that was very disquieting. One evening, in accordance with the custom of the great Byzantine nobles, she had received until a very late hour persons who wished to speak with her or to pay their respects. Afterward she went to the top of a tower that rose high above her palace to watch the moon come up over the horizon. She was standing there, lost in thought, when all at once she saw at the foot of the tower an armed man on horseback, who was measuring the height of the castle keep with his lance. Terrified, she called her servants, and ordered them to go and find out what this mysterious horseman wanted. But they found no one; all the doors through which a horseman could enter the palace were shut. Profoundly impressed by this apparition, which seemed to her an alarming omen, the noble lady, says Gregoras, "filled with sadness, was on the point of tears."

She was right. Her son's fall from favor was near. By order of the Emperor, Cantacuzene received letters dismissing him from office. At the same time, his goods were confiscated and divided among his enemies, and all those who had insulted him were rewarded. His friends, brought down with him in his fall, saw their houses pillaged. His mother was arrested and thrown into one of the Palace prisons. There was only one thing left for him to do—offer armed resistance and proclaim himself Emperor. Before taking this step he wanted once more to recall to the Regent's memory the late Emperor's will, and the solemn oaths by which she had bound herself with regard to him, Cantacuzene. She answered him only with insults. And he made his decision.

At Didymoticus, on the feast day of St. Demetrius (the 8th of October 1341), he placed the imperial crown on his own head. To emphasize, however, the fact that he was not a rebel, he decreed that in the acclamations saluting his name and that of his wife, the first place should be given to the Empress Anna and her son John, and during the religious ceremony he also had mention made of the Basileus and his mother, and even of the Patriarch John. Further, he declared that his sole aim was to defend and consolidate the throne of the young sovereign confided to his loyal care by Andronicus III; and three days after his coronation, he discarded the purple to attire himself in white, "as is the custom when in mourning for an Emperor." By this he meant to demonstrate his loyalty to the memory of a Prince whom he had loved "as a brother," and he continued to wear mourning for five years, until the day when he entered Constantinople as Ruler. He reminded the Empress once again of her husband's last wishes, and told her how dangerous it was for her to ally herself with advisors who "were pursuing only their own interests, thinking only of overthrowing the old constitution as soon as possible, in short, of ruining the Empire." All this consideration, all these warnings, must have gone unheeded in Byzantium. To the usurpation of Cantacuzene, the Patriarch responded with the precipitate coronation of the young Emperor John. The civil war was beginning.

. . .

This is not the place to relate the prolonged vicissitudes of the struggle that lasted for more than six years and ended in victory for Cantacuzene. We need only to grasp its essential outlines and note its serious consequences. At the same time we shall see how it brought out all the weaknesses, passions, and faults of Anna of Savoy.

To make war, money was needed. Now the Treasury was empty, the Empire drained. The Regent used all possible means to obtain resources. The churches were subjected to confiscation, the holy images were sold or melted down; the valuables of the Imperial Palace, the dishes of gold and silver, the precious jewels, were parted with; the wealth of the great families was confiscated, and those who refused to fall in with this were arrested and imprisoned; in order to lay hands on the recalcitrant, even the ancient privilege of sanctuary in St. Sophia was not respected. The heaviest fiscal tyranny weighed down the capital and the Empire. And what was worse, the money collected in this way was not wholly consecrated to the needs of the war. Anna, who was very avaricious and her Counselors, took scandalous advantage of the circumstances to enrich themselves personally. In the general confusion, it was easy for them to cover up these malfeasances by juggling the accounts and recording fictitious expenditures; it was still easier for them to misappropriate precious objects, or to buy at absurdly low prices the most beautiful pieces of the imperial treasure that they decreed should be put up for sale. Anna of Savoy found a double satisfaction in this, it gratified at one and the same time her passion for gold and her petty jealousy; if ever Cantacuzene were to be victorious, she said, at least he would not lay hands on all those splendors that enhance the glamor of power.

To carry on the war, neither of the two adversaries had the slightest scruple over appealing for foreign aid. To obtain the

support of the Prince of Serbia, Stephen Dushan, Cantacuzene did not hesitate to offer him the strongest fortresses of
Macedonia. To obtain the support of Orkhan, the Turkish
Sultan of Nicea, he did not hesitate to give his daughter in
marriage to the infidel. Anna did as much on her side. She offered to cede the whole of Macedonia as far as Christopolis
to the Kral of Serbia, and to give her daughter in marriage
to his son, if he would deliver Cantacuzene into her hands
alive or dead. The alliance with the Emir of Aidin was
bought with gold. For years the Turks were to be seen cross-
ing the Hellespont, penetrating into Thrace as if it were their
own territory, and ravaging the country horribly. They plundered friends and enemies indiscriminately. They carried off
the flocks and the oxen, and even the inhabitants, dragging
them along by ropes tied around their necks. They came with
their spoils right up to the walls of Constantinople, where
Anna, deliberately indifferent to the fate of her subjects, ignoring the crowd of captives whose pitiful cries rose to high
heaven, received them with the greatest friendliness. What
did it matter that the land should be uncultivated and deserted, that thousands of Romans should be massacred or
sold like slaves, if by this means Cantacuzene could be defeated? What did it matter that Stephen Dushan should
ravage Macedonia and push his conquests as far as Christopolis? These were just so many fortresses that would not
belong to Cantacuzene. On this point, moreover, the two parties could not reproach each other. If Gregoras rightly brings
up the inhumanity, the cruelty, of Anna of Savoy, the hatred
that she seemed to feel for her people, we should not forget
that she was, as he says, a foreigner. So what terms shall we
apply to the conduct of Cantacuzene, which was no better
than that of the Empress?

While all this was going on, Anna of Savoy, in the depths

of her Palace, was allowing herself to be ruled by her favorites. With the support of the Patriarch, Apokaukos had become the real master of the Empire, and the Regent, to free her mind of all care, willingly abandoned the public welfare to him. The favorite took advantage of this to enrich himself; he thought more and more of marrying his daughter to the young Emperor; and even though his rivals attempted to discredit him with the Empress, his influence at the Palace held firm. All the same, he was uneasy, and felt himself surrounded by enemies. Although he took endless precautions to protect his person, although he never went out unescorted by soldiers and set a guard around his house, although he had imprisoned most of his political adversaries, he knew he was very unpopular and he was always afraid of an insurrection. He was not altogether mistaken. He was in process of having a formidable prison constructed inside the Great Palace for the incarceration of his victims. One day, when he had come to inspect the work and hurry it on, he made the mistake of entering, without a guard, the court where the prisoners were exercising. Aware of his plans for them, they did not let the opportunity pass. Armed with a stick, one of them threw himself upon Apokaukos and beat him almost to death; others joined in, and one, with a hatchet wrested from the hands of a workman, split his head open. It was the 11th of June 1345. Terror-stricken, the guards fled. The prisoners announced the death of the tyrant to the capital by hanging his bloody corpse from the battlements of the Palace, and entrenched themselves there to await events.

Anna of Savoy was to avenge her favorite cruelly. Upon the news of the murder, she had the great Palace surrounded, then she authorized the widow of Apokaukos to launch her adherents to the attack. A crowd glutted with gold and with wine flung itself into the assault. The order had been given to

kill everyone, some as perpetrators and others as accessories
to the crime. Unable to put up any real defense, the prisoners,
seeing the walls breached, fled into a neighboring church.
There they were pursued and pitilessly massacred, even on
the altar. Afterward, the severed heads and hands of the victims were carried through the streets of Constantinople. Terror reigned for several days. Anyone who dared to pity the
dead, to utter a single word of commiseration, even though
he was a friend or a relative of the condemned, was immediately arrested and beaten with switches, "as a traitor and an
enemy of the Empress Anna." It is said that in her rage the
Regent even entertained the idea of leaving the bodies unbur-
ied and having them thrown into the sea. Fearing the wrath
of the populace, she gave up this idea; but she did not conceal
her joy over the cruelties and bloodshed with which the death
of Apokaukos had been avenged. Then she looked for another favorite to help her resist Cantacuzene.

She was possessed by a fierce hatred for her adversary,
and was prepared to do anything rather than make peace
with him. When, in 1346, the Patriarch advised her to come
to terms with her rival, the mere suggestion was enough to
throw her into a frenzy. From then on, she looked on the
prelate as a traitor, and she did not rest until she had overthrown him. She succeeded in 1347. By her order he was deposed without a hearing; and with the exaggeration that was
the hallmark of her every act, Anna decided to celebrate with
a great feast the downfall of the man who had for so long
been her most loyal and intimate collaborator—so much so
that it was said of them that they were "one soul in two bodies." She invited to this banquet all those who had assisted
her in getting rid of the Patriarch, "and the repast," says
Gregoras, "was notable for the merry stories and the somewhat unseemly laughter that enlivened it. But that same

night at cock-crow," adds the historian, "all this jubilation was turned to sorrow." At that moment, Cantacuzene was entering Constantinople.

It had been obvious for several months that resistance was becoming impossible. The Regent's new favorite, the Italian Facciolati, realized it, and on the 3rd of February 1347, he opened one of the gates of the capital to Cantacuzene. Anna, however, stubbornly refused to face the facts. Entrenched in the Palace of Blachernae, she wanted to go on with the struggle. Through her emissaries she endeavored to rouse the populace; she asked the Genoese of Galata to come to her assistance; and she replied with coarse insults and violent outbursts of rage to the proposals of Cantacuzene, who invited her to surrender with a good grace and offered her in return a share in the government and all the honors due to her rank. Finally, however, on seeing a part of the Palace taken, and an assault about to be made, she consented to negotiate. After deliberating with the last of her partisans, she resigned herself, on their unanimous advice, to making peace. But she had no intention of admitting that she was guilty of anything that called for forgiveness. "Her proud, hard spirit," says Gregoras, "would have considered such an admission humiliating and unworthy of her." Haughtily she demanded solemn promises, special pledges; she claimed the right to reign alone, without even accepting Cantacuzene as a colleague. It was pure insanity. Anna should have been happy to accept the offers of the conqueror; she remained Empress, she was even given precedence over the new Basileus.

Cantacuzene flattered himself on disarming his enemy by means of courtesy and charm. He gave the imperial apartments over to her and her son, and contented himself with the more or less ruined portion of the Palace next to the great Triclinium of Alexius Comnenus. But these courtesies accomplished, he set himself to take possession of the power in earnest. As a precaution, he married his daughter, Helen, to the young Emperor John, and, in the sanctuary of the church of Blachernae (the recent fall of St. Sophia's cupola had turned the Great Church into a ruin), he had himself solemnly crowned all over again.

The coronation festivities were lamentable. "Such," says a contemporary, "was the poverty of the Empire, that among the dishes and cups used at the feast, there was not a single one of gold or of silver. Part of the service was of pewter, the rest of clay or seashells. Anyone who knows anything about the usual customs will know by that, and by other details that were not in conformity with etiquette, to what dire straits everything had been reduced. I must add that the glitter of gold and precious stones on the imperial robes and diadems worn at this festival was, for the most part, false. The gold had been replaced by gilded leather, the gems by bits of colored glass. Only here and there could be seen stones with an authentic sparkle, pearls whose water was not an optical illusion. So utterly ruined was the antique splendor of the Roman Empire, so utterly vanished its former prosperity, that I cannot tell of it without shame." The coffers of the Treasury were empty: "there was nothing to be found in them but air and dust." This was the condition to which the Empress Anna had reduced the monarchy by her rashness, her greed, and her folly.

Anna of Savoy was defeated, and she was never to forgive the man who had defeated her. He was well aware of this. So his first care was to disband the Empress's Italian court, to send away all the foreigners and the women who had made the Gynaeceum into a perpetual hotbed of intrigue. In addi-

tion, he tried to free the young Emperor from the evil influence of his mother by sending him to live in Thessalonica. It
was wasted effort. The Princess never forgot her grudge.
Always full of contempt for Cantacuzene and his friends, always secretly hostile, she maintained a constant opposition to
the new régime. Somewhere Cantacuzene speaks of the
friendship she displayed toward him; it is difficult to believe
that she was sincere, or that he should have thought her so.
True, she acceded to his request that she should intervene to
smooth out the awkward situation that arose in 1351 when
her son John, who also privately detested the new Emperor,
thought of repudiating his wife to marry the sister of the Serbian Tsar Stephen Dushan, and begin, with foreign aid, a
war against Cantacuzene. She went to Thessalonica, says a
chronicler, and "broke up all the intrigues as if they were
cobwebs."

She considered her son's idea premature and that she saw
in Cantacuzene's difficulties an opportunity to extract from
him a promise to abdicate in the near future. Like her son,
she was waiting for her revenge. She got it in 1354. With the
support of the Latins, John Paleologus took Constantinople
by surprise and forced his father-in-law to abdicate. Curiously resigned, Cantacuzene, who had always been so ambitious, quietly entered a monastery, and his wife, the grave
and intelligent Irene, remarked, not without irony: "If, in the
past, I had defended Didymoticus [where she distinguished
herself in 1342 by an admirable defense] as you have defended Constantinople, we would have found salvation twelve
years ago."

Cantacuzene, in spite of his outstanding qualities, and
Anna of Savoy, because of all the mistakes of her rule, were
largely responsible for the decadence and final ruin of the
Byzantine Empire. In unleashing, by their rivalry, an inter-

minable civil war, and especially in appealing for aid from the worst enemies of the Empire, they both erred with equal gravity; and perhaps the Grand Domestic, capable of foreseeing the results of his acts, is more guilty than the stupid, heedless Empress. Never, before his day, had a Byzantine Princess been known to marry a Moslem; never before had the Turks been seen to all intents and purposes permanently established in Thrace, nor had the treasures of the churches been used to satisfy the demands of infidels. But all that, and more, took place. Gregoras relates that even in the Imperial Palace, the Turks, received as friends, did exactly as they liked; they even danced and sang during the celebration of the Divine Liturgy, to the great indignation of the Christians. Realizing that they alone had gained by the civil war, they felt they had the upper hand. They were proved to be right. One hundred years later, in captured Constantinople, in plundered St. Sophia, the crescent was to replace the cross for centuries. The seeds of this final catastrophe were sown during the reign of Anna of Savoy. In contrast to the many obscure and unobtrusive Western Princesses who moved across the scene of the Byzantine throne, Anna wanted to, and did, play an active role. It is to be regretted that for want of intelligence she should have played it so disastrously.

A NOTE ON THE TYPE

The text of this book is set in Monticello, a Linotype revival of the original Binny & Ronaldson Roman No. 1, cut by Archibald Binny and cast in 1796 by that Philadelphia type foundry. The face was named Monticello in honor of its use in the monumental fifty-volume *Papers of Thomas Jefferson*, published by Princeton University Press. Monticello is a transitional type design, embodying certain features of Bulmer and Baskerville, but it is a distinguished face in its own right.

Printed and bound by The Haddon Craftsmen, Inc.,
Scranton, Pennsylvania.
Typography and binding design by
GEORGE SALTER

A NOTE ABOUT THE AUTHOR

Charles Diehl died in his native France in 1944, at the age of eighty-five. During the course of his long and distinguished career as a historian and teacher, Charles Diehl explored virtually every aspect of Byzantine civilization and did much to shape the modern image of the Byzantine Empire—an image that had been previously distorted by the influential writings of Montesquieu and Gibbon. His remarkably extensive knowledge of original source material, combined with his lucid and graceful prose style, has made him one of the most respected and widely read authorities on Byzantium. Among the many academic honors that crowned his career were honorary degrees from Harvard University and the universities of Bruxelles, Athens, and Bucharest. He was Professor of Byzantine History and Archaeology at the Sorbonne, a member of l'Académie des Inscriptions et Belles Lettres, and a *Grand Officier* of the Légion d'honneur. Diehl's *Byzantine Portraits*, from which a number of the chapters of this book are drawn, was published by Knopf in 1928.